Revolutionary Premiere 6

Christian Darkin
Joe Allen
Mark Schaeffer
Corné van Dooren
Alan McCann

Cover photograph of Pathe 35mm splicer appears by kind permission of Michael Rogge.
Collecting Cinematographica http://www.xs4all.nl/~wichm/cinemat.html

friendsof

DESIGNER TO DESIGNER™

Revolutionary Premiere 6

© 2001 friends of ED

First published December 2001

Trademark Acknowledgments

friends of ED has endeavored to provide trademark information about all the companies and products mentioned in this book by the appropriate use of capitals. However, friends of ED cannot guarantee the accuracy of this information.

Published by friends of ED
30 Lincoln Road, Olton, Birmingham. B27 6PA. UK.

Printed in USA

ISBN: 1-903450-49-7

Revolutionary Premiere 6

Credits

Authors
Christian Darkin
Joe Allen
Mark Schaeffer
Corné van Dooren
Alan McCann

Technical Reviewers
Corné van Dooren
Ben Forman
Matthew B. Hein
David Martin
Ian Plater
Michael Watson

Index
Fiona Murray

Proof Readers
Jon Bounds
Andy Corsham
Alice Myers
Gavin Wray

Content Architect
Andrew Tracey

Editors
Alan McCann
Rob Tidy

Author Agent
Mel Jehs

Project Managers
Thomas Stiff
Simon Brand

Graphic Editors
Matthew Clark
Katy Freer
Chantal Hepworth
Deb Murray

Cover Design
Corné van Dooren
Deb Murray

Christian Darkin

Christian Darkin is a writer, animator, and filmmaker. He has written on video editing for dozens of magazines including Computer Arts, Camcorder User, and Digit. as well as the Times, The Guardian and the FT. He's written, directed, and edited several short films and written two plays for the Edinburgh festival, and comedy sketches for TV and BBC radio. He's also the author of the Darwin Plug-in for 3D Studio Max, and a desktop version of Prime Minister Tony Blair.

Joe Allen
picture accreditation: Mark A. Raynes

Joe Allen shoots and edits video for AudioVision in Overland Park, Kansas. A small company that specializes in corporate training and marketing, the only thing they don't do is wedding videography. Joe originally came from an audio background – working as a live sound and recording engineer, and designing and installing sound systems. An interest in graphics, combined with the audio engineering experience, led to a position as a video editor – which started by editing (with the client) on a linear A/B roll system the first day on the job! Stress levels continued to escalate from there with the introduction of non-linear editing systems.

Joe would like to thank Stephen and Lorie Foster, Doug Chandler, and Barbara Lindstrom for the gracious contributions of their time and talent for the tutorial footage.

Mark Schaeffer

Mark Schaeffer has been in the audiovisual business for more than 20 years, most of that time with his own company, Schaeffer and Goldentyer. His clients have included educational publishers such as McGraw-Hill and Houghton Mifflin, nonprofit organizations such as Catholic Charities and the Sierra Club, and industrial clients such as Apple Computer, Levi Strauss, and Kaiser Permanente. He is the author of an Adobe Premiere 6.0 training CD for Virtual Training Company. He currently teaches multimedia courses at San Francisco State University and the Center for Electronic Art.

www.cornevandooren.com **Corné van Dooren**

Born Autumn 1979 in Hooge Mierde, a village in the south of the Netherlands, Corné is a graduate Interactive Multimedia Developer. Currently building his skills in Hunterskil Howard, an international B2B communications agency in Eindhoven. With a colourful background as a cartoonist, Corné discovered the infinite world of multimedia when he was 17 and hasn't stopped discovering. He spends much of his time with most of the well-known packages from Adobe and Macromedia, for online / offline use. There are many other visualisation packages on his desktop too, along with Corné's mantra: the only limit to multimedia is the imagination.

Alan McCann

Alan McCann has been a full-time friend of ED for over 10 months now, his enthusiasm for video finally satisfied by the launch of the DVision books. Whilst working towards a media studies degree in Glasgow, he co-produced a number of documentary features including a well-publicised and acclaimed community video on public facilities in the city, and also an extended drama piece which he wrote, produced, edited and directed.

He currently lives in Birmingham, about 250 miles from the sweetest girl in the whole world.

Revolutionary Premiere 6

Table of Contents

Revolutionary Premiere 6

00 Welcome

You won't have missed the fact that digital is taking over, but you'd be wrong if you thought that all that those 1s and 0s can do for you is make your pictures a little bit clearer and your soundtrack a bit crisper.

Digital video gives you complete control over every frame of your production. You really can just drag and drop scenes, clips, still, music, anything you want, onto the versatile timeline where you compose your final video. And if you make a mistake, you just hit Undo. Digital video editing really can be that easy, and this book will take you from start to finish learning how to digitally edit using Adobe's premier league desktop video solution.

Windows 2000, MMX detected, v6.0

Adobe® Premiere® 6.0

Sylvain Francoeur, Eric Sanders, David McGavran, Bill Bachman, Matt Douglas, Jerry Scoggins, Nick Schlott, Russell Zornes, Enzo Guerrera, Dave Wise, Trent Happel, Larry Lozares, Steven Warner-Swirsky, Paul Young, David Vasquez, David DiGiacomo, Matt Davey, Tod Snook

Initializing...

You can tuck the manual away from now on, because we'll show you everything you need to know, and much much more. Over the course of the next 500 pages you'll learn all the essential ways to use Premiere like a pro:

- Importing your footage into Premiere – digitising and organizing your material.

- Editing scenes together in Premiere – composing your video.

- Dealing with sound and music in your production.

- Transitions and Filters – making your scenes flow together and enhancing your video.

But it doesn't stop there. This book is designed not just to show you what Premiere does, but also what more it can do for you with a little application. Learn tips and tricks from the pros and make that final video a polished masterpiece.

- Learn about pre-production techniques and also how to shoot your video. Get a view of the whole video production process.

- Using Premiere with other tools, such as Photoshop to enhance scenes and create effects.

- Adding titles and credit sequences to finish off a professional production.

By the time you get to the index you'll know enough about Premiere to put together stunning digital videos, as well as being able to correct some shooting problems, plan out your videos and even perform the all-important export to whatever format you need your production to be in.

Working Through the Book

For the bulk of the book, we'll be using tutorials and exercises to show you what Premiere has to offer your digital productions. You can either use your own footage or, for **Chapters 5**, **6** and **7**, you can use the footage available from our web site to follow the main editing tutorials step by step.

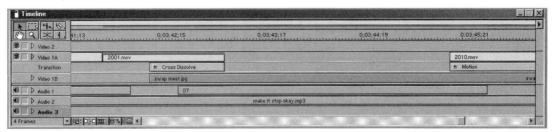

If you're interested in producing and shooting your own videos, we also have a special DVision production pack downloadable from our web site; this provides you with samples and templates for common production and pre-production tasks such as storyboarding and scripting.

So come visit us at www.friendsofed.com/dvision for information on new DVision books and more free downloads.

How the Book Looks

We use a few layout conventions to make things clearer throughout the book.

- If we introduce a new **important** term or reference another **Chapter No**. then these will be in **bold**.

- We'll use different styles to emphasize things that appear on the screen, KEYSTROKES or SHORTCUTS and also hyperlinks.

> *If there's something you shouldn't miss, it will be highlighted it like this! When you see the bubble, pay attention!*

- Finally, as the book is tutorial driven, much of the practical content will be built into examples and exercises which you should follow through:

  1. If you see the exercise numbers, switch on your computer and get ready for action.

  2. Follow the steps through and check the screenshots and diagrams for more hints.

  3. When you get to the end, give yourself a pat on the back.

Support – Just In Case

friends of ED DVision books aim to be easy to follow and error-free. However, if you do run into problems, don't hesitate to get in touch – our crack team of reader support professionals will have you sorted in no time at all.

You can reach us at support@friendsofed.com, and even if you're not running into difficulty we'd still love to hear from you; send us your comments about the book and any requests for future titles, or just fill out the little reply card at the back and pop it in the post!

Well, that's all you need to know before launching into **Chapter 1** – our pre-title sequence is over and it's time to learn a little more about what desktop video entails and what this DV revolution can do for you.

01 Introduction to Desktop Video

Premiere 6.0 is Adobe's popular video-editing software, redesigned to work with the latest generation of digital video hardware and the latest streaming video formats for the World Wide Web. Premiere is powerful, easy to use, and adaptable to a wide range of computers and video equipment, making it an ideal tool for video makers who have big imaginations and limited budgets.

This book will introduce you to the major features of Premiere by offering detailed explanations, plentiful illustrations, and hands-on exercises. Even if you've never edited video before, you'll be able to bring your ideas to life through the skills you acquire in the coming chapters.

What Is Premiere Used For?

Though Premiere is generally referred to as a video-editing application, it actually does much more than simply edit video. Premiere is, in fact, an entire video (and audio) post-production suite in a single, easy-to-use package. Here are some of the things that Premiere can do:

- **Video acquisition** – When used with the proper hardware, Premiere automates the process of converting video from its original source (a camera, a camcorder, or a video deck), to a digital file on your computer's hard drive. This is a necessary first step in the video-editing process.

- **Visualization and storyboarding** – Premiere now includes a Storyboard window that enables you to arrange video clips in a comic strip format, allowing you to plan your movie before you begin to edit. Once you're happy with your storyboard, Premiere can automatically transform it into a rough edited version of your movie.

- **Video editing** – Premiere offers a wide set of tools that allow you to trim, arrange, and rearrange video clips to get your movie just the way you want it. These are **smart** tools that do complicated calculations behind the scenes, allowing you to accomplish in seconds what would have taken hours in a traditional video-editing suite.

- **Audio editing and mixing** – Whether you're working with synched audio (that is, audio that was recorded at the same time as your video) or stand-alone audio (such as music and sound effects), Premiere allows you to adjust the timing, relative levels, equalization, and panning of up to **99** simultaneous audio tracks.

- **Transitions and effects** – From the simplest dissolve or wipe to the most complex warping effects, Premiere gives you the power to reshape and re-imagine the images on your screen. You can customize effects, add multiple effects to individual video clips, and control the means by which one clip leads into another.

- **Motion control** – Premiere allows you to add movement to your images, whether they're still photographs or full-motion video clips. You can zoom in and out, pan, rotate, skew, and even make an image dance around your screen in a precisely executed motion path.

- **Title creation** – Premiere's title window allows you to design and create on-screen text and graphics, incorporating gradient color, shadows, and transparency. You can make titles that stand still, roll vertically, or crawl horizontally across the screen. Once a title is complete, you can effortlessly superimpose it on any background or video clip.

- **Compositing** – The process of superimposing one image on another - allowing, for example, an actor shot in a studio to be placed against a background shot somewhere else. Premiere offers a full selection of compositing tools, which allow up to 99 layers of video to be combined smoothly into a single shot.

- **Output** – When your video project is complete, Premiere allows it to be exported in any of the most common distribution formats. You can output your movie to videotape, save it as a digital video file that can be burned to a CD or DVD, or create streaming files that can be played in real-time over the Internet.

How Video Works

Because Premiere is a video application, it's important that you learn a little bit about video in general, even those aspects that aren't related to Premiere directly. Premiere has the ability to work with a wide range of hardware and software, from the most old-fashioned to the absolute cutting edge - but to make the best use of this versatile tool, you need to understand what your hardware and software are doing.

> *You may be tempted to skip this section, since you probably don't really care how video works. After all, to use a car, you don't need to know how the car works - you just have to know how to drive it, right?*

Sure – but unlike driving, which has pretty much stayed the same over the course of a century, the process of video editing is in a constant state of change. The vast shift from analog to digital is still going on, and there isn't yet an agreed standard for video technology. The sheer amounts of options for video, which now include various Web streaming formats, further complicate things. So, while all cars and roads are basically the same, Premiere's configurations and uses can vary widely. This short, crash course in video technology will help you make the most of Premiere's potential.

The following explanations may seem a bit daunting, but we've simplified them so it is easier to understand. For one thing, they don't deal at all with color or audio - but they should give you enough of a foundation to be able to make informed decisions when using Premiere. Even if the significance of each of them isn't apparent right now, you'll see why it's important when you get to later chapters.

The Basics of Video

You're probably familiar with how a movie camera works: it takes a series of snapshots in quick succession and records them on a strip of film. When these snapshots - known as **frames** - are projected on a screen at the same very fast rate (generally 24 frames per second - but can vary), they give the illusion of motion.

A video camera works somewhat differently. Instead of photographing an entire frame at a single moment, it scans the scene **line-by-line**, working gradually from left to right and from top to bottom. It then jumps back to the upper-left corner and starts all over again. When the output from the camera is sent to a video monitor or TV set, the TV's picture tube recreates the image in the same way. An electron gun sweeps across the screen line by line, from left to right and from top to bottom, shooting electrons at a phosphor-coated screen and causing those phosphors to glow.

Early experiments with television showed that this line-by-line redrawing of a video image was difficult to watch. By the time the electron gun reached the bottom of the screen, the phosphors at the top of the screen had already begun to fade. The resulting image was always uneven, with bands of brightness and darkness that rolled down the screen.

Some clever guys solved this problem by using a process called **interlacing**. Instead of scanning every line of an image, a video camera would begin by scanning every *other* line, in other words, line 1, line 3, line 5, and so on. When it reached the bottom, it would jump back and fill in the missing lines - line 2, line 4, and line 6. This process allowed the TV's electron gun to cover the screen twice as fast, illuminating the phosphors at the bottom of the screen while those at the top were still glowing brightly. The result was a more uniform, stable image. Despite vast improvement in picture tube technology, today's broadcast video still uses interlacing.

Each complete sweep of alternate lines is called a **field**. Two interlaced fields - the odd lines combined with the even lines - make up a frame.

| Field 1 | Field 2 | Full Frame |

Several different video systems have popped up throughout the world, each of which uses a different number of lines, fields, and frames. **PAL**, the standard used in the UK and most of Europe, uses a 625-line screen at 25 frames (50 fields) per second. **NTSC**, the standard used in the United States and much of the western hemisphere, uses a 525-line screen at approximately 30 frames (60 fields) per second. (There are other video systems as well, but these are the only two that are supported by Premiere.)

Analog video

In a video camera, each line of an image senses variations in brightness and darkness. These variations are converted by photovoltaic sensors into a fluctuating electric current; the brighter the light, the stronger the current; the dimmer the light, the weaker the current.

Basically, the electric current takes the form of a **wave**, which is a direct representation of the image that the camera sees.

This fluctuating current may be sent to a video deck, where it creates a fluctuating magnetic charge on a strip of videotape. Or it may be sent to a transmitter, where it's converted to fluctuations in an electromagnetic carrier signal.

Eventually, the signal is converted back into electricity, which is fed to the TV's picture tube. The variations in the strength of the electric current are translated into variations in the firing of the electrons - and hence the brightness of the phosphors - as the electron gun sweeps across the screen.

> *There are no numbers or calculations involved. The video information is encoded in the simple, continuous movement of a series of waves. The waves may take different forms - light, electricity, magnetism - but in every case, the wave is an analog of the patterns of light and darkness that the camera detected in the original scene.*

This system worked fine for over 50 years, even today, most of the video that you see in your daily life is analog video. Let's say you turn on your television and tune into a local broadcast station, you'd be receiving an analog video signal. If you rent a movie on VHS tape and pop it into your VCR, you're viewing analog videotape.

While there's nothing really wrong with analog video, it's becoming obsolete because video editing is subject to constant pressure to become faster and cheaper. In today's cut throat information age, the fastest and cheapest way to do things is to use a computer, and to use easily available software like Premiere.

Digitization

Computers can be fickle and don't work well with analog waves. Computers need discrete bits of information that can be represented by simple binary code - a series of zeroes and ones. Therefore, in order for a computer to work with video, the video information needs to be encoded in a digital format. (There are a number of different digital formats, with names such as D1 and DV. Each differs in the details of how it represents video digitally, but they all follow the same basic principles.)

It's important to note that the real world is analog, not digital. Visual images reach our eyes - or a camera if you like - in the form of **light waves**. Video cameras and picture tubes make use of various forms of electromagnetic waves. Therefore, the process of digitizing video information always requires turning a wave into numerical information.

In order to do this, a computer examines - or **samples** - the wave at regular intervals (The frequency of sampling is generally thousands of times per second - any parts of the wave that fall between the fixed intervals don't get sampled, and therefore don't survive the conversion from analog to digital).

Each time the computer takes a sample, it measures a precise point on the wave and records those measurements as a string of zeroes and ones. Those zeroes and ones can be used later to reconstruct the original wave, and thus to recreate the video image.

These points get sampled

Sampling a wave

Digital video

Digitization – the conversion from analog to digital - can take place in several places in the video production process. The original practice is for video to be shot with an analog camera and recorded to analog videotape. (Professionals generally use a high-quality format such as Betacam, while home users favor VHS.) When it's time for this video to be edited, the output from the camera or deck is plugged into a **capture card** that's installed in a desktop computer. The capture card contains all the hardware that's needed to digitize the video and store the digital information on the computer's hard drive.

More recently, it's become popular for video to be shot with a digital camera and recorder (which are often combined into a single unit known as a **digital camcorder**). With this type of equipment, the conversion from analog to digital occurs directly within the camera. In other words, the camera scans an image line by line just as older cameras did, but it **samples as it scans**, producing a string of digital information instead of an electrical current. The digital information is saved on videotape, but this kind of videotape is related much more to a computer hard drive than to VHS or Betacam - it's designed to store numbers, not waves.

With all these changes in technology, the use of the term **digital video** has become a bit confusing. For example, it's often said that Premiere 6.0 is designed to handle "digital video," while the previous version, 5.1, was not... Obviously, this isn't true, because **all** video that's edited on a computer is digital video. What this really means, however, is that Premiere is now equipped to handle the **newer** type of digital video - the type that's shot with a digital camcorder, in which the *digitization occurs much earlier in the process.*

Are you confused yet? Well, adding to any confusion, are the now popular video formats called DV and DV-CAM. **DV** is an abbreviation for Digital Video, but not all digital video is DV. Premiere can handle a number of digital video formats, including some that are not DV, so don't feel that you must buy only a DV or DV-CAM camcorder in order to shoot digital video.

Lines vs. pixels

Anyone who works with video on a computer must learn to straddle the worlds of digital and analog. There are some video projects out there that are 100% digital - for example, those whose images are created entirely on a computer and are distributed by streaming over the World Wide Web - but such projects are rare. (Even the latest digital camcorders are still designed to use NTSC or PAL standards, since whatever they shoot is likely to end up being shown on a traditional analog TV.) For this reason, it's important to understand the differences between how video is displayed on a television screen and how it's displayed on a computer, since you'll be dealing with both.

- As you know, analog video is made up of discrete horizontal lines. Each line is continuous and unbroken, with lights and darks flowing together in classic analog style. Digital video, however, is made up of an array of dots, called picture elements or **pixels**. Each pixel is an individual unit, with its own location, brightness, and color. An analog video image that's been converted to digital is typically 640 pixels wide by 480 pixels high.

- An analog video image is interlaced, with two fields coming together to make a frame. A digital video image, since it's not made up of lines, is not interlaced. Since there is no interlacing, there are also no fields - in digital video, a frame is simply a frame.

- An analog video image has an **aspect ratio** - a ratio of width to height of approximately 4:3, since those are the proportions of a standard TV screen. Digital video can have any aspect ratio, but since most digital video is still viewed on analog TV sets, most digital video conforms to the 4:3 aspect ratio as well.

(Apart from the aspect ratio of the video image, there is also a variation in the aspect ratio of the pixels that make up the image. Some digital video formats, such as DV, use rectangular pixels that are taller than they are wide. The standard pixels used by most computer software are square.)

In most cases, you won't have to be concerned with these differences between analog and digital video. If you have an external TV monitor hooked up to your computer, Premiere is smart enough to display the same video analog-style on the TV monitor and digital-style on the computer monitor. But if you're converting from one format to another - for example, if you're capturing analog video and outputting it as a streaming Real Video file - you will have to pay attention to these issues when you define your capture settings and export settings. But we'll cover this in more detail later in the book.

Video editing

In the earliest days of television, there was no such thing as video editing, because all TV was broadcast live. Videotape recording didn't become practical until the mid 1950s, and wasn't widely used until the early 1960s.

Originally, videotape was edited the same way audiotape was edited - it was cut with a razor blade and stuck back together with splicing tape. While this technique was fine for audio recordings, it was not especially suitable for video. The tape had to be matched precisely line-for-line and field-for-field, or else the picture would become unstable, not looking too good!

Therefore, a more complex system was developed for editing video. It required two videotape recorders: one called the **source deck** and one called the **record deck**. (Each had a monitor connected to it; they were called the **source monitor** and the **program monitor**.) The two decks were connected to a device called a **controller**, which allowed a human editor to operate both decks at once.

The original videotape - called the **source tape** - was played on the (you got it!) source deck, while the record deck held a blank videotape. The editor would look at the source tape, find the scene he or she wanted, and mark the beginning of this scene by punching an **In point** button on the controller. The editor would then locate the end of the scene and punch the **Out point** button on the controller. Finally, the editor would find the place on the **record tape** where he or she wanted to begin the scene, and would punch the **In point** button on the record side of the controller.

To perform the edit, the editor would press the **take edit** button on the controller. The record deck would switch into record mode, allowing a copy of the scene to be made on the new tape. When one of the decks reached the **Out point**, the recording would stop.

In this painstaking way, video programs would be pieced together. This process was called **linear editing**, because everything had to be done in order: the first scene had to be copied to the record tape, then the second scene, and so on. If the editor had edited several scenes and wanted to change something near the beginning of the program, all the edits following that change would have to be done over again!

As you probably realize, this traditional method of video editing is rarely used anymore. Just about all video is now digitized and edited by computer, in a process called **non-linear editing**. The advantages of non-linear editing are clear: scenes can be edited in any order; edits can be performed instantly, without waiting for decks to rewind or sync up; and anything that's done can be easily revised or undone.

Still, vestiges of the old system remain, and they explain much about Premiere's interface. As you'll see, Premiere still uses source and program monitors, and still requires In points and Out points. Just as most word processors still use an old-fashioned typewriter as their point of reference, Premiere, still uses the two-deck editing system as its desktop metaphor.

Video on the desktop

Personal computers have been around for quite a while, but it's only in the past decade or so that it's become practical to edit video on them. That's because video is hugely data-intensive. Thinking about it for a second: for a computer to display an average, full-color, 640 x 480 digital image requires about 200 kilobytes of information. Now, imagine the computer having to display 25 or 30 such images per second. That comes out to about **5 megabytes** of information that have to be transferred from your hard drive, loaded into memory, and displayed on your monitor, **every second** for as long as your video plays. Until relatively recently, hard drives and computer processors were not fast enough to process that much information that quickly.

In fact, they're still not really fast enough. The only way it's possible to play video on a standard desktop computer is to use compressors that reduce the amount of information required to reproduce a movie.

A **compressor** (also known as a compressor-decompressor, or **codec**) is a program that analyzes video images and throws away any information that isn't necessary for reconstructing the image. For example, if a door is shown in the same place in each frame, it's only necessary to store the door's visual information for one frame. The same information can be used for each succeeding frame - at least until the camera moves or the door opens.

There are many different compressors that are useful for different situations, but all of them reduce image quality to some degree.

Even with compression, some very simple video-editing tasks put a strain on desktop computers. Let's suppose you want to superimpose the title "THE END" over video footage of a car driving off toward the horizon. For each frame of video, the computer must figure out which pixels in the title are transparent, throw them away, and replace them with the constantly-changing pixels of the moving car.

This is not something that a desktop computer can do on-the-fly very easily. Instead, it takes whatever time it needs to do all the calculations, stores the results in a separate file, and then plays the video. (This is the process called **rendering** or **creating a preview** in Premiere.)

These kinds of problems can be reduced or eliminated by using specialized video-editing hardware. Ordinarily, a computer devotes much of its processing power to following the instructions it receives from software such as Premiere. But if some of those instructions can be carried out by a piece of hardware, the computer is relieved of much of its load.

For example, the process of compression and decompression can be handled by **hardware compressors**, in which the necessary compression formulas are hard-wired into specialized computer chips.

The ideal situation is to have all the major video-editing functions handled by specialized pieces of hardware, and to use software just as a means of controlling them. Software/hardware hybrids such as **Avid** and **Media 100** take this approach, and the benefits are immense: almost everything, including complex video effects, can be viewed in **real-time.**

For people who need to do serious video editing - such as long programs intended for broadcast – Avid is usually the solution of choice. But the disadvantage of a hardware-based package such as Avid is that it is extremely expensive to acquire and maintain.

Premiere - along with its rival, Final Cut Pro - is known in the trade as a **software-only solution**. It lacks the real-time capabilities of Avid or Media 100, and it may require patience if used for long projects. But it compensates by being inexpensive, easy to upgrade, extremely flexible, and usable on practically any off-the-shelf computer.

The Video Production Process

Video production is typically divided into four stages:

- Pre-production

- Production

- Post-production

- Distribution

Premiere can help with many of these tasks, but others will require the use of other tools and skills. Here is an overview of the entire process:

Pre-production

Pre-production is basically *planning*. This is the stage that many people would rather skip. ("Can't we just get to the fun part?") But by paying proper attention to pre-production, you can make the rest of the project much easier - not only for yourself, but for your clients and collaborators.

Some of the elements of pre-production are:

- **Budgeting** – whether you're doing a high-end corporate presentation or a small project just for fun, there are going to be costs involved. How much will you need to pay for equipment rental, travel expenses, or blank videotape? Do you need to upgrade your hardware or software? If you plan to hire people, how much will you have to pay them?

- **Scripting** – even a totally improvised drama requires some writing beforehand. What scenes will you need in order to tell your story? If there are actors involved, where will they be and what will they be doing? If you'll be interviewing people on camera, what questions will you need to ask them? (There's nothing worse than sitting down to edit your video and discovering that there's something you needed to shoot, but didn't.)

- **Hiring** – it's a very rare video production that's done entirely by one person. If you're going to be behind the camera, who's going to be in front of it? Who's going to take care of lighting, sound, continuity, and snacks? Whether you're paying a cast and crew or just getting volunteers, it's important to find people you can count on and communicate with.

Production

Production is the process of creating all the elements that you plan to include in your finished program. At the very least, this means shooting video - taking care to get all the angles, alternate takes, and transitional shots that you might need later when you're editing. (For more about shooting, see Chapter 2). But production may also include the making and recording of animation, music, or sound effects.

Post-production

This is the phase in which you gather all the elements that were created during production and assemble them into a finished product. As you might have figured out, this is where Premiere comes in. The post-production stage incorporates nearly everything in the list at the beginning of this chapter: **Digitizing video** (if necessary) and loading it into your computer; **rough** and **fine** editing; **adding motion**, **transitions**, and **effects**; creating and inserting **titles** and **graphics**; **compositing video** and **mixing audio**. All of these topics will be covered in depth in Chapters 3 through 12.

Many film and video producers will tell you that post-production is most important part of the creative process. The footage that was shot during production is simply raw material; it's the editing and the effects that make it come alive! Unlike the production phase, which has a definite conclusion, post-production can go on endlessly. There are many different ways to put a video program together, and you'll probably want to try most of them.

The good news is Premiere makes this easy. You can easily experiment, make alterations, and change things back to the way they were. You can even create several variations of your project and decide later which one you like best. Eventually – when you and your clients are happy (or when you run out of time or money) – you'll accept that the latest version of your project is the final one, and declare the post-production phase to be over.

Distribution

Once your video program is finished, there remains the problem of getting it to its intended audience. How is your program going to be distributed? Whatever option you choose, Premiere allows you to accomplish it easily.

- **Videotape** – With its Export to Tape and Print to Video options, Premiere allows you to make a master tape in the analog or digital format of your choice. This master may just be a VHS tape that you send to your relatives, or it may be in a professional format such as Betacam or DVC-Pro. If you opt for a professional format, the master tape can then be used for broadcast, or it can be sent to a duplication house to make multiple copies for sale, rental, or free distribution to the public.

- **CD or DVD** – You can't burn a CD or a DVD directly from Premiere, but you can export a QuickTime or AVI file that's specially designed for CD or DVD. You can incorporate the file into a multimedia program (using an authoring application such as Macromedia Director), or you may decide to distribute a disk containing just your movie. Once you've output the appropriate file from Premiere, your disk burner and its accompanying software will do the rest.

- **Web** – There are now many ways to distribute video over the Web, including QuickTime, RealMedia, and Windows Media formats. Premiere allows you to export your video program in one or more of these formats, specially configured for streaming over low or high-bandwidth connections. Once you upload these files to your web server, you're ready to go.

All of these distribution options (and techniques for adapting a single project to more than one distribution method) are covered towards the end the book.

How Premiere Fits into the Process

As you've seen, Premiere can play a major role in both the post-production and distribution of a video program. However, depending on your preferences, needs, and technical requirements, you may decide to use Premiere in different ways for different projects. Here are some sample workflow scenarios and the circumstances in which each might be appropriate.

Sample Workflow 1: Entire project done in Premiere.

After you've shot all your video, you connect your camcorder to your computer and use Premiere to control the importing (and, if necessary, digitizing) of the footage. You then use Premiere to edit the footage and to add whatever effects you desire. You create all your titles and graphics in Premiere's title window and incorporate them into the project. Finally, when the project is complete, you reconnect the camcorder to the computer, insert a blank tape, and export your video.

Obviously, this is the simplest way to get the job done. This option has some drawbacks, however.

- First, it limits you to using only hardware that you can personally connect to your computer. You can't create a master tape in Betacam format, unless you can get your hands on a Betacam deck (and even then, may not have the right connectors on your computer to hook it up properly).

- Second, it limits the "bells and whistles" you can include in your video program. For example, if you want your titles to include text on a curved path, you're out of luck - Premiere's title window can only create text on a straight line.

- And third, it limits the length and complexity of your projects. Keeping in mind that Premiere needs time to render each frame individually in scenes where you use titles or effects (see Video on the Desktop, above), you may have to be prepared to wait several hours to preview a medium-length program, or overnight to preview a longer one.

For these reasons, the best circumstances for doing everything in Premiere are if you're producing relatively short projects (such as a collection of two- or three-minute clips to be included on a multimedia CD or streamed over the Web), or relatively simple projects (such as those that include mostly cuts and few titles or effects). Otherwise, you may want to look at other options such as those described below.

Sample Workflow 2: Rough cut done in Premiere; final output done on another system

After you've shot your footage in a professional format such as Betacam, you have a professional duplicator make copies for you in a format that you can play on your own equipment (such as VHS or DV). You then import the footage into your computer and edit the project as in Scenario #1. When the project is finished, you export it to videotape. This videotape is a **rough cut** - a model for what the final program will look like, but with lower technical quality.

You then export an edit decision list, or **EDL**, from Premiere. This is a text file that lists every In and Out point for every edit and all transition and audio levels that's included in your program. You take your EDL, your original Betacam tapes to a professional video editing company.

There, the editor imports your EDL into a hardware-based system such as Media 100 or Avid, and recaptures your footage directly from the Betacam tapes. Your edited program is automatically recreated on the new system according to the information in the EDL, and is exported to a Betacam master.

The advantages of this scenario are that:

- You have much more flexibility in the video formats you can use for shooting and mastering, and that many of the effects that take hours to render in Premiere can be recreated in real time on a hardware-based system.

- Also, a professional editing suite will be equipped with the necessary engineering tools (such as waveform monitors and vectorscopes) to produce a broadcast-quality videotape, which you can't easily do on an ordinary desktop system.

But there are disadvantages:

- First, not all professional systems are equipped to import EDLs. And even if they are, the EDL doesn't include all the information needed to reproduce the project you created in Premiere.

- Second, not all of Premiere's features have equivalents in other systems. For example, if your movie uses an unusual feature such as the **Difference Matte**, you may not be able to duplicate that effect on a system such as Media 100.

- And third - if it's not already obvious - time spent in a professional editing suite costs money, particularly if you need to pay an operator as well!

Sample Workflow 3: Editing done in Premiere; other tasks done with other tools

You shoot your video on a DV camcorder, import it into Premiere, and edit it as in scenario 1. You design graphics in Photoshop, export them in Photoshop format, import them into Premiere, and use them as backgrounds for special-effect sequences. You create animated titles in Flash, export them in QuickTime format with an Alpha channel, import them into Premiere, and composite them with your video.

You export all your audio tracks, 'sweeten' and mix them in Pro Tools, and import them back into Premiere. You export portions of your movie as QuickTime files, apply effects to them in After Effects, and re-import them into Premiere. Export your movie to DV, take your DV tape to a professional duplication house, and have them convert it to Betacam (for broadcast) and DVD (for home use).

The main point of this scenario is that, even though Premiere can do many things, it can sometimes pay to consider using more specialized tools for specialized tasks. In some cases, you can get better-looking titles in Photoshop, possibly better audio in Pro Tools, and a broader range of effects in After Effects than you can by using the corresponding tools in Premiere. Fortunately, Premiere is flexible enough to accommodate this sort of workflow by importing and exporting a variety of media formats.

The secondary point is that digital video is a robust format. It often looks good when it's originally shot, it can be made to look even better in Premiere, and it can be converted to other formats with little or no loss in quality.

You may rarely use as many external tools as are mentioned in this scenario - time and expense are definitely limiting factors. But if you do have other tools available, it's often worth considering what's to be gained by using them. It is always a good idea to search around and experiment.

These scenarios are just basic examples, of course. In some cases, your project may contain elements from all three. But if you plan to be doing a lot of video production work, you may want to think about these options as you decide what hardware and software you want to acquire and what outside resources you want to look into.

Using this Book

To make the best use of this book, you'll want to make sure that Premiere is already installed on your computer. The early chapters will guide you in getting Premiere set up and in learning your way around its interface. After that, each chapter will include step-by-step tutorials along with explanations of Premiere's features. We will be using general footage that can easily be shot by yourselves and captured on to your computer.

This book is not intended to be an exhaustive reference or bible of everything 'Premiere' - it doesn't include information on every single sub-menu item and dialog box. (For that information, your best source is the manual that came with the software.) Instead, this book will guide you through the tasks that you're most likely to perform in Premiere, and show you the best and easiest ways to do them.

Because this book is designed as a guide and not an encyclopedia, it's recommended that you read the chapters in sequence. If you don't have time to follow the tutorials, you could skip them and come back to them later, though this may cause you problems in later chapters, so be careful not to go too far ahead of yourself. You should definitely follow all of them at some point in order to get the full benefit of this book.

Most important, give yourself time to play! As you read about each new feature, follow along on your computer, try it out, and see what you can do with it. You can't learn to use any piece of software just by reading about it - least of all Premiere, which is geared toward using your senses and your creative impulses. Teaching yourself Premiere is one of those rare occasions when the learning process can be as fun as it is rewarding.

Summary

This chapter has served as a brief introduction to what Premiere is and how it fits into the video production process. We've seen:

- An outline of the tasks that can be completed within Premiere

- An introduction to analog and digital video, and the differences between them

- An overview of the video production process and how Premiere fits into it

Before we fully immerse ourselves in Premiere, it will be useful to know more about what happens before we edit our movie. Therefore, the next chapter covers exactly this topic.

02 Shooting Video

We've all heard that every picture tells a story and every film or video tells one too. But often the most unbelievable and fantastical story is the one that you don't see on-screen; the story of how the video came about the days; months or years of sweat, blood and tears that go hand in hand with the idea of putting together a video.

You've seen the 'behind the scenes' documentaries about big feature films, but you'd be wrong if you thought that your own smaller scale productions would be free of such backstage dramas. Producing a video of whatever length is a *big* challenge, but one you'll rise to with some planning, foresight, plenty of scribbling and of course, a little help from this chapter!

We saw a brief outline of the whole process in **Chapter 1**, and we'll go into a little more necessary detail later on, so you already know what part your forthcoming new skills in Premiere have in the grand scheme. But what if you're not just going to be editing this 24-frame masterpiece? What if you're being asked to plan and shoot it or what if you're not being asked, but just *want* to? Well, this chapter is designed to show you the rest of the process, empowering you to shoot the vid as well as edit it, and explaining how to make your life a little easier through sound production practices early on.

The Editor's Role

Depending on your circumstances, there are a number of positions you might find yourself in as a newly skilled video editor.

You might be intending to:

- Get hired as a freelance editor, brought in at the final stages of the production to put the piece together. Your involvement in the earlier stages of conception and production might be very limited, but your skills might add a final veneer to a polished project.

- Work as part of a production team from the outset, mainly involved in editing but with input in the earlier stages. You might work as an editor within a production company, or you might just work with a regular group of colleagues or friends to produce a video.

- Go it pretty much alone. You won't be the only person working on the video – that would be tough – but you could still be the director, producer and maybe even the cameraman all rolled into one!

As far as reading and benefiting from this chapter goes, the same applies whichever category you fall into, you'll just be approaching the issues covered here from a slightly different angle, and whether you're shooting the video yourself or getting someone else to do it, you'll need to understand these issues equally to make sure that the footage you find yourself working with is the best it possibly can be.

> *Remember, it doesn't matter how good your editing skills become by the end of this book, you'll still need great footage to work with. An editor is often only as good as his material and any editor worth his fee knows that without the right amount, type and quality of footage, you're editing blind!*

Let's have a brief look at the two main categories your editing will fall into: **editor-for-hire** and **one-man-show**.

The Editor as Post-Production Producer

In many production situations, the editor is in effect the post-production producer, overseeing this particular stage of the process. Yes, the director or producer may still be there supervising you, but you're on your home territory here and will have a great deal of control over the content of this stage both technical and creative.

The director may look to you to fix problems, improve sound (see **Chapter 8**) or design and apply visual effects (**Chapter 10**). As editor, you come into your own here, and although you fall into the first category above, you're a major force in the post-production stage.

It's important that at this early stage of your editing career you realise that whatever your overall role in the team, you form a huge part of the finished product, and wield an enormous amount of creative control, even if it's just in the latter stage of the video.

Maybe working as an editor might also encourage you to do your own thing at weekends, promoting yourself to director on your very own independent project.

The Editor as Director

If this video is going to be your baby, you'll want to know a lot more about how to plan and produce your video, so pay extra attention to the rest of this chapter. With Premiere you can easily and quickly edit your own desktop movies, and later, I'll show you the shortcuts to conceiving and creating your scenes for the edit.

If you fall into this category, then all creative control is yours, but so is the responsibility to turn your idea into a viable production, and you could say that once you're sitting in front of your computer with Premiere open, most of the work will be done!

For the rest of this chapter, I'll assume that you either plan to perform most of the main roles yourself or guide others and take a supervising role. For those of you who know a little about the production side already, you'll see how a little forethought for the edit can save you hours or days in editing time once the footage comes in.

You also might want some footage to work on throughout the book, so this is the best place to dream up an idea for a vid that you can work on for the next 450 pages. I'll be reminding you at every stage to take each piece of advice in this chapter and apply it to your own productions.

The Path to the Edit Suite

In **Chapter 1** we saw just how diverse the production process in full can be – from initial conception through to delivery of a coherent video, it can turn out to be an intensely long and drawn-out journey. The planning and execution of the many different phases we saw listed in the previous chapter can dictate how rough or smooth your days or weeks in the edit suite will be, and only a firm understanding of how it all comes together can save you from the gremlins and surprises that can turn a three-day edit into a fortnight of mayhem.

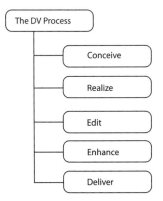

Work through the rest of this chapter as if you're planning and preparing for a production of your own, even if you don't need footage for the book, and you'll begin to understand how the footage arrives in the edit suite. Once you start thinking how your director or cameraman is thinking, those insights will serve you well when managing the final stage of the production process, and ensuring that your few days alone in the dark are a walk in the park.

Contextualizing Your Video

We established earlier that every video tells a story, and we all know that every story needs a beginning. Well, this is it, this is where your video project, whatever kind it is, takes its first breath.

If you're producing a video, you'll need to start by asking yourself two key questions:

- **Who** am I producing for?

- **What** kind of video am I producing?

> *You might think that "what kind of video am I producing?" would be the first question, but as you'll discover, video production (beyond those produced for your own amusement) is a highly audience-driven process. Once you know **who** it's for, everything else comes more naturally.*

Who Am I Producing For?

This is your first question. Who will be watching this video? Who asked you to make it? This often defines what kind of video you are producing, and usually defines how you produce it. Think about your audience and you have the key to making a great vid.

Certain audiences carry certain expectations. If you're producing a video for a company, for example, you'll need to gather background information about what the company does and who their audience is, because when you start producing a video for them, and when you start using your skills to tell their stories, *their* audience becomes *your* audience.

Be aware of the sensibilities of your audience and/or client and do your research. It'll save you time in the long run. Draw the line from an early stage between your creative powers and those dictated by your audience; be clear from the outset where you stand and how much scope you have.

In the edit, these factors will play a huge role. The same constraints and audience requirements that shape the conceptual stage and the shoot will impact on how you edit the piece together.

> *As an editor you can never have too much information. At whatever stage you're brought into a production, gather as much info as you can about the goals and about the audience of the production. The responsibility to fulfil those goals will often be largely down to you, even in a production where you've had limited pre-edit involvement.*

Once you have it in your mind who your vid is for, you need to give some thought to the shape your production will take. Very often, this too is dictated by the client or the intended audience, but often, such as the case of corporate videos, you might have scope to get across a certain message, with the exact delivery and nature of the video at your own discretion.

What Am I Producing?

OK, you've invested in Premiere, and maybe some camera equipment, and you're looking to DVision from friends of ED to teach you the ins and outs of the software. You must be quite serious about video, and this is a major step in your video career.

Throughout this career, you'll work on a variety of video projects, so now's the time to get familiar with the scope and the limitations of each.

Whether someone's said to you, "Hey, wanna edit my vid?" or you've thought to yourself, "Hey, I've got a great idea for a vid!", you'll want to know just how different each genre is, and how crucial it is to be familiar with these differences before you go any further.

If this is your baby project, you've got to test feasibility at this stage. It's no use writing a script with three dozen characters on a zero budget if you don't have that many actor-wannabe friends! And if you've been asked to produce by a client, you don't want to promise what you can't possibly deliver.

Video productions usually fall into one of the following categories:

- Instructional video

- Promotional video

- Documentary (aka Factual)

- Drama

These types overlap and contain many sub-types, so let's get a little more familiar with each in turn.

> *Later in the chapter, we'll look at the more practical aspects of shooting in various circumstances, including an in-depth look at filming interviews.*

Video to Teach

I won't dwell on this it's probably the least common of the types described. From an editor's point-of-view, this is not a type that'll cause you much in the way of problems. This type of production will be aiming to teach and instruct, usually of short duration, usually to the point and straightforward to produce, shoot and edit.

You have a pre-supplied narrative dictated by the process you are instructing on, and so your editing options are limited. Similarly, during production, you'll be mainly filming "things going on" without a huge degree of creative input. However, this only means that the conceptual stage of production is even more important.

You'll be looking to think about visual aids and graphics, possibly to be composed in Premiere, to spice up the production, and because you're dealing with reality, like two of the other categories listed, you'll have to pay special attention to the organisation. From an early stage, think about *who* you'll be filming, *what* they'll be doing, and what constraints these place on your shooting and editing.

Instructional Video – Suggested Components

- Demonstrations / Tutorials

- Graphics and text illustrations

- Narration

Video to Promote

As a video editor, you'll probably find a lot of your time is spent on material that promotes in one way or another. You could be promoting a cola company, your friend's band, or your own skills by way of a showreel. Either way, producing promotional video is very tricky, involving in-depth pre-planning and knowledge of your subject.

> *Promotional video, corporate or non-commercial, is about message delivery more than it is about message presentation.*

When taking on or devising a promotional project, in addition to the target audience, you'll need to think about:

- ■   What the core message is

- ■   What you need to show to get that message across

- ■   How best to show it

And also...

- ■   How much live footage will you need?

- ■   How to stage material "as live" so you can exert greater control over it

Now, you might be the thinking the last one's a little sneaky, but I can guarantee you, practically every promotional video will take liberties with actuality. It's not sneaky, it's vital, and often it will simply mean recreating something that would otherwise be impossible or difficult to film.

From an editor's perspective, promotional video is always difficult to cut together, because you will need to rely heavily on editing techniques to best get that message across. In effect, just like with an advertisement on TV, you're selling something – a company, a person or just an idea – and before you start arranging shooting dates, you'll have to think ahead to what you'll need to achieve that.

Promotional Video – Suggested Elements

- Live shots of subject

- Dramatised shots

- Graphics

- Considerable effects shots

- Narrative

- Music

*For these last two types of video, you're likely to be working for a client and from a document known as a **Brief**. This will outline the objectives of the project, and in order to earn your fee from this project, you'll need to stick to that mandate. Sometimes, you'll prepare this brief yourself and pitch it to your client, other times, you will be provided with this. When working with a client you might be expected to pitch a few ideas for their approval, and the success of this presentation might be the difference between you getting the contract or losing it to another producer.*

Documenting with Video

Video documentary is one of the most widespread kinds (heck, there's even two Oscar categories for it!) and in your career as a video editor or producer you'll probably have to put together a documentary or two.

Documentary is less about creating and more about **capturing**. You're still painting a picture on video but reality provides the palette. As an editor, you'll need to make sure that you have enough footage to tell the story you've set out to tell. How you arrange that footage in Premiere is hugely important; you can sway your audience one way or another just by organising your clips differently. Usually, you also have to balance the storytelling with **objectivity**.

Your subject might be a person, a place, or a general theme. Your angle is also up to you, but subjective documentaries need to be backed with plenty of research and hard facts to maintain credibility.

> We'll look at conceiving a short documentary in more detail in our case study in the next section.

Documentary – Suggested Elements

- Testimonies/interviews

- Narration

- Occasional music

- Stills/photographs

- Illustrative footage

- Occasional effects shots

Dramatized Video

This is maybe the section you've been most looking forward to. The majority of videographers relish the chance to do drama of some sort – their own scaled-down feature film – and if as an editor you start having ideas about your own productions, then this is probably how they'll take shape. Drama is the sexiest and most exciting video genre to work in, but it is undoubtedly the one most fraught with pitfalls and obstacles.

The world is a big and complex place, and much as it's difficult to *capture* the world in a video documentary, it's even harder to *recreate* that world in fiction. You need people and places and words for them to say you have to do it all. The drama is a blank canvas, and every second of the time spent planning, organising and worrying over a drama production is worth it once you've painted your own little piece of imagined reality on the little or big screen!

Video drama throws away the rules you have to work with in the other genres and introduces a few of its own, mostly relating to resources. Can you afford actors, can you customise sets and locations, or do you have to work within the constraints of a next-to-zero budget?

Drama – Suggested Elements

- The sky's the limit it's up to you! You'll probably need actors, more cameras and crew, and a script this time (maybe even some music) but it all depends on the scope of your story!

Conceive Your Project

A big part of shooting and editing a drama comes from the script, and we'll be going through this in more detail in the next section. Firstly, though, it's about time I gave you something to do!

OK, blah blah blah with the theory; let's get you thinking about a project you can work on for the remainder of the book. I'm going to have to make a few assumptions, so let's say the most viable projects here for you are either documentary or drama. For the purposes of a consistent case study, let's go for a short drama. It'll give you all the scope in the world and it needn't be very complicated.

1. Start by having an idea.

What do you mean, it's not that simple? Everything has to come from somewhere; sure you can wait for the flash of inspiration, but why not spark up that flash yourself?

Here's some starting points:

- Think of your last scene. Imagine a really cool ending. OK, at this stage maybe it's a mish-mash of bits of other films you've seen, but once you've worked out who's in that scene and why they got there, you have the basis of your own little picture, and by the time you get to scripting the end, you'll have changed it to something more original anyway.

- Flick through your address book, and pick a name. This is your main character. What does he or she do? Why is he or she interesting? This may form the basis of your plot!

- Think of a place or a landmark and build a scene around it, then work your story backwards or forwards from that. Keep it small but interesting for the time being.

- Think of an unusual situation for an opening scene. Anything will do; what would get your interest if you were a viewer? Think of a hook! A sci-fi story I once wrote began with an image of a Rover 75 car racing through the streets of Victorian London; maybe not a viable low-budget video but you get the idea. Think of something to confuse or intrigue the viewer to begin with. It'll draw them into the story and it'll set your imagination racing onto page two of your script.

2. Next step; write it down. Typing up a document in Word outlining your idea simply isn't fashionable. Write it on a bus ticket or on a scrap of paper, that's much more creative.

3. That's it for now! OK, so that wasn't a huge exercise, but if you now have an early idea of what your video is going to be about, then you're well on your way.

> *Conceiving a documentary is a little different to drama, so let's sit down and open our notebooks for the first of several mini-masterclasses.*

Mini-Masterclass – Preparing a Treatment

Whereas the drama begins with an idea and a plot, a documentary has the idea and then a **treatment**. This is a short one or two page document outlining the subject matter and the source materials for the production. This short section will give you all the information you need to prepare one in a flash.

- The treatment should only be written after some research. You'll know what your video is about and you'll have already thought about what it would contain. The treatment is made up of the following elements.

- **Program Information** – the title and duration of your project.

- **Focus** – this encapsulates the theme of your documentary in one sentence. Narrow everything down until you have one definitive line to describe the programme you are going to make. Examples might be "An examination of the psychology of cats" or "A retrospective of the career of actor Paul Eddington". Your video will need a solidly grounded focus if it is to stand out.

- **Audience** – define and describe who you are aiming the documentary at. If it's easier, try to think about where it would fit into the TV schedules; is it primetime, is it late-night, is it mainstream or niche? Use a few sentences.

- **Resumé** – the real meat of your documentary. Describe in 10-20 lines what the video is about. To carry on our examples, describe what's so interesting about cat psychology or who Paul Eddington played during his career.

- **Sources** – where are you going to get material from? This might be the findings of a new report on cat thought processes, or diaries and letters from the family of Paul Eddington. Anywhere you might gather information from people to interview, records, archive footage, and so on...

- **Suggested Elements** – finally, this is where you list the central components of your video. These might include a presenter or narrator, interviews, reconstructions, or film clips, and these form the creative basis for telling your factual story.

Once completed, you can present your documentary treatment to TV companies for commissioning or if you plan to produce it yourself, it will form the basis for a storyboard and shot list in the next section.

> We've put together a production pack (downloadable from our web site) to take away some of the tedium from your planning process; you'll find some templates and printable documents commonly used in the pre-production stages of professional video, from storyboard sheets which you can print out and use, to an empty treatment template you can fill in.

From Script (to Storyboard) to Screen

We're now officially into the proper pre-production stage. You're definitely producing a video in a set genre, you just need to figure out how! Ultimately, it's here that you determine the shape your video is going to take, and how many of your original creative ideas will be eaten up by harsh shooting realities.

As a video producer, your greatest skill has to be balancing **idealism** with **pragmatism** – what you really want to do balanced with what you can realistically achieve. In pre-production you'll start asking the questions that help you perform that balancing act later on!

We've covered the framework in which you'll be making your video, and the options you have, whether chosen or imposed by a client or other producer, let's start developing the project idea you scribbled down in the last section (what do you mean, you've lost it?).

Writing a Script

All dramas need to start with a script, in the same way that other types of videos follow a treatment or a brief. If you're writing this yourself, you've got a great opportunity to think ahead and save yourself some time later on down the line.

Once the idea is there ("diminutive cop joins circus to infiltrate crime ring" or "girl wakes up to find she has amnesia and can't remember how she got it") you need to flesh it out. We're beyond the realms of bus tickets and scraps of paper here, you'll need much more structure for your script.

However you write this little masterpiece, there are some ingredients you'll need, and they're fairly obvious:

- Plot

- Characters

- Narrative (beginning, middle and end, not necessarily in that order though!)

And tying it all together...

> With a great story you can enthrall your audience every bit as much as the latest Hollywood blockbuster. Stories are what drive movies, and video dramas too; good watchable characters, a good plot and some humour, and your viewers will never notice that the picture quality's a bit grainy and that the cast are all members of your family!

- Motivations – the driving forces which carry your characters or the situations they find themselves in, forward towards the conclusion of the story.

The path from start to finish is up to you. Many editors-turned-director naturally like to play with flow and narrative, using editing skills in the script to jumble events and build up complex sequences and interwoven story strands.

Put yourself in the viewer/reader's place; what's happening in this story to make it interesting, what's keeping you hooked? If your friends weren't your friends, would they still be interested in seeing your video? Don't worry, your project doesn't always have to be a life-changing cinematic experience, but always keep the viewer in mind – keep them glued to the edge of their seats.

> Remember that it's not just wholesale dramas that have scripts. Documentaries and promotional videos might all have reconstructed or dramatised elements. All the following tips apply whatever kind of vid your scripted scenes are for.

Your plot and your characters make your script come to life, so once you have a few people in the story and a few scenes, you can start writing it down. With that in mind, let's get straight back into your own project, and carry it forward a little more.

Fleshing Out Your Idea

You have your idea, but you now need to turn it into a great but workable script.

1. A script generally has three main components:

- Dialog
- Stage directions
- Technical instructions

The first one is obvious. The stage directions are instructions to your cast; movements, expressions, anything. The technical instructions tell the filmmakers what's going on; they might refer to locations of scenes, some background music, or sound effects.

2. Time to plan out your first scene. Even if you haven't totally finalized your story, drafting a first (or even last) scene could give you the flash of inspiration you're waiting on.

3. Open up a new text document in your preferred word processor or text editor and follow the layout of the diagram.

Now, let's pencil in the scene you have in mind.

4. Start with the scene number or some kind of identifier – for example, a pre-title sequence. You'll need to refer to scenes somehow in the shooting and editing stages, and maybe also include the approximate length.

`SCENE 1 - PRE-TITLE SEQUENCE - APPROX. 1 MIN`

5. Start off with the **location** and the **time of day**. You will also need to note any other major scene factors here. For example, are the characters going to be talking about the awful weather? In that case, it had better be cloudy or rainy!

You should also note whether it's indoors (INT.) or outdoors (EXT.)

`EXT. NIGHT. SATURDAY NIGHT ON BUSY CITY STREET`

6. Is there any **music** or **sound**?

`AMBIENT BACKGROUND NOISE OF NIGHTCLUBS AND DISCOS SPILLING ONTO THE STREETS. ECHOES OF DANCE MUSIC.`

7. Where is your camera; what's it looking at?

```
TRACKING SHOT TWO GIRLS WALKING ALONG STREET TOWARDS CAMERA
```

8. Now, after establishing what the camera is watching, establish what is happening. We now lapse into **stage directions**, which we'll keep in lower case (with character names in CAPS).

```
Two girls, PAMELA and JULIA have just left a disco and are laugh-
ing and giggling. As they get closer to the camera, a third girl -
CHANTAL - comes into view from the right, out of breath. PAMELA
and JULIA clearly know her.
```

> *Also remember to include any important facts about your cast, just as you would if you were writing a short story or novel. But before you write "PAMELA is wearing jeans", ask yourself if it actually matters? If there's no relevance to what the characters are wearing then you don't need to worry about it for the moment, but if the video is called "Pamela's Jeans" then you might want to establish them early on!*

9. Next, your **dialog**. Dialog's tricky, in that very few people generally ever write in a manner that people would speak. Try it, and what you'll have will be virtually unreadable. Rather, plenty of practice and rehearsing will allow your cast to naturalize any dialog you give them.

```
JULIA:          Chantal, what's wrong?

CHANTAL:    You'll never guess who I just saw!
```

And so on...

10. Other optional things to include in your scripted scenes:

- Captions

- Effects

- Transitions

These are all things handled in Premiere, but as an editor/producer you'll know to plan them as far in advance as possible. For example, if you plan on a title fading up over the last few seconds of that piece of dialog, you'll need to ensure that your cast don't stop performing after the last word.

As you'll see when we cover shooting in more detail, you need to think about the edit at every stage, to make sure you get yourself enough footage, of the right quality, to do your job in Premiere.

11. OK, I'll leave you to get working on your script. It might be one scene or a feature-length drama, but whatever it is, think carefully about these last few pointers:

- For a first drama, generally keep it short. A page of script usually works out to about a minute on-screen, so keep your first script under ten if you can. The experience you gain while seeing this one through to a polished final production will serve you well when you turn your attention to 90 – or – 120 page monsters!

- What is this whole script going to require, in terms of people, money, locations, effects and so on? Can it be done?

- What resources do you have? Back to the old question of size-of-cast vs number-of-willing-friends.

- Be adventurous; it really is true that the sky's the limit, but scout out adventurous locations (see later) before making them an inseparable part of your script.

- Think in pictures. We're about to look at storyboarding, which is essential whether you're working on your own script or producing someone else's. But if you're writing your own, it pays to think visually. If from the start, your words on the page accompany images in your head, then you've got a headstart on the whole production process.

> *Above all, remember that you shouldn't rely on Premiere for editing out unwanted material from your video. If there are scenes you're not going to use, best to decide that at the script stage, then you don't need to go to the bother or expense of shooting. Don't edit your **script** in Premiere!*

Thinking in pictures is great, but planning in pictures is essential, so let's have a look at the filmmaker and videographer's greatest planning tool – the **storyboard**.

Storyboarding Your Video

Storyboarding is an essential creative tool, the stepping-stone between those words on the page and the screen; a trigger for ideas and a place to store them. It's also an essential planning tool.

Much as you can build shooting instructions and details into your script, the storyboard animates those ideas for you and gives you a visual frame of reference.

Whether or not you're a good artist, the storyboard is equally useful. It's not about how well you can draw, it's about what you convey, and there's no rule that says your storyboards need to be understandable by everyone. As long as you know what you're getting at, then you've hit the mark.

> *Many modern feature films now use* **animatics** *to plan out and visualize complex scenes; these are short animations, often quickly computer-generated, which also show pace in addition to movement and camera angles.*
>
> *Something else you might want to think about is a* **sketchbook** *where you can jot down ideas and suggestions for shots, angles, scenes ... anything you like. It could be that a hastily drawn shot in your sketchbook could form the beginnings of your next big script!*

You could approach a storyboard in one of two ways:

- Storyboard everything, practically shot by shot – big feature films do this, but when single shots can take weeks to get and thousands of dollars to shoot, you kind of need this level of planning.

- Storyboard only the key scenes – this is your path for the time being, unless you're planning an expensive or particularly complex video. Scenes best for storyboarding in this way are those which involve a very special location (where rehearsals and reshoots might be limited by time), action scenes that will false-start unless planned properly, title sequences, or any other scene which involves choreography (and I don't just mean dancing!)

Take this end shot from my first drama.

Now, although a kiss isn't something you can storyboard to death, without it getting icky, that shot was only the last stage of a very mobile sequence.

- **Stage 1**: Camera facing straight along bridge – Lisa and Eldon hugging

- **Stage 2**: Lisa and Eldon part, still holding hands

- **Stage 3**: Camera gently approaches and swings round Lisa's shoulder

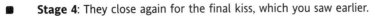
- **Stage 4**: They close again for the final kiss, which you saw earlier.

The scene was shot in a large park in Glasgow, and we were at the mercy of the weather and the general public. If we didn't know exactly what we wanted before we got there, we could never have achieved what we had to shoot in those few minutes that we managed to clear the bridge for the long shot.

Later, we'll be covering how to scout out your locations, and in some instances this will need to come before the storyboard, depending on the kind of things you hope to shoot. You'll be using storyboards often to plan an exact framing of an exact shot, and sometimes you'll find that all you have to do is follow the storyboard and set the camera rolling.

This is the final shot from the same film, where the characters walk over the horizon. Once there was a storyboard, it really was as simple as telling Nicola and Andy (my lovely actors) to walk and pressing REC on the camera. That sequence pretty much shot itself as a result of a little scouting and forward planning.

The last thing you'd want to feel, though, is constrained by a storyboard. It's only a guide and you're allowed to change your mind. It's there to encourage you to think your production out in pictures and to save you time on the day. In one video I worked on, the most finely planned storyboarded sequence was binned in the edit suite, because it looked rubbish when we put it together! The storyboard is your friend, but don't let it boss you around. Take an eraser and some blank storyboard sheets with you on the shoot and improvize if you need to!

What to Include in a Storyboard

The level of detail you include on a story is up to you. We've provided a blank storyboard sheet for you in the downloadable production pack, but you can just use this as a guide if you want something with more detail. Some storyboards have boxes where you can record video and audio elements needed for each shot – this is often a great idea!

The basic elements are:

- **Framing** – where is the camera? You should be experimenting with shots when you scout out your locations (see later) so unless things change on the day, the position of your camera in the storyboard is how it'll be on film.

- **Placing of characters** – where are your cast, where are they looking, what are they doing? Check your script, but give them scope to improvise on set. If they move, draw some arrows.

> *Don't let your storyboards get too static; remember you're producing a live action piece of work. This isn't still life or a photography exhibit. Bring your pictures to life; make them show action, motion and transition.*

- **Environmental factors** – what else is there in shot that you need? Is it a bright or dark shot? If it's outdoors, are there any 'actors' in the environment; clouds, trees, buildings? In this next shot, we specifically wanted the building in the background – a later sequence is set there – and we wanted a grim mood. Translated into reality on the day of the shoot, we balanced the shot of the building with the clouds provided courtesy of Mother Nature to achieve a great effect.

> *If you're banking on uncontrollable forces, like the weather, or if you have a wishlist in that area, show them on your storyboard – record everything you need, want or hope for, then on the day of the shoot you can be more focused on how to achieve it all.*

- **Camera motion** – you've seen from our example how important it was to plan and choreograph camera actions. Usually, you do this with arrows. It's especially important to plan where the viewer's "eye" will be going because if you're moving the camera around, you'll need to keep crew, microphones, lights and other cameras out of shot.

The more of your video that you plan out like this, whether on paper or even partly in your head, the greater the sense you'll have of the look, feel, style and flow of the final video. If you've thought your whole picture through, you might be thinking, "If I can only get exactly what's in my head onto the screen, it'll be great." If that's the case you're on the right track, and whatever the shooting problems and unforeseen traumas, if you stick to your ideals, and back them up with resolute planning, you'll get there!

Storyboarding for Documentary

You might be thinking that storyboarding is exclusively a dramatic necessity. Well, you'd be wrong. Most documentaries are (or could benefit from being) storyboarded. In the same way that you set out to produce scenes and shoot footage for drama, so you do with documentary. We've seen how to produce a treatment, and set out our suggested elements and sources. Well, you'll want to plan out how you're going to get them.

As well as interviews and testimonies, you'll have background shots, footage of whatever your subject is, and you'll need to storyboard what material you want to get.

Assisting you and reinforcing the storyboard in a documentary production is a **shot list**. This is exactly what it says it is – a list of shots you want to get. On occasions when it doesn't really matter how you shoot your subject (the angle, the camera movement and so on), a shot list features all the shots you hope to get when you go filming.

Because you're documenting reality, in many ways you need a better idea of your intentions, because your chances for reshoots might be limited. As with drama, the best way to make the most of your shooting time is to plan it to death and save yourself a lot of time and money.

If you work from a storyboard and shot list together, you can quite easily reconcile these to keep a record of all the footage you've shot; this can be crucial if you end up with a dozen tapes full of material.

Drafting a Storyboard

Let's get back to your own project, which you can hopefully work on throughout the book. Whether your video has one scene or twenty, you'll want to draw some pretty pictures.

1. Decide whether you want to storyboard the whole video or just the key scenes. If you have mainly static shots, you might want to leave them off the storyboard, but if there are complex sequences of any kind, even just with a few actors at once or with a moving camera, get them on paper!

2. Print off and photocopy the blank storyboard sheet provided in the production pack, and pick your first storyboarded scene. It's usually best to always storyboard the first scene, as it's normally pretty important to the overall vid.

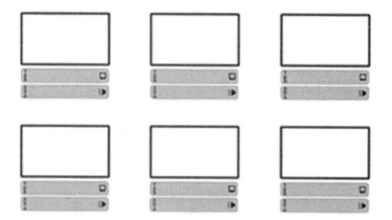

3. Make sure your pictures include all the elements that each shot *needs* – it's no good having a blank background if the shot needs to take place in a certain place.

4. Gather as much information as you can about your prospective locations – if you'd rather, leave certain storyboards until we cover locations and scouting in the next section.

5. Once you've done a few frames on the storyboard, you'll begin to get a sense of how your vid, however simple or complex, will look on screen, even if the cast are only matchstick characters at the moment.

   Often running concurrently with the development of your storyboard are the remaining pre-production elements of casting, finding crew, getting equipment, and managing choice of locations. Once you've decided on all these things, maybe you can add some more colour to your storyboard!

Turning Your Fiction Into Reality

Hopefully you've been shamelessly ambitious and idealistic in your script ideas and your early storyboards, but you've probably also been keeping a pragmatic eye on what's feasible for your production.

Although it's no use thinking, "Oh well, I only know one actor friend so I can only make my video a monolog." The time is now upon you to start putting faces to parts and filling in those blank backgrounds in your storyboard with real locations.

Whatever genre you're producing for, you'll need to take these steps to make it happen:

- Nail down where you need to film, how to get there, and how to customize the location for your shooting.

- Pinpoint who you need to film and when, and think about how to organise your cast and crew's time.

- Figure out what equipment you need to physically pull off the shoot. Aim high, and you should hopefully always get the bare minimum.

Finding the Money

You'll be saddened but not surprised to hear there's no sure and fast way to get finance for your video. If you're working *for* someone there may be a budget, but if you're producing on your own, it's a little more tricky.

Producing on a zero budget is done so often that you shouldn't be disheartened, but if you can find money from somewhere, then the production will be the better for it. For a short video that you might be entering into competition, for example, sponsors are often the best way. The winner of the BAFTA for best short film two years ago was one such production; backing from a raft of small sponsors gave the production team the money they needed for cameras and the like, but you're never going to have enough.

The money issue reinforces just how important it is not to waste shooting time. If you're hiring equipment by the day, you'd better not. Get there, get your shots, as dictated by the script, storyboard and shot list, and get the equipment back.

As a video producer, even more so than as an editor, you'll also find your life heavily constrained by time; yours and other people's. That said, you'll be surprised just how cooperative people will be, and how responsive they can be to the camera. That piece of equipment can be your ticket to a host of freebies, so be ambitious and be audacious and you'll be amazed what you can get for free

Finding the People

The next obstacle you have is finding the people. If you're working as part of a production company, you'll more than likely have colleagues to work on camera/lights/sound, but if you're freelancing or working on your own project, you'll need a crew – and in the case of drama, you'll need a cast.

Take the time to sit down and figure out *who* you'll need to carry the production through. In many ways, the cast is the easy part; at least you know how many people you need. The crew can be a deceptively large contingent. It all depends on the scale of your production, and often can be as much about sheer manpower than skills. Even if you are trained to use camera, sound and lighting equipment, you can't hold a big microphone and the camera at the same time. And what if you need more than one camera?

This is often where friends come in, but beware not to fray good relationships by putting your friends under too much pressure. If you have the resources, you might be able to hire other freelancers, or you might have the resources to hire actors. It's often mutually beneficial to all parties to work on a decent video project. For budding or training actors, it's a notch on their acting belt, for technical crew (maybe also training), it's something else on their showreel.

A small checklist of likely people would include:

- Cast

- Cameraman (unless it's you!)

- Soundman

- Lighting Technician

- Production Assistants – to help out with equipment/organisation

You probably want a driver amongst those – getting equipment around the place can be an unexpected production pain! But where are you going? That's next on the list...

Finding the Places

Many producers and videographers underestimate the need for good (if not great) locations in any picture. At the very least they need to be accommodating and suitable for your purposes, but with a little effort, you can end up shooting in some great places.

If you're working on a documentary or promo vid, these are kind of decided for you, but if you're making drama, they fall into the scope of your script, and it's another great asset of the old storyboard – it gets you thinking about setting and locale!

Whatever your genre, you need to get permission and cooperation to use most locations (unless you happen to own large amounts of property). Again, you'd be surprised how helpful people can be, but don't take advantage. If you need to film on private property, contact the owner of the property or location well in advance and discuss the project; it's generally best not to just turn up. You'll usually find that people will be quite responsive to a request to film, and usually go out of their way to assist. If there's anything else you need, let them know.

Filming in public places is usually a bit trickier. Always try to find a quiet spot to film; try to pick a quiet time, or have some members of the production team politely ask passers-by to wait a few moments till the shot is finished.

This video was shot in the busiest park in Glasgow, but in the script it was supposed to be empty. A little patience and a spare production member on hand to deal with the public, and we pulled off quite a deception.

At all times, bear in mind the following:

- Always speak to whoever's in charge

- If it's a public facility (like a swimming pool) you may be asked to sign that you take responsibility for the shoot

- Remind whoever you speak to that their assistance is appreciated

- Don't overstay your welcome

- Don't make things awkward or difficult – remember, life goes on for others whether you're filming or not

- Pay attention to safety at all times;

- Lastly, thank them in the credits!

Mini-Masterclass – Reconnaissance

Scouting your locations can make or break your production. You don't want to carry £5000 worth of equipment to location ten miles away only to find they don't have power sockets for your lights and there are no windows!

Here's what you need to know:

- Visit your location well in advance, especially if a large part of the production relies on it. If, for example, you're doing a documentary about a library, then as well as getting permission to film there, make sure it's practical!

- The last thing you want are any surprises, so think about this scouting mission as if it were the actual shoot; if possible, take some of the equipment with you – if that's not practical, make a list of what conditions you'll need to pull off the shoot (sound, lighting, backdrops and so on).

- If it's not possible to take along your production camera with you, try to take some kind of camera – a camcorder or even a still camera – to get some shots of the area, as much for reference back home as for testing purposes.

- Pay particular attention to lighting conditions. What are the natural lights like? How many windows are there? Grab a member of the production team, or a random person in the vicinity, and place them in some likely areas, checking how the camera picks them up.

- Also pay attention to background noise and sound conditions. If there's too much noise, ask around to see what can be done about it. Is there music in the background of your location – can it be turned off? Do some sound-recording tests with your microphones, if you have them with you.

- When you get back with the test footage, you'll want to be able to see how your subject (which on the day may be your actor) appears *and* sounds. If the results are bad, you may have to think about a new location, or about returning to tweak the conditions as much as circumstances permit.

- Wherever you're planning to film, *what*ever you're planning to film, make a quick map of the room or immediate area. Sit your lights on that map, and place your cameras. Test different arrangements. Lighting conditions and even furniture will often dictate where your equipment can go, depending on how portable it all is. Position all your cameras on the map, and try out angles. If you're planning some moving cameras, work out a motion path. Where can your cameraman move? Will he cast shadows? Will he trip over and break your (or worse, someone else's) camera?

> In this example, when we were filming in a potentially very awkward situation for a documentary about a pub quizmaster, we made a map of where our lights, camera and microphones would go, and also planned out where quiz participants (and also the furniture) would be.

- It's so important I'll mention it twice – make sure there's adequate power sockets for your equipment. If there aren't, you need to know *now* so you can stock up on batteries and go to plan B.

- Think *safety* above all. You'll be using cameras, maybe power cables for lights, tripods and other accident-prone pieces of hardware. Keep anyone who's not in the production out of harm's way, and be sure to inform any local first-aiders that you're there.

- Lastly, if you haven't fully decided on exactly where in your location to shoot, this reconnaissance is vital for scouting out possible parts of the building/street/whatever to use. Look for nice backdrops and well-lit spaces; you'd be surprised at the great video locations hidden away in the most unlikely of places!

After the reconnaissance or scout, you might be getting a better idea of the look of your video. Suddenly, your vid looks that little bit more *real*. But there's one more thing to think about...

Finding the Equipment

This is largely down to what kind of project and your current set-up. But give some thought to the kind of things you'll need for the task at hand.

How many cameras will you need? For a drama, you'll need more than one for it to be convincing – it's the multi-angles and reverse shots that will make your drama come to life. For documentary or any other type, you can get away with just the one, although you'll still require a varied amount of shots to make it interesting. A common practice is to take along a smaller, maybe lower quality camcorder to shoot cutaway shots and background footage. Often, such shots are treated (maybe slowed down or reduced to black-and-white) for effect, so the slightly poorer quality of the footage won't matter.

Depending on your locations you might need some kind of lighting equipment, but this doesn't necessarily need to be heavy (although the high-end stuff certainly is!). Portable hand-held lamps or the kind that can sit on top of your camera might be enough to light a single subject. The same goes for sound, and we'll be covering the different types in the sound section shortly, but the most important thing is to make sure you use it wisely, and practice with what you have to get the best results.

The great thing about DV is that it's making the whole video process a lot easier to break into, and for the price of a DV camera and Premiere you can really make waves in video. If you want or need more high-end equipment, you don't have to buy it. You can rent it economically, or join a local film club and benefit from special hiring rates. If you're a student in the field, you could always ask to borrow equipment from your college or university – they'll usually be very helpful (hey, that's what I used to do!).

*Remember, the less equipment you can afford, or carry, the more creative you need to be with what your surroundings and locations naturally provide, and the craftier you need to be with your application. Don't ever feel constrained by your equipment or lack of it – if you only have a tiny camera and nothing else, some ingenuity and the delights of Premiere can still help you make a mini-masterpiece. Think **big**, aim **high**, and remember that begging and borrowing can get you anywhere!*

Getting Your Shoot Together

Let's think about your own video project for a moment and apply what we've seen to the vid you might be preparing for the rest of the book.

1. Jot down what you'll need to carry your video off. Think about money, people, locations and equipment. What do you have immediate access to? Who could you rope in to help you?

2. Start taking steps to bring it all together. Contact your crew and consider your cast. For this little project, you'll probably be looking at friends, but if not, put the word round local drama schools that you'd like to shoot a film.

3. Decide on your locations and scout them out. Bear in mind all the things we've discussed – stay focused on the reality, be practical, and visit *all* your locations to test out footage, to practice and to assess suitability.

4. OK, we've spent aeons planning this thing, but it'll serve you well on the day. Time to gather all that stuff together. Looking at your polished storyboard, your shot lists, your roster of cast and crew, focus on what *needs* to be achieved on the day. Get your equipment ready, check your batteries, make sure you have enough tapes (these are common pitfalls!) and ensure you have transport to and from the location. Make contingency plans for bad weather – take along some protection for the equipment and some umbrellas just in case. Find somewhere you and the rest of the team can have lunch, all this kind of thing – last minute stuff we always forget!

Enough talk, time to start shooting! But do make sure you test *all* the gear before leaving home!

Shoot the Video!

There are three areas you'll need some knowledge of if you're going to shoot your own video, even if you actually intend someone else to be physically holding the gear. These are camera, lighting and sound – you guessed those, right?

At all times, aim for the perfect shoot, and you'll always get, at the very least, what you came for. The best general shooting-day tip I can give you is to manage your time properly. If you have five minutes of footage to get in one particular place, it will *not* just take five minutes to get! You have to arrive there, set up, check out the equipment, put the batteries in, angle the lights, warm up your actors or interviewee … the list is endless.

The great thing is, the amount of planning you've put into the thing will start paying off here, because you'll have a much better idea of what needs doing and how long it'll take. Extra shooting days can be a pain though, and expensive if you're hiring people or equipment, so make the absolute most of what you have and get on with shooting some great material.

If there's drama happening on this shoot, then you need to think about spending quality time with your cast in the role of director. There will also undoubtedly be lots of retakes. You probably can't afford to be there all day getting that perfect single take, but again, do balance your ideals with reality and get the best take you can without sacrificing the quality of the rest of your scenes.

However much you've planned, there will be some surprises, good and bad. Be prepared to improvize and make the best of what you're presented with. If the weather's bad, are there back-up scenes you can shoot indoors instead? You might even want to storyboard a few versions of key scenes if they rely heavily on the uncontrollable.

React to the unexpected and think on the fly. In the scene illustrated here, we had been filming a character scene with our angel character – Lisa – indoors, and when we left, we noticed a huge stone angel atop the building across the street!! Needless to say we concocted a short scene to make the most of that!

Getting the Most from the Camera

The camera itself is your ticket to great-looking material in Premiere. As you know, once the footage is there on your desktop, you have a huge amount of control over it, but carefully and skilfully shot material is essential if you want a polished video. The editor is powerless to 'invent' a great shot that was never filmed, or fill in the gaps when the provided footage doesn't quite fit together or gel.

Tip number one – *get enough stuff*! On a basic scale, this means shoot some extra at the start and end of each scene; don't just turn the camera off when the last line is spoken – what if you want to fade out and need a few seconds more? To a wider extent this means making sure you get enough background footage, illustrative shots and establishing shots. These should form part of your storyboard or shot list, but as a rule, when you shoot somewhere, grab a few minutes of general footage of the surrounding area – if it's a building, get an exterior shot to establish where your characters are. As an editor, you'll need these shots to build a flowing and coherent piece in Premiere.

Practice with the camera and get used to the **focusing**; you'll want all your shots to be properly focused. If you're shooting an interviewee or actor, try zooming in on the eyes, and focusing there, then pulling back. This should ensure that the whole figure is properly focused before recording begins.

Before you start shooting, zoom in on the closest part of your subject you expect to film, usually the eyes - then focus the camera.

Now zoom out and from now on, no matter how much you zoom in and out during shooting, your focus will stay accurate!

If your camera has a feature known as white balance, this is a great tool for improving the color of your footage – something many ignore. The white balance feature involves demonstrating to the camera what "white" looks like in the conditions you're in; from there it extrapolates what other colours should look like! Ordinarily you'll need something white to calibrate it, so keep some white paper or card with your camera.

Following your storyboard, choose the right kind of camera angle and handling for the shot you want. If you want a rugged look to the vid, you might go for handheld throughout, but for documentary this would generally be unusual, so keep a tripod at the ready. Be prepared to engage with your scene if the action dictates it, but *have someone spot you* to make sure you don't trip or fall when your eyes are on the viewfinder!

The key to good camerawork is **framing** – put simply, how you frame the action in your viewfinder, and how the camera sees your scene.

Mini-Masterclass – Framing

The basics of capturing the action with your camera, however big or small:

- Arrange the action within your shot. In conjunction with your storyboarding efforts, place your cast and your scenery in shot the way you would brush them into a painting. Composing the scenes and arranging the 'actors', whether living or not, is one of the keys to getting a good shot!

- Give your subjects headroom and keep them central unless the scene dictates otherwise.

- If there's any extra information your shot needs to convey, pointers as to a location for example, frame the shot appropriately to include all the viewer needs to see.

■ Think about how your scene needs to be viewed – how close should you be, from what angle. Do we want the camera to appear to be 'watching' the characters or just plainly recording events?

■ Use the right distance of shot for the right occasion. Zoom in to capture an emotion, or keep your distance to observe objectively.

The next mini-masterclass on interviews also includes some more documentary-specific framing tips.

Mini-Masterclass – Shooting Interviews

Interviews will form an integral part of your video career in almost every genre except drama. Here's the core information to help you get that perfect interview:

- Prepare your questions well in advance and if it's a pre-arranged interview you're shooting (as opposed to interviews on the street), send a copy to your interviewee.

- You'll need to get the answers you want, so be sure to word each question so that the interviewee needs to give more than just a yes or no answer. For example, instead of "do you like cats?", ask "what is it you like about cats?". The phrasing of your question will determine how much information a potentially shy interviewee will give you.

- Once you're with your interview candidate, be sure to warm them up, and make them feel at ease with the situation – they might well be nervous.

- Decide where to place the interview and set up your camera (almost certainly on a tripod) accordingly. Perhaps get some footage of the interviewee arriving at the location or other material to intersperse with the talking.

- Before or after the interview, get some reverse angle shots of the interviewer – they're a bit tacky but almost everyone uses these at some point. Get the shots anyway in case you need to cutaway material in the edit.

- When framing your subject, give him or her "looking room"; that is, a little extra space on the side they're facing. Allow space for hands and zoom back if they need to show anything to camera.

- Also, take any opportunities that arise, to think ahead to the editing and compositing of your video. In this next shot, myself and my co-producer thought our interviewee's monitor might be a good place for a superimposed graphic, so we specially line it up to be pretty much square to camera.

- You might find the need at some point in your video career to collect and edit vox pops (shortened from the Latin *vox populi* – 'voice of the people') – these are short sharp interviews collected from the general public – you must have seen them. They require a few special preparations.

- From an editing perspective, if these are going to be cut together, you'll want the "looking room" and the interview angle to alternate sides, like so:

Sound Recording

Generally, you'll be using one or more of a number of microphone types. The normal, **hand-held** reporter-type microphone is usually used for interviews only, and will have no viable place in your drama. Nor will the more intimate **tie-pin** or **lapel** mic, but these are great for recording voices during interviews. The most likely candidates for any drama shooting are the **rifle** mic – a long, thin, highly directional mic – and the **boom** mic, the big fluffy one on a 'boom' fishpole that you've undoubtedly seen hanging around film sets.

Whether it's one of these, or just the microphone on the camera itself, you need to be aware of just how essential sound is to any production. Sound is probably the most neglected aspect of the shoot but it's absolutely crucial in any scene. Poor sound distorts the message of your video and pollutes any emotion you hope to create in your audience. It's no more preferable to having an extremely fuzzy picture. The same attention you pay to framing and recording the *video* of your vid needs to be paid to the *audio*.

I've got two main pieces of advice for the sound on your shoot – keep the microphone (whatever kind it is) as close as possible to your subject, and test to death before the actually shoot. If you've scouted your locations well enough, you'll probably have honed your sound conditions as close to perfection as you can, and if you haven't then you really should!

Placing really is the key. If you're in an enclosed space you should avoid placing the mic near corners, walls or on the centre horizontal and vertical lines of the room. Where's left, you're thinking? Well, to keep your microphone smiling, it's best to keep to one of the four quadrants you see in the diagram:

Above all, keep it as close to your actor/speaker as possible, and know the range of your mic. If it's too far away, all you'll hear is a hiss!

If you're outside, background noise is your worst enemy. Try to minimise it as much as possible through tact and polite requests, but you can also minimise its *effect* by narrowing the pick-up range of your mic so it won't pick up much more than your subject.

> *Whenever you shoot a scene, **always** record a buzz track – a track of background noise – which you can then use later in the edit to overlay on top of scenes, transitions or establishing shots.*

Be reactive, and get your subjects to speak up if there's excessive environmental noise. Make sure, however, when you're recording your sound, that you've got a pair of headphones on and you're listening to what you're getting. There's nothing worse than getting back and discovering that your beautifully framed visual masterpiece has an inaudible soundtrack!

Lighting Your Video

Like sound, your lighting set-up is as complex or basic as you want it to be. And like sound, good or bad lighting really can make or break your video. Taking care of the obvious first, you won't need much in the way of lighting if you're shooting outside in daylight, but if you're indoors or outside at night, there are some issues to consider.

> *Don't forget the tips featured in the special interviews masterclass earlier in the chapter!*

The all-important thing is that your *subject* is lit well enough. Although good general lighting is always a boon, on a limited scale or budget, focus your lights on what the viewer will be looking at; if your centre of attention is lit to perfection, shades of light and dark in the surroundings won't be noticed quite so much.

Take for example these shots from a video I produced with some colleagues about a pub quizmaster. The nocturnal setting was a nightmare to shoot in, but we emphasised two factors lighting our entertainer, and lighting the table of participants.

Of course, we didn't light up every competing table in that quiz – only the one we had planned to film, and we had asked the quizzers earlier in the evening if that was OK. So we set up lights around them, as per our floor plan drawn during the scout.

If it's drama you're lighting, be careful though if people are moving around. It looks pretty bad to have people moving in and out of the light, so keep a wider area covered if possible or follow the subject with the light as accurately as you can.

If you have the resources to set up large-scale lights, position them to fill the scene, and keep them out of sight this doesn't just mean physically out of shot; reflections of large bright lights can bounce off spectacles, windows and the like. Keep your artificial lighting *invisible*.

Of course, if possible, use natural light from windows to light your subject or your scene. Have the subject facing the light and if possible keep the camera (and your crew) at an angle to it you don't want to be causing any awkward shadows! See the diagram below for a typical set-up:

Keep your camera beside (but never in front of) a window to maximise light on your subject without risking shadows!

Just as I've advised you about getting constrained by other factors, don't feel too put-upon by the demands of lighting. Adequate lighting is when your scene and your subject are lit appropriately and just enough for the action to be clear, but exceptional lighting comes from your own applications. Don't be afraid to flaunt any of the rules for effect; they are there to be broken if the scene demands it. Take this shot for example:

If you can make him out, this is the character Eldon from my earlier video. Following on from the dark clouds of the shot I showed you before, he has now been deliberately placed against the light (causing him to be in near-complete silhouette). Also deliberately silhouetted, the junction of a lamppost and railing behind him divide the shot into four and illustrate the indecision and choices of the next few scenes, involving the also-shadowy building still in shot behind him.

Play around with light and see what you can get. Once you've mastered the basic lighting of your shots, you can start getting more adventurous. A pan (horizontal camera movement) across the sky in this next shot produced a highly animated and visually striking series of flares.

OK, you're on your way to a great shoot, but technical aspects aside there are a few more things to focus on before setting off with your cameras, and these are the basis of two final mini masterclasses...

Mini-Masterclass – Managing Footage

On the shoot and leading up to the edit, you need to keep track of what you shoot and where it is, or your life as an editor will be hell! Here's the information you need:

- In the same way as you make a list of the shots you plan on getting when you head out to shoot, make a list of what you *actually* get when you return. Your footage is your most valuable asset, so don't let the best shot in the world get forgotten about at the end of tape no.14b. Make this list of shots on the day; note them down as you shoot them! Tick each shot off the shot list or storyboard and mark it down on the tape log, that way nothing will ever go missing!

- Keep this list of shots achieved alongside the tape itself, and clearly mark the tape, e.g.:

  TAPE 3 – DAY TWO – KELVINGROVE PARK – SCENES 6, 12 & 13

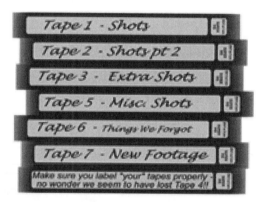

- If you're working on DV tapes, you might be planning on digitizing your footage as you shoot it (see **Chapter 4**). However, I'd also recommended keeping your tapes as a back-up, and make sure you pay equal attention to organizing your material on your hard drive.

- Spend serious time checking back over what you've filmed. Watch it all! Check that the sound is OK, that the shots are well-composed and that the scenes are as you desired them. You're bound to find some things that aren't ideal, and you'll have to assess whether or not you need to re-shoot any of your material. If not, you should start thinking ahead to how you can maybe use Premiere to sharpen up any flagging footage.

Mini-Masterclass – Continuity

Boy, is this a pain! Most prevalent in video drama, continuity will strive to find new and undiscovered ways to mess up your video, no matter how much you try to foil it. No-one, not even the best, are immune to this nasty c-word, so here are the facts you need to know:

- Your **buzz track** is a great weapon against continuity glitches. In the edit, you'll be able to use this continuous track of background noise to smooth over bad cuts and jumps in the soundtrack, adding a seamlessness to the polished production.

- But not even a buzz track can solve some sound mistakes. Music is a particularly troublesome one. I once shot various individual dialog scenes which I was planning to cut together, until I realised Billy Ray Cyrus' *Achy Breaky Heart* had been playing in the background all along – after the edit, the song would have been jumping around all over the place!

- A basic one, but often the last thing on your mind when you're booking up people for a shoot – if you're filming consecutive scenes on different days, make sure your cast are wearing the same clothes. You might want to mark up in your cast members' scripts what they need to wear and when. And in a similar vein (and this did happen to me once) try to make sure your lead actor doesn't go get a haircut between shooting days!

- Now onto some of the more sneaky continuity gremlins. Cigarettes and glasses of orange juice are the classics; the cigarette whose length varies from shot to shot and the orange juice whose fill level does likewise. Keep track of every last thing on set. If your cast pop out for lunch, see to it that they don't acquire a mustard stain on their shirt that they didn't have before.

- If you have the luxury of any production assistants, you might want to ask him or her to keep track of such things for you – as the director/producer you might have a lot more on your mind.

- Shoots that span over a few days or even longer, would benefit from a few timely photographs of cast and locations, for continuity purposes. That way, you can easily match the situation to exactly how you left it a few days back when the shoot continues.

Continuity problems have the potential to make your life a misery when you start piecing together your final video in Premiere, so keep a watchful eye out for anything out of place.

Shooting Your Project

What do you mean you haven't shot your video by now? You're not waiting for me to give the go-ahead, are you? Get on out there and capture the material you'll need to bring into Premiere.

1. Take all that you've planned, and all that I've taught you and add a little bit of on-the-day improvization and inspiration and you'll garner yourself some first-class footage.

2. When you get back with the footage, watch everything over carefully, and make sure that by this stage you've logged every shot and marked every tape.

3. If necessary, go out shooting again and again until you get all the material you need, and a little bit extra just in case.

4. You're now pretty much ready to import your material into Premiere in the coming chapters!

Conclusion

You've now seen the ins and outs of the pre-production and production stages and how a little effort in these can save you some time in the edit suite. And if your video's going to be a one-man (or woman) show, I've hopefully given you some pointers as to how to conceive, plan and shoot some Grade A material that Premiere will just love you for.

There's nothing left to say except get out there and shoot as much material as the days allow, because in the next 450 pages, as you learn Premiere from start to finish, you'll be glad of all the practice you can get, and you'll see the greatness that good footage and good editing combined can produce.

Whatever your genre, or however you plan to use Premiere, it's a tool towards telling stories and you've now learned how to first paint the scenes of those stories onto the screen. Whether you're capturing fact, fiction or just *life*, you're only limited by your imagination and your audacity.

03 The Premiere Interface

Whenever you buy a sophisticated tool – a VCR, let's say – you need to do two things before you can use it. First, you need to get familiar with its controls – learning what all those buttons on the remote control do. Second, you need to set it up so it works with all your other hardware – such as your TV and your cable box.

This chapter will allow you to do both those things with Premiere.

First, you'll be introduced to Premiere's interface, so you'll know what to do with all the buttons, icons, menus, and palettes. And second, you'll have a chance to customize Premiere to fit your preferred way of working, your computer's requirements, and the requirements of your other video hardware.

As you read this chapter, it's recommended that you follow along on your computer. Try out the interface elements as they're introduced, and adjust the various preferences and settings. By the time you're finished, you'll be ready to use Premiere for some serious work, and Premiere will be ready to handle the workload.

> *One useful feature that Premiere shares with many other graphically-oriented programs is its use of **tool tips**. These are labels – usually black text on a yellow rectangle – that pop up automatically when your mouse pointer rolls over an icon or button. If you see something in Premiere and you're not sure what it is, point to it with your mouse and look for the tool tip. Once you've identified the item, you can look it up in this book, in the Premiere manual, or in the* Help *system.*

Starting Premiere

When you first open up Premiere, it will ask you to choose an initial workspace. You'll learn more about workspaces later in this chapter. It doesn't matter very much which one you choose for now, since you can easily change your choice later. Pick the Single-Track Editing workspace for the moment, since that will give you the dual-monitor layout that's described in this chapter.

Next, Premiere will present you with a dialog box called the Load Project Settings window.

The Load Project Settings window

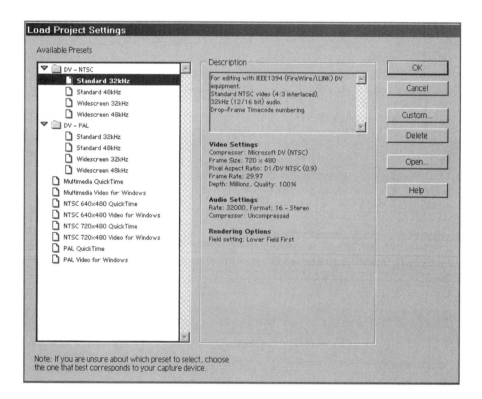

Every time you start Premiere – and every time you open a new project in Premiere – the first thing you'll see is the Load Project Settings window by default, although you can actually change this in the program Preferences (see later).

The Load Project Settings window is where you give Premiere some initial information about the technical requirements of the project you're working on. There are additional settings that you'll have to make as the project continues, and we'll look at these later in the chapter – but for now, the best way to get started is to select from the list of Available Presets at the left-hand side of the window.

Choose the preset that best corresponds to the type of hardware from which you'll be capturing video. For example, let's say you're using a standard digital camcorder. If you're in the US, you're most likely using an NTSC camcorder, so you'd choose from among the presets in the DV-NTSC folder. If you're in the UK, you're most likely using a PAL camcorder, so you'd choose from among the presets in the DV-PAL folder.

In either case, the preset to choose depends on the characteristics of your camcorder. Standard 32 kHz will be suitable in most cases. (32 kHz refers to the rate at which audio is recorded. If your camcorder records audio at 48 kHz, you'll need to use that preset.) If you're using a special widescreen camcorder, you can choose one of the two widescreen presets.

If you're not using digital video, and you'll be capturing from an analog video source, you'll want to select a preset that corresponds to the characteristics of your capture card. In fact, many capture cards come with their own software that's designed to work with Premiere.

Many of these software installations add a custom preset to the Load Project Settings window. If you have such a capture card, be sure to choose the custom preset that's designed to work with that particular hardware. We'll be covering capturing video in full in the next chapter.

Otherwise, you'll need to choose one of the generic presets. If you're using an NTSC capture card that uses square pixels, the appropriate setting is NTSC 640 x 480. If you're using an NTSC capture card that uses rectangular pixels, the appropriate setting is NTSC 720 x 480. If you're using a PAL capture card, simply choose PAL.

If you're not planning to capture video at all, but will simply be editing video files that were captured elsewhere, choose the preset that best corresponds to the hardware on which the video was captured. If the video files aren't in a standard PAL or NTSC broadcast format (for example, if they're not interlaced, or if they run at a frame rate of less than 30 frames per second), the best preset to use is Multimedia.

Once you've selected a preset, click the OK button, and you'll be taken into Premiere's editing workspace.

Premiere's Interface

If you've done any video editing before, Premiere's interface may feel a little more friendly. But even if you haven't, there are certainly elements that you'll find familiar.

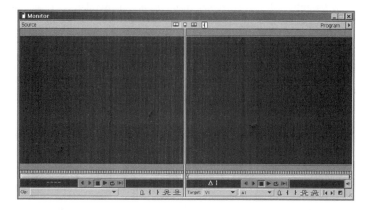

For example, the two black rectangles are Premiere's version of TV monitors. Underneath them, you'll find Stop and Play buttons that are recognizable from any tape player or VCR. To the left of the monitors, you'll see a window (with a folder in it) that looks much like the navigation windows in the Windows or Mac operating systems.

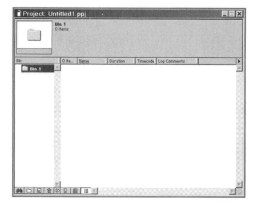

Down at the bottom of the screen is a Timeline, which is similar to the timelines found in other time-based applications such as Flash. You probably already have some idea what these windows do.

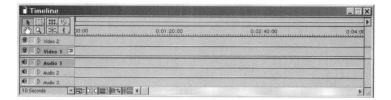

We're about to take a tour through Premiere's interface. You'll find out how to use most of the controls that Premiere gives you, and you'll also find out what's on all the menus. Since you haven't actually used Premiere yet, some of the details may be hard to absorb, but take in whatever you can as you go along. You can always come back to this chapter later for reference.

Project Window

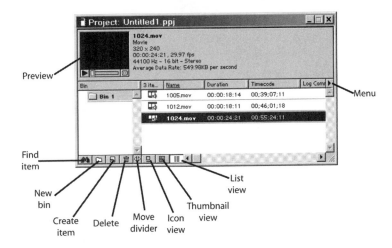

The Project window is where you store the various elements that you'll be editing into your movie in Premiere. Those elements might include video clips (with or without attached audio), still images, audio files, titles, and backgrounds. We call these elements **clips** (or **assets**).

At the upper left-hand corner of the Project window is a small, rectangular preview box. Whenever you select an item in the Project window, it appears in that box. If the selected asset is a video or audio clip, you can play it by clicking the Play button (a rightward-facing triangle) underneath.

Project Window Views

The first time you run Premiere, the Project window appears in its default configuration, which is called List View. List View arranges your assets in a simple text column. To the left of each item is an icon showing you what sort of asset it is. If you scroll to the right, you can see other information about the item, such as its type, duration, and size.

There are two other views that you can use in the Project window. You can select the view you want by clicking the appropriate button at the bottom of the window. One of them is called Icon View, which is a much simpler and bolder way of looking at your assets – it shows a big thumbnail image of each clip, labeled with its name and duration.

The other is called Thumbnail View, which is sort of a cross between List View and Icon View. It shows a slightly smaller thumbnail of each clip along with its name, type, and dimensions, all in a neat column format. You can add other kinds of information for each clip by filling in the additional blank fields, and – as you're about to see – you can even decide which labels go on the fields.

> *These views are explained more fully in chapter 5.*

Bins

For convenience, the assets in the Project window may be sorted into **bins**. A bin is simply Premiere's word for a folder (and, in fact, is represented graphically by a folder icon). When you open a new project, Premiere automatically gives you a default bin called Bin 1. You can also create new bins at any time by clicking on the New Bin button.

> *To see the contents of a bin, you can double-click on it. You can also drag and drop clips from one bin into another, or even drag an entire bin into another bin. In other words, you can work with bins in Premiere just as you would work with folders on your computer's desktop.*

If you wish to adjust the proportionate amount of space given to the bin area and the file list, you can move the divider by dragging the double-arrow icon at the base of the divider. You can also choose not to display the bin area at all by selecting Hide Bin Area from the Project window menu.

Other Buttons

At the bottom left of the Project window, you'll see a binoculars icon. This is the Find button. Clicking it brings up a dialog box that allows you to find an asset by a combination of criteria such as its name and media type. This is a useful feature when you have hundreds of assets and can't remember in which bin you placed a particular clip.

Most of the assets in the Project window will have been captured from videotape or imported from other programs. But there are certain types of assets, such as titles or colored backgrounds, that can be created directly within Premiere. There are several ways to do this, but one of the easiest is to click the Create Item button at the bottom of the Project window and choose the type of asset you want to create.

The Trashcan button allows you to dispose of a single clip, multiple clips, or an entire bin. Of course, you can do the same thing by selecting the items you want to dispose of and pressing the BACKSPACE (Windows) or DELETE (Macintosh) key.

Monitor Window

If you've ever edited video on an old-fashioned linear editing system, the layout of the Monitor window probably looks familiar to you. It consists of two monitors – the Source monitor and the Program monitor – and associated controls.

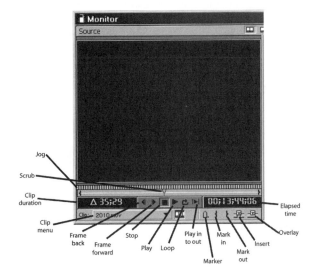

Source Monitor

The Source monitor is where you look at clips before you incorporate them into your movie. You can drag any clip from the Project window into the Source monitor. You can then view it and set the **in** and **out** points (the places where you want the clip to start and end).

You can view a clip either by clicking on the Play button or by dragging the playhead manually in either direction (a procedure called **scrubbing**). The hashed area above the scrubbing channel is called the **jog tread**. Dragging your mouse pointer back and forth in this area allows you to scrub through your movie in a slower, more precise manner, even a frame at a time if you like.

The numeric field at the lower left-hand corner gives the duration of the clip. It's preceded by the Greek letter delta, which stands for "difference" – in this case, the difference in time between the in point and the out point.

The numeric field at the lower right-hand corner tells you where in the clip the playhead is currently located. By default, the location is given in standard timecode format – that is, as a series of two-digit numbers representing the number of elapsed hours, minutes, seconds, and frames. The display format can be changed in the Preferences settings, as described later. In addition to simply reading this number, you can edit it. For example, if you want the playhead to jump to the timecode 00:01:02:03, you can enter this timecode in the field and press ENTER (Windows) or RETURN (Macintosh).

Centered beneath the Source monitor are the standard Stop and Play buttons. To the right of the Play button is the Loop button, which causes a clip to play repeatedly until the Stop button is pressed. The two arrows next to the Stop button are the Frame Back and Frame Forward buttons. They allow you to move one frame at a time in either direction.

The last button in the row is the Play In to Out button, which plays from the in point to the out point. At first, it behaves no differently from the Play button, since the default in and out points are the physical beginning and end of the clip. But the in and out points of a clip can be changed. If they have been changed, this button plays only from the designated in point to the designated out point, while the Play button plays the entire clip.

The buttons that look like curly braces (below the timecode field) are the Set In and Set Out buttons, used to mark the in and out points. To set the in point, move the playhead to where you want the clip to begin and click on the Set In button. To set the out point, do the same with the Set Out button. This process will be described in more detail in **Chapter 6**.

You can drag any number of clips from the Project window to the Source monitor. Each one that you drag will be added to the drop-down menu under the Source monitor, so you can instantly recall a clip by selecting it from the menu.

Program Monitor

When you add a clip to the Timeline and thus make it part of your movie, the clip becomes visible in the Program monitor. The purpose of the Program monitor is to display what's happening in the Timeline as you play or scrub through your movie.

> *The playhead underneath the* Program *monitor corresponds to, and moves in unison with, the playhead in the* Timeline.

Layouts

The Monitor window's default layout – with the Source and Program monitors side by side – is most useful for beginners to Premiere or for people who have had experience with linear editing. But just below the Monitor window's title bar is a series of buttons that allow you to choose other layouts.

The Single-monitor layout, which can be selected by clicking the middle button, displays only the Program monitor. It's still possible to edit source clips when using this layout. If you double-click on any clip in the Project window, the clip will open up in its own free-floating Clip window, which looks exactly like the Source monitor and has all the same controls.

Next to the single-monitor button is the Trim Mode button, which converts *both* monitors to Program monitors as a means for performing very precise edits.

Timeline Window

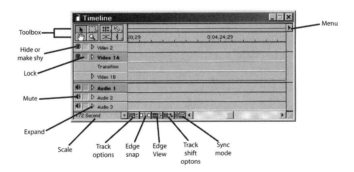

The Timeline is where your movie gets put together. It's where all the clips get assembled and moved around until everything looks the way you want it to look. Simply by moving clips around in the Timeline (or by dragging their in and out points) you can change their order, their duration, and their relationships to other clips.

It's called the Timeline because it's marked off horizontally in time increments, moving from left to right. Vertically, the Timeline is divided into channels or **tracks** – two tracks for video and three for audio. These numbers can be increased, as you'll see later. At the lower left-hand corner is a scale menu that allows you to zoom in or out of the Timeline so you can see more or less of what's in the Timeline.

Work Area

There are many ways to get clips into the Timeline, but the easiest way is to drag them from the Project window or the Source monitor. Video and graphic clips go in the video tracks; audio clips go in the audio tracks. If the clip has an audio track attached to it, the video track and the audio track automatically get dragged at the same time. When you drop the video portion of the clip into a video track, the audio portion ends up directly beneath it in the first available audio track.

As soon as you drag a clip into the Timeline, a yellow bar appears above it. This bar marks the **work area**, the segment of the Timeline that's currently in use. If you want to preview your movie, you can press ENTER (Windows) or RETURN (Macintosh) and Premiere will play the part of the movie that's within the work area. By default, the work area encompasses all the clips in the Timeline, but you can change the extent of the work area by dragging the endpoints of the yellow bar. You can also CONTROL-SHIFT-CLICK (Windows) or COMMAND-SHIFT-CLICK (Macintosh) within the work area channel to move the in point of the yellow bar, and CONTROL-ALT-CLICK (Windows) or COMMAND-OPTION-CLICK (Macintosh) to move the out point.

Working With Tracks

The tracks in the Timeline are in a collapsed state by default, but they can be expanded to reveal additional controls. To expand a track, click the triangle to the left of the track name.

If you expand an audio track that has a sound clip in it, you'll see a waveform representing the sound. You'll also see a red *rubberband* that allows you to set the track's volume.

If you expand a video track (any track except Video 1) that has a clip in it, you'll see a red rubberband similar to that in an audio track. This is used to adjust the clip's transparency.

You can see this in the following screenshot:

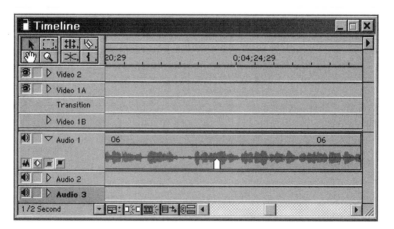

The Video 1 track is a special track. If you expand it, you'll see two separate Video 1 tracks (labeled Video 1A and Video 1B). These two sub-tracks allow you to create transitions, which will be described in **Chapter 7**.

Any track in the Timeline can be temporarily disabled by clicking the "eye" icon at the very left edge of the track. When a track is disabled, all clips in that track will be invisible and inaudible in the movie.

Toolbox

At the upper left-hand corner of the Timeline window is a toolbox. The rectangular frames in the toolbox hold a variety of tools that allow you to manipulate clips in various ways. Note, however, that a single frame may hold more than one tool, only one of which is visible at a time. If there's a tiny arrow at the lower right-hand corner of the frame, position your mouse pointer over it and hold down the left mouse button. You'll then see the alternate tools that are available in that frame. Still holding down the mouse button, drag your mouse pointer to the tool you want and release. That tool will then become visible, and you'll be able to click on it and use it.

Unfortunately, tool tips (text labels on a yellow rectangle) only appear for the tools that are visible in the toolbox at a given time. If you're holding down your mouse button and dragging over the alternate tools in a frame, you won't get any tool tips to identify them. To find out what an unfamiliar tool is you have to drag-select it to make it visible in the frame, and then roll your mouse pointer over it to see the tool tip.

You'll learn more about the contents of the toolbox in later chapters. For now, the most important tool to know about is the default Selection tool, represented by a mouse-pointer arrow. This is the tool you'll be using for most of your work in the Timeline. After you use any of the other specialized tools, be sure to go back and click on the Selection tool, to regain your ability to move and drag clips.

Other Buttons

At the bottom of the Timeline window is a row of buttons. The left-most button, Track Options, allows you to add or delete video and audio tracks. Any tracks you add can be deleted, but there must always be a minimum of two video tracks and three audio tracks.

The next three buttons – Snap to Edges, Edge View, and Shift Tracks Options – affect the way clips behave when they're moved around in the Timeline.

The last button, Sync Mode, allows the audio portion of a clip to be linked to or unlinked from the video portion. You'll learn more about linked audio in **Chapter 8**.

Customizing Your Workspace

By default, Premiere senses the size of your computer screen and arranges its windows in a way that will be convenient for most people. However, you're free to rearrange the windows in any way you like. The arrangement and selection of windows on your screen is called your **workspace.**

Premiere offers four preset workspaces, which you can select from the Workspace item on the Windows menu. If you wish, you can choose one of these presets based on the way you plan to use Premiere for a particular project or session. The preset workspaces are Single-Track Editing, which is a good all-purpose layout; A/B Editing, which is best for projects that will contain many transitions; Effects, which makes it easy to apply effects to clips; and Audio, which puts the Audio Mixer front and center. You can easily switch from one workspace to another without affecting your assets or your movie.

Using any of these workspaces as a starting point, you can rearrange elements on the screen to create our own customized workspace. When you've found an arrangement you like, you can name it and save it by choosing Workspace > Save Workspace from the Windows menu. From that point on, Premiere will allow you to select your custom workspace from among the other presets on the Workspace submenu.

The Menus

The top-of-the-screen menus in Premiere are, to some degree, superfluous. Most of the functions in the menus can be accessed more easily elsewhere – from controls in the various windows and palettes, from each window's drop-down or context menu, or from the keyboard. However, having a nearly complete collection of commands in one place can be convenient, especially for beginners.

To this end, you can find a reference guide to the menus in Appendix B.

Palettes

Premiere's interface includes a number of **palettes** – small, free-floating windows that provide access to a group of related commands or features. Some of the palettes have specialized functions (such as effects or transitions) and therefore will be introduced in the chapters that deal with those features. Others, however, are useful throughout your work sessions in Premiere. Those are described here.

Navigator

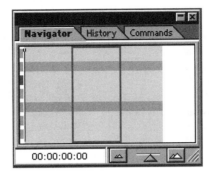

This is a thumbnail version of the Timeline, with a green rectangle indicating the portion of the Timeline that's currently visible. By dragging the green rectangle, you can move easily to a different part of the Timeline. This is a handy alternative to scrolling through the Timeline using the scroll bar.

You can also jump to a particular place in the Timeline by typing a timecode number into the numeric field at the lower left-hand corner of the palette. (Of course, you can do the same with the timecode field underneath the Program monitor.)

In the lower right-hand corner of the Navigator palette, there are controls that allow you to change the scale of the Timeline. You can click on buttons to zoom in or out incrementally, or move a pointer on a sliding scale to make finer adjustments. As you may recall, there are other ways to do the same thing: you can use the Scale menu in the Timeline window, or select the Zoom In or Zoom Out commands from the Timeline menu.)

History

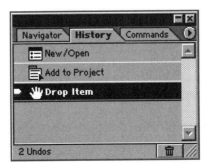

This is a recent addition to Premiere, and it makes you wonder how Premiere users ever managed without it. Every time you perform an action – whether it's editing a clip, applying an effect, setting a marker, or anything else – that action is listed on the History palette. At any time thereafter, you can find that action on the list and click on it, thus restoring your project to the state it was in at the time you performed that action.

> *In other words, the* History *palette acts much like the* Undo *command – except that instead of having to click* Undo *multiple times to go back step-by-step, you can accomplish the same thing with a single click.*

Info

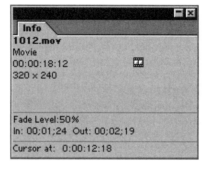

The Info palette displays information about any clip that's selected in the Timeline: where the clip starts, where it ends, and how long it is. It also tells you the exact location of your mouse pointer in the Timeline. Most people find this information indispensable while editing, and so it's a good idea to keep the Info palette visible at all times.

Command

This palette gathers the most common and useful commands in Premiere – collected from menus, buttons, and on-screen controls – and puts them in one place where you can execute them with a single mouse click. If you don't like the default selection of commands, there's a drop-down menu that allows you to add and delete commands or to save and load entire sets of commands.

Setting Preferences

Before you can start using Premiere for serious work, there are a number of preferences that you need to set. To begin the process, select Preferences from the Edit menu. You'll find several submenus there, which we'll look at one by one.

General and Still Image

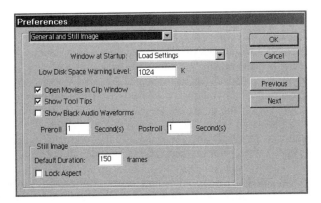

The first selection you're asked to make is Window at Startup, which determines what you see when you first start Premiere. The default is for Premiere to display the Load Settings window. If you wish, however, you can elect to have Premiere open a new project, present you with an Open File dialog box, or show you nothing at all.

Low Disk Space Warning Level

This is the minimum amount of free space that must be left on your hard drive in order for Premiere to operate. If the amount of free space drops below this level, Premiere issues an alert and offers you an opportunity to clear some extra space on your drive before continuing. In general, the default of 1024 kilobytes (one megabyte) works fine.

The next settings are toggles that can be turned on or off.

- If Open Movies in Clip Window is selected, then double-clicking a video clip in the Project window – or opening a video clip from the File menu will cause the clip to open in its own clip window rather than in the Source monitor. If you're using a workspace which has no Source monitor, then this setting has no effect.

- If you are using Premiere on a Macintosh, you will see Deactivate Appletalk when Recording. If this is selected, then background networking activity will cease whenever Premiere is capturing video or audio. For best capture quality, it's recommended that you select this option.

- Tool tips, as noted earlier, are the labels that pop up when your mouse pointer rolls over an icon or button. If you find these useful, select Show Tool Tips; if you find them annoying, deselect it.

- When you expand an audio track, you see your recorded sound represented visually as a waveform. By default, these waveforms are blue, but you can make them black by selecting Show Black Audio Waveforms.

- Preroll and postroll are the number of seconds for which a clip is played before the in point and after the out point. The Preroll and Postroll settings in Preferences are misleading – regardless of what numbers are entered here, Premiere's default behavior is to play clips with *no* preroll or postroll. If at any time you wish to play a clip with preroll and postroll, you can hold down the ALT key (Windows) or the OPTION key (Macintosh) when you click the Play button. The number of seconds that you specify in Preferences take effect *only* if you use this keyboard modifier.

The last two settings are for still images – graphics that you might import from programs such as Photoshop, or titles or color mattes that you might create in Premiere.

- Default duration determines how many frames the image will encompass in the Timeline – in other words, how long it will appear in the movie. Keep in mind that the setting here is just the default. Once you've placed an image in the Timeline, you can easily make its duration as long or short as you want by dragging its in and out points.

- Lock Aspect is short for "lock aspect ratio". It means that Premiere will keep an imported image at its original proportions, even if its ratio of width to height is different from the 4:3 proportions of a standard TV screen. If this option is selected, a non-standard image will be "letterboxed", but if the option is not selected, the image may appear distorted. Note that this is simply the default setting. It can be overridden by selecting Video Options > Maintain Aspect Ratio from the Clip menu.

Auto Save and Undo

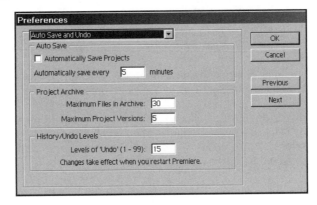

The best defense against making unrecoverable errors is to save your project frequently, and to save it under a different name each time; that way, if you mess up a project, you can open an earlier version of the project that still worked the way you wanted it to. Since most of us don't have the discipline or patience to save our work in this way, Premiere will do it for you if the Automatically Save Projects option is selected. Without interrupting your work, Premiere will save your project at whatever interval you specify in the Automatically save every X minutes setting.

The first time Premiere automatically saves a project, it will append a number to the filename, and on each subsequent save it will increment the number by 1. As a result, previously saved versions will remain on your hard drive – each with a unique filename – in case you want to return to them later. The Maximum Files in Archive setting determines how many files Premiere will allow to accumulate before it starts overwriting older files. This number encompasses files from *all* projects you've worked on in Premiere. To specify how many files to keep from each individual project, enter a number for Maximum Project Versions.

The Undo Levels setting determines how many steps backward you can take by repeatedly issuing the Undo command. The default is 15 levels, but you can specify any number up to 99. The more levels of Undo you specify, the more memory Premiere will need to store all the information. Unless your computer has an extraordinarily high amount of memory installed, you're better off staying with a lower number.

Scratch Disks and Device Control

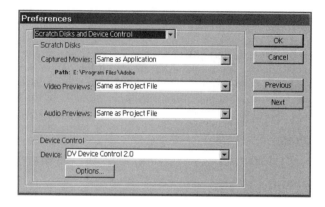

In the course of doing its work, Premiere often has to create temporary files on your hard drive. These files can be quite large, particularly the video preview files that were discussed earlier.

The **scratch disk** is the drive on which Premiere creates and stores these files. If you have only one hard drive attached to your computer, then it will automatically act as your scratch disk, so setting this preference isn't necessary. You may, however, want to specify a folder in which the temporary files should be stored.

If you have more than one hard drive, you'll need to specify which one Premiere should use as a scratch disk. You can, in fact, specify three different scratch disks – or three different folders – for three different kinds of temporary files: captured movies, video preview files, and audio preview files. Captured movie files remain temporary only until you name and save the movie; they're then converted to permanent files.

Whichever disk you choose as a scratch disk should be fast and should have lots of available space. Ideally, you'll want to use a disk other than the one that Premiere is running on, but this isn't absolutely necessary.

Device control is Premiere's ability to operate a camcorder or video deck that's attached to your computer. Not all camcorders and video decks are designed to be controlled remotely, and not all computers have the hardware needed to control them. But if you have the necessary hardware (which, in the case of many digital camcorders, is simply an **iLink** or **Firewire** port and an appropriate cable), device control makes the process of capturing video much easier.

The Device Control menu in Preferences allows you to select the type of device control that's appropriate for your hardware (you'll need to check the documentation that came with your camcorder or video deck to find the proper selection). If you don't have a camcorder or video deck attached to your computer, or if your hardware doesn't support device control, stay with the default selection of None.

Online Settings

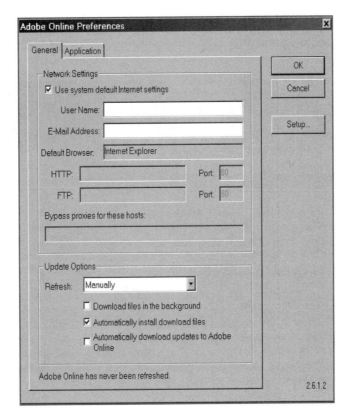

The Adobe Online preferences allow Premiere to communicate automatically with Adobe over the Internet. There are two tabs in this preferences window – one labeled General and one labeled Application. The settings on the General tab apply to all Adobe programs that are installed on your computer. Those on the Application tab apply only to Premiere.

The initial General preferences have to do with your Network Configuration. The exact settings here will depend on your particular internet hardware and software, but they'll no doubt be similar to the settings you've previously entered in your e-mail client and Web browser.

Also on the General tab are Update Options. Adobe periodically issues minor updates to its software that fix bugs and add features. Here, you can specify how you'd like to handle these updates. The default setting is for manual refresh, which requires you to periodically check for updated software by choosing Updates from the Help menu. But if you choose a Refresh interval – once a day, once a week, or once a month – Premiere will automatically check for updated software and download it if it's available. If you select Auto Install downloaded components, Premiere will even install the updates for you.

The Adobe Online service offers tips and support for Premiere users. If you want Premiere to download new additions to Adobe Online whenever they're posted, you can select Automatically Download Updates to Adobe Online.

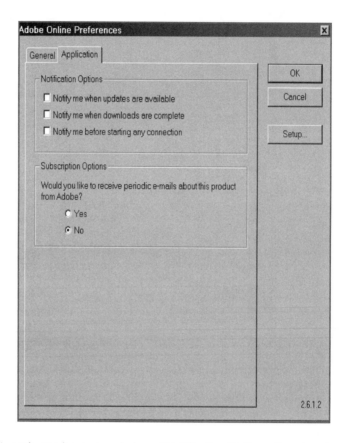

On the Application tab, you have your choice of Notification Options. If you've chosen any of the automatic options on the General tab – that is, automatic updates or automatic downloads – these settings control whether Premiere will interrupt your work to let you know what's going on, or simply go about its online business in the background. Under **Subscription Options**, you can also choose whether or not to receive periodic emails from Adobe.

Now that you've learned your way around Premiere's interface and have set your preferences, you're ready to begin some actual work with video. The next chapter will take you through the process of capturing video from a variety of external sources. That captured video will eventually end up in your Project window, where you can use it to build a movie in the Timeline.

04 Capturing and Importing Media

Adobe Premiere is an excellent tool for editing and producing high quality video files. However, this isn't much use unless you have the actual video files to edit in the first place. Premiere has the ability to import various source files into your projects. These can be movies, audio, and still images, material from videotapes or your digital camera, giving you a wide range of media to work from.

The one thing to remember about all the files you import is that they *will* have to be digital. If you are looking to do some work with the home movie of your last vacation recorded on a VHS tape, it isn't digital, so in its current format you won't be able to use it in Premiere. But there is a simple way to convert your taped VHS into a digital file. This is a method called **capturing**.

This chapter will show you how to capture and import media into Premiere. We will look at the whole process, as capturing is more than just clicking a few buttons. We'll start by explaining some basics, and then we'll look at how to connect to, and capture, your media. At the end of the chapter, we'll show you how to create a project and import your **digitized** media.

What is analog media?

Analog media is simply media that isn't digital. We covered this earlier on in the book, but just to recap; a computer can't store analog video (such as VHS tape). To use footage that is stored in this way, it has to be digitized, which means having to capture the analog footage and convert it to a series of zeros and ones so it can be stored on your computer's hard drive.

There are various capture cards available on the market that can help you with your digitizing needs – we'll have a look at these later in the chapter.

What is DV?

DV (Digital Video)files are stored in a file format that computers can understand. Recognizing this, the latest camera and audio technologies actually record and save information as digital files. Premiere 6 has acknowledged those possibilities by providing some new options for using DV.

The biggest advantage of DV is that you don't need to spend time digitizing your material, as it's already digital. As a result, it can easily be stored on a computer.

How to connect analog media

Capturing analog media is only possible with a capture card installed. There are various cards available on the market, produced by companies such as **Hauppage**, **Terratec**, and **Pinnacle Systems**.

If you're installing a card, here is a diagram that roughly shows you how it works:

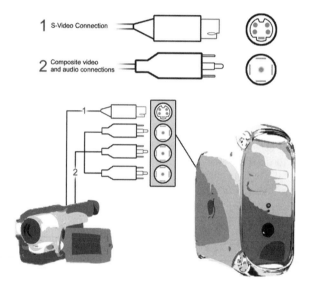

The Hi-8 camera used in this diagram can also represent your VCR. As you can see, there are two types of plugs:

- One of them is the S-Video connection; this cable transfers your video information.

- The other tulip-cables are for transferring composite-video and audio information.

The manual enclosed with the capture card will describe how you can also connect to a TV, giving you a valuable opportunity to view your edited material as it will appear on an actual television.

How to connect DV

Digital video can only be captured and used to its full potential if your computer is able to connect to your camera (or other digital device) using **FireWire**. FireWire is a really fast standard that can transfer data at up to 400Mbps, and because of this, FireWire is a real good choice when working with large video and audio files. You may also hear FireWire referred to as **IEEE 1394** or **i.Link**.

However, DV cameras and other digital devices are not cheap. The big advantage of these expensive components is that the video is really clean and no quality is lost when you transfer it to your computer, since it doesn't need to be specially digitized.

As FireWire technology was invented by Apple, a Mac user would be at a slight advantage as all the latest Mac machines have built-in FireWire/i.Link ability. FireWire is becoming common on recently built PCs, but when buying a new PC do check to ensure FireWire compatibility. This diagram shows how to connect a DV camera to a Mac via a FireWire connection:

IEEE 1394 connection

For a Mac, this is just a plug and play principle. You can look at FireWire as an extended USB port. Extra documentation on using FireWire/i.Link and DV is available when you purchase either the DV camera or the Mac or Windows PC.

File sizes

One thing to be extremely careful of when working with video files is the ease with which you can run up a huge file of 1GB or more. Video files are an extremely memory intensive format, so keep an eye on the amount of footage you capture and the quality setting at time of capture.

Premiere can handle up to three hours of video. This is something that is not really determined by the software package, but more by the **capture card**, **system setup**, and the **size of your hard disk**. The Premiere manual tells us that Premiere considers 'large' files to be those that are 2GB or more.

You should really read the information supplied with your capture card to check how much it can handle. Adobe has a list that shows you what you need when using large files in Premiere 6.

To make use of large files (2GB and more) in Premiere:

- ■ You'll need to have Mac OS 9.0.4 installed with QuickTime 4.1.2 or later.

- ■ You will also need Mac OS Extended volume format (HFS+).

If one of these components is missing, Premiere will create a **referenced** movie and not one large movie file.

Referenced movies are movies that consist of a series of files (under 1.99GB) where each file leads on to the next one. For instance, if you are working with a file that is 7GB, you'd possibly get four files, which would appear something like this: myfile(1.98GB), myfile01(1.98GB), myfile02(1.98GB) and myfile03(1.06GB).

In these cases the first movie (in this case myfile) is called a **parent**. If you try to open a parent in Premiere it will automatically open the other three files – called **child files**.

You can't open a child file separately, because the parent contains all the essential information and a child is simply placed after the parent. Premiere handles parent and child files really well. If you import the parent into a project for instance, it doesn't only import the parent, it imports the parent with all its child files. It will also show the parent (with child files) as one large file – the complete movie.

However, if you always work with files which are under 2 GB in size, you won't need to worry about referenced movies.

Timecodes

Now we know a bit about the options for video capturing and editing, there are two more important aspects we must cover before we start capturing the images and sound. These are **timecodes** and **pixels**.

Most VCRs don't keep track of frames and the timecode often the timecode is reset to 0:00:00 when the VCR is turned on after being switched off. However, professional cameras *do* keep track of the timecode, which is a major step forward. The DV camera also has this feature; in fact, you can even rewind or fastforward the tape in your DV camera with the tools of Premiere!

If you are working with a normal VCR for analog capturing, it's best to make a clear list. Make sure your VCR timecode starts at 0:00:00, then make a simple list that shows you what you want to tape, how long it takes to record, and what you want to use.

For the movie *Gladiator* the list could look like this:

Timecode	Description	Why use this	Video or Audio
1:14:37 – 1:20:55	Battle for Carthage	Shows anger	video & audio
1:22:40 – 1:23:50	My name is Gladiator	Maximus tells name	audio
1:34:18 – 1:41:02	A man for the people	Maximus becomes a hero for the crowd	video

What I often do is save the captured clip by the description title. For example, the first clip would be called `Battle_for_Carthage.mov`. The list shows you what you've captured and it can also be used as an edit-list.

We will discuss timecoding a bit more when we are about to capture, because analog and DV use various ways to set the timecode.

It's all about the pixels

You should always capture your movies at the same **pixel aspect ratio** as the original source. This way you'll get the best quality because the computer doesn't need to perform any mathematical tricks.

The pixel aspect ratios can be set to the following values:

- **Square Pixels**
  Uses a **1.0 pixel aspect ratio**. You can use this setting if your video has a **640 x 480** or **648 x 648** frame size.

- **D1/DV NTSC**
  Uses a **0.9 pixel aspect ratio**. You should use this setting when you've got a video that has a **720 x 480** or **720 x 486** frame size. This is a 4:3 frame aspect ratio. As you may

already know, NTSC is the American standard for working with video, as opposed to PAL, the British and dominant European standard.

- **D1/DV NTSC Widescreen**
  For that 'movie' effect. This uses a **1.2 pixel aspect ratio**. You should also use this setting when your video has a **720 x 480** or **720 x 468** frame size. The image below shows the difference between D1/DV NTSC and D1/DV NTSC Widescreen (same applies for PAL and PAL Widescreen):

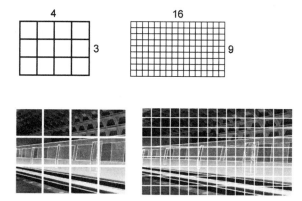

- **D1/DV PAL**
  Uses a **1.0666 pixel aspect ratio** and is the European standard for video. You should use this setting when you're working with a **720 x 576** frame size. This is also a 4:3 aspect ratio.

- **D1/DV PAL Widescreen**
  Uses a **1.4222 pixel aspect ratio**. You can use this setting if your video has a **720 x 576** frame size. This is a 16:9 aspect ratio, shown in the previous image.

- **Anamorphic 2:1**
  Uses a **2.0 pixel aspect ratio**. You should use this setting when your video was shot using an anamorphic film lens.

- **D4/D16 Standard**
  Uses a **0.9481481 pixel aspect ratio**. You should use this setting if your frame size is **1440 x 1024** or **2880 x 2048**.

- **D4/D16 Anamorphic 8:3**
  Uses a **1.8962962 pixel aspect ratio**. You can use this setting when your video has a frame size of **1440 x 1024** or **2880 x 2048**. This results in an 8:3 frame aspect ratio.

Capturing

As we're now ready to start our capturing, we'll discuss the various capturing methods involved, as it's more complicated than just capturing analog video or digital video. There's also the option to capture audio and the option to **batch capture**.

Premiere has a feature called **Device Control.** This is a method of controlling your camera or video deck from within Premiere. This is tremendously useful, but it's dependent on your particular hardware setup, so check the documentation of your equipment to see if device control is supported. Most DV cameras will be supported through Premiere's built in support for DV device control

Setting up for analog capturing

You need to make sure that the setup process for analog capturing is recognized by Premiere. Most of the capture card packages will appear in Premiere. If you are having any problems with your capture card, it is best go to www.adobe.com/premiere where you can find solutions to many common technical problems.

OK, let's set up the properties for capturing analog video.

1. Once you've opened Premiere, a pop-up message will appear, asking you for the Project Settings. Click the OK button for now; this will open an unnamed project and we'll come to this later.

2. From the toolbar, select Project, and click Settings Viewer. A Settings Viewer window will appear:

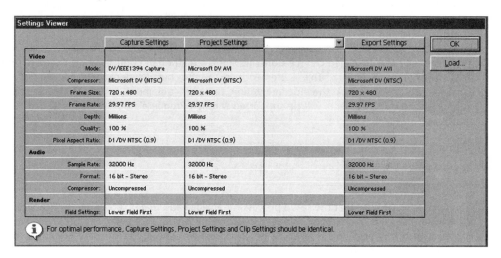

Settings Viewer	Capture Settings	Project Settings		Export Settings	OK
Video					Load...
Mode:	DV/IEEE1394 Capture	Microsoft DV AVI		Microsoft DV AVI	
Compressor:	Microsoft DV (NTSC)	Microsoft DV (NTSC)		Microsoft DV (NTSC)	
Frame Size:	720 x 480	720 x 480		720 x 480	
Frame Rate:	29.97 FPS	29.97 FPS		29.97 FPS	
Depth:	Millions	Millions		Millions	
Quality:	100 %	100 %		100 %	
Pixel Aspect Ratio:	D1/DV NTSC (0.9)	D1/DV NTSC (0.9)		D1/DV NTSC (0.9)	
Audio					
Sample Rate:	32000 Hz	32000 Hz		32000 Hz	
Format:	16 bit – Stereo	16 bit – Stereo		16 bit – Stereo	
Compressor:	Uncompressed	Uncompressed		Uncompressed	
Render					
Field Settings:	Lower Field First	Lower Field First		Lower Field First	

For optimal performance, Capture Settings, Project Settings and Clip Settings should be identical.

The Settings Viewer box contains the following columns – Capture Settings, Project Settings and Export Settings. Column 3 is empty.

The most important thing about this window is that when all the information shows up in black text, your settings are optimized. If some information appears in red then a problem will arise when you are capturing, editing, or exporting.

The next column along from Project Settings is used if something is incorrectly used in Premiere, such as importing an MPEG video.

MPEG videos are compressed video files, which means they cannot be reused. Importing an MPEG file will show a lot of red information since Premiere won't be able to work well with this file:

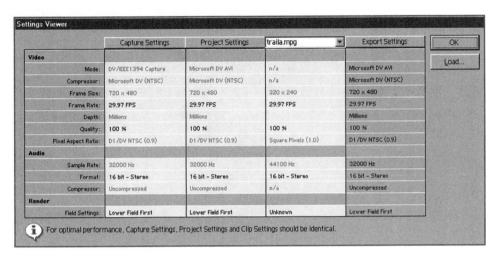

3. If you have one, import an MPEG to see this in action. As you can see, the third column along also contains some information now. Most of the information cannot be read and comes up with the letters n/a, because it is a compressed file. You can also see a lot of items don't match, such as Mode, Compressor, and Frame Size).

When Premiere displays information in red like this, it indicates that I have to adjust one or more settings to make this file usable for Premiere

> The information in the bottom of this window explains that, for optimal performance, Capture Settings, Project Settings, and Clip Settings should be identical. This ties in with our earlier discussion about pixels.

There is still more information that we can look at.

4. If you click the Capture Settings button, you'll get the following window:

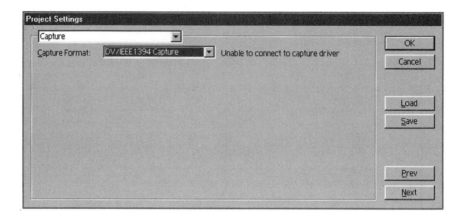

To select a card (if you have one installed), from the drop down menu click on the Capture Format drop-down menu and select the card.

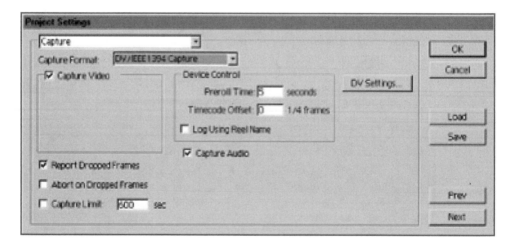

Having selected your capture card in the Project Settings window, a lot of new options will appear:

■ **Capture Format**
Select your format here. Changing this format changes the available options in the window.

- **Capture Video**
  Select this option to enable video capturing. You will also get an extra option to select the size of the video (for instance, PAL would be 720 x 576 pixels).

- **Preroll Time**
  Capturing with the device control, enables you to specify the amount of time Premiere winds the tape before the **In point** (the point from where you start to capture). This is only possible if Premiere understands the format in which the tape's timecode is being played.

- **Timecode Offset**
  When capturing with the device control, you can type the number of quarter frames to adjust the timecode. This way the timecode on the captured video corresponds to the correct frame on the source. Again, this is only possible if Premiere understands the format in which the tape's timecode is being played.

- **Log Using Reel Name**
  In Device Control, you can also check this option to select the reel name you specified in the Batch Capture list.

- **Capture Audio**
  Select this option to capture audio. This option is sometimes unavailable, as we will see later on when we take a look at audio capturing.

- **Report Dropped Frames**
  Selecting this option means Premiere will let you know whether one or more frames were dropped. A Get Properties window will pop-up at the end of capturing letting you know how many were dropped.

- **Abort on Dropped Frames**
  Select this option if you want to cancel capturing as soon as Premiere drops a frame.

- **Capture Limit**
  Here you can specify the time limit (in seconds) you want Premiere to capture.

Setting up for digital capturing

After you've connected the DV source, you'll need to set it to VCR screen mode. Your DV source probably has three standard modes: Camera, Off, and VCR. After you've set this, you can start Premiere. The following message box will open up:

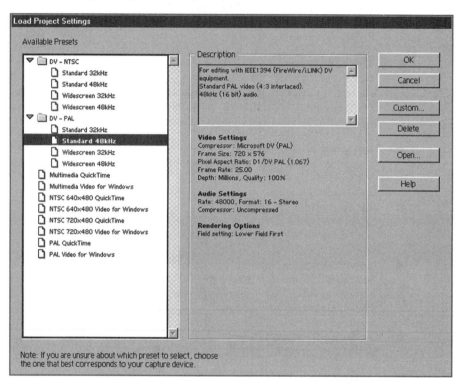

1. Select the desired DV preset from the Available Presets box (remember that the standard for America is NTSC and for most of Europe it's PAL). This will start a new project.

2. Now in your toolbar go to Project > Project Settings > General. The following window will open up:

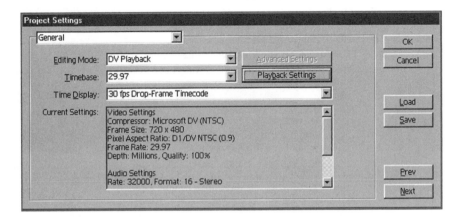

3. Now click on the Playback Settings button to activate a new window, giving more options:

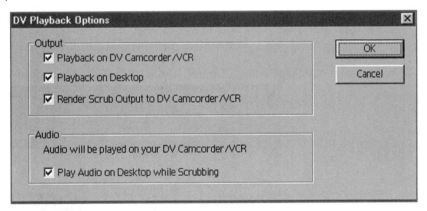

■ **Playback on DV Camcorder /VCR**
This option plays back all the compressed video to the source (either your video monitor, LCD screen, or camcorder). This is a Windows only option.

■ **Playback on Desktop**
This option plays back all the compressed video in the Monitor window or Clip window on your desktop.

- **Render Scrub Output to DV Camcorder /VCR**
  Select this option to display rendered frames on the output device when you render scrub the timeline. Render scrubbing is a nice option in Premiere, to activate this, press the OPTION button on your keyboard (Mac) or the ALT (PC) and then drag your cursor through the Time Ruler in the timeline Window.

- **Play Audio on Desktop while Scrubbing**
  Select this to play the audio through the desktop when you are render scrubbing.

> *As well as these, there are also some options available that depend on your operating system. It is best to refer to the Premiere manual to see which options they are. With certain DV camcorders/sources, other problems can crop up; as before, refer to the documentation of your DV source for solving these problems or go to* www.adobe.com *for technical support.*

Audio capturing

Audio has the same kind of rules as video, in Premiere: we can use both is analog audio and digital audio. Again, analog audio will need to be **captured**.

Windows

In the main toolbar choose File > Capture > Audio Capture. The following window will open up:

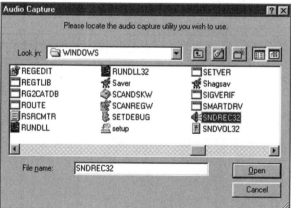

The Audio Capture box asks you to select a utility for capturing the audio. Windows supplies you with the **Windows Sound Recorder**, a nice little program that will do fine for capturing audio. But if you have a third-party application (such as **SoundForge**, **Cool Edit Pro**, **WaveStudio** or **Audio Grabber**), select it here.

Mac

On a Mac choose File > Capture > Audio Capture > Sound Input. Select your source from the menu. The number of options depend on your system and installed cards.

The Sample Rate is determined by what you want to do with the audio. I suggest keeping the quality of the source equal to the capture settings. You can also select a Bit Depth from the left menu. If memory is an issue, 8-bit sound is adequate for medium-quality sound recordings and possibly voice recording, but I would recommend 16-bit sound – however, this would need more disk space.

Don't forget to select the channels you want to use from the right menu.

Importing digital audio

Digital audio is stored on formats like **compact discs**, **DAT** (Digital Audio Tape) or your **DV Source** with a FireWire/i.Link connection. A normal audio CD uses **CDA** as a format. Premiere cannot understand the CDA format, so you will need to digitize this to a format Premiere can understand, such as **AIFF** or **WAV**. On Macs there is an option to import an audio-track from CD, which we will come to later.

AIFF and WAV are the audio formats in Premiere, and they are also common outside of Premiere. **AIFF** stands for **Audio Interchange File Format**, is the standard for a Mac. It will work on a Windows PC where QuickTime 4 or later is installed. **WAV** stands for **Windows Waveform**, the standard for the Windows PC, WAV files can also be used on a Mac.

Importing audio CD tracks on a Mac is possible straight from a CD. Once Premiere is opened go to File > Open. Find your CD drive, select a track and click Options > Play to check whether you selected the track you want to import. You can set various options that will allow you to set the audio to the desired settings.

Other options here are Rate, where you can select the number of samples per second for your recording. CD quality is 44.100 KHz. Size is the bit-depth – remember that CD quality is 16 bit. In Use, you can choose whether the track is mono or stereo. Mono uses the same track for both channels, whereas stereo has a separate track for both the left and right audio channel.

The last thing you need to do is name your file and specify a location to save it.

The Movie Capture window

Now we know what analog video is, and what digital video is, we need to know how to connect these resources and how to capture them. To do this, we'll take a detailed look at a window you will use a lot when capturing – the Movie Capture window.

This window gives you control over the video or audio you want to capture, especially when you've got device control or if you are using a DV resource.

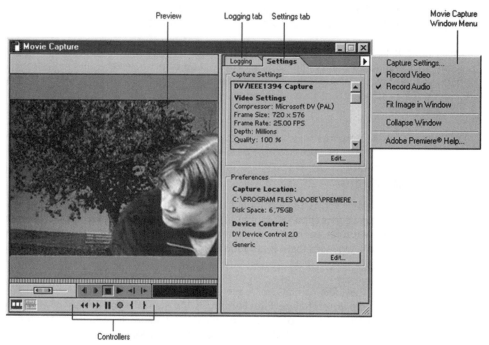

This is how the Movie Capture window looks like when you open it by going to File > Capture > Movie Capture.

In the image above the window is divided into five sections: Preview, Logging tab, Settings tab, Movie Capture menu and Controllers.

- **Preview**

  The Preview shows the current position on your resource device. In this case the DV device is at a frame showing someone sitting in front of a tree.

- **Logging tab**

  The Logging tab is where you can manually designate clips for capture. It will be described more fully when we come to discuss batch capturing.

- **Settings tab**

  This tab shows the settings that Premiere uses for capture. You can change these settings by clicking on the Edit button in the Capture Settings section or by going to the Movie Capture window menu and clicking the Capture Settings option. For the best quality during capture the settings should match the original Source settings.

■ **Movie Capture menu**

In this pop-up menu you can quickly specify some settings. The Capture Settings option changes the settings for capturing video or audio.

If you want to capture video or audio, you should check the Record Video or Record Audio options respectively. If necessary, you can check both. Fit Image To Window makes the view fill the whole Preview window.

Collapse Window will hide the tabbed controls: if you select this option the Logging tab and Settings tab will not be shown. If you already have the tabbed menus off, Collapse Window will be replaced by Expand Window.

There's also the option to go to the Adobe Premiere help files.

■ **Controllers**

There are many controllers in the controllers section. Here is a list of what the various icons stand for:

If you don't have device control, these options are unavailable. If this is the case, your Movie Capture window will look a bit different. Since you won't be able to scroll through your video, it doesn't have the scroll controller:

This is what the Movie Capture window looks like when you don't have the device control options. There are only four buttons. In the bottom left we can still see the Capture Video and Capture Audio buttons. All the others are replaced by two other buttons: Enable Device Control and Record.

- **Enable Device Control**

  If you are not using the device control you will see the previous picture. Hit the Enable Device Control button to use this device control. If you don't have the ability to use device control, the option will not be available in the drop-down window. If you *do*, select your device from the menu.

- **Record**

  This button begins to record/capture. Make sure though that you've already started playing your source before you click this button. It is best to capture *too much* as it is more difficult to edit a capture that starts exactly at the proper point and ends at the proper point.

  To stop capturing, click the mouse or press the Esc key. Again, it is a good idea to record a little too much, so when you've reached the final point you want to capture, keep recording for about five seconds longer.

There is also a second reason to have some extra seconds at the beginning and end of your capture: Premiere sometimes gives a flicker at the moment recording began. This isn't always the case, but to prevent it from happening, it is best to capture more than you need, giving you more freedom in the edit cycle.

Once you've stopped recording, a dialog box will appear asking you for a location to store the file in and a filename. If you already have a project open, the captured video will appear in the Project window.

Batch Capturing

If your device control set up is good and the tape has a timecode, making a batch file is relatively easy. **Batching** means that you create a list of items you want to digitize from the source. You can use a batch list with analog and DV sources, though you'll need to have a good setup for the device control.

Let's take a look at the batch list to get a better idea of what it is and how it looks in Premiere. To get the list up, click on File > Capture > Batch Capture.

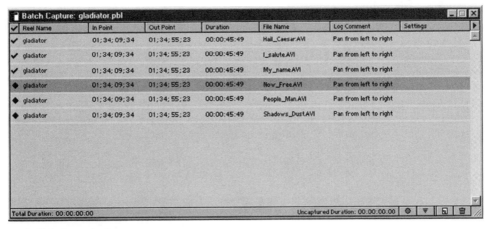

✔ = Clip has been captured
◆ = Will be captured when the record button is pressed
● = Record or Capture button
▼ = Sort
🖫 = Add new batch list entry
🗑 = Remove selected entry

This is what your batch capture should look like. There is a lot of information, so let's take a look at all we can read from this window:

- **Check-mark column**
  The check-mark column shows you whether an item:

  - was captured

  - is not yet captured

  - failed to capture.

  When an item has been captured you will see a tick. When it is not yet captured you will get the diamond sign and if capturing failed you'll see a cross.

- **In Point**
  The In Point indicates the second that Premiere started capturing.

- **Out Point**
  The Out Point shows the last second that was captured.

- **Duration**
  Shows the number of seconds captured.

■ **File Name**
The captured file was/will be saved as the name specified in this row.

Creating a batch list

Now we know what batch capturing is, we need to know how to create the batch list we've been talking about. We've looked at the Movie Capture window already in this chapter. Now we'll examine the Logging tab, which is used when batch capturing.

1. Click File > Capture > Movie Capture. The following window will pop up:

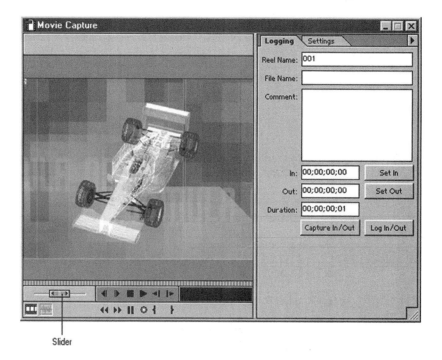

Slider

By default it will open the Settings tab, but for batch capturing we'll need the Logging tab. As mentioned before you'll need device control to be able to batch capture: if you don't have this you can't control the **screen**. This allows you to scroll through your source; the buttons next to the slider allow you to fine-tune the frames. The last two buttons are for slow play backwards and slow play forwards.

2. Scroll to the point where you want to start capturing and press the { button to create an In Point. You can also set an In Point by clicking the Set In button at the right of this window.

3. Then scroll to the point where you want to stop capturing and click the } button or the Set Out button.

4. After that click the Log In/Out button, making a log.

5. Now enter text in the text boxes Reel Name, File Name, and Comment. Normally you can use one Reel Name for everything you record.

6. In the box that asks for a file name you can type in the name you want to give a certain capture – it is a good idea to give it a name that corresponds to the capture.

7. That's nearly all, we've made one item for our batch list. Now click File > Save As and save the batch list.

It is useful to save your batch list just in case Premiere crashes while batch capturing – saving the batch list means Premiere can continue from where it crashed before.

Projects

Now we know the various options for video, connecting to its source, as well as capturing the video and audio, we will now learn how we can use this material in Premiere. Premiere works with **projects** to make it easy for you. A project contains all the information about your movie, not the finalized movie, but more of a *working file.*

One way to think of project is to liken it to going to a supermarket to buy food. Here, you make a list that tells you what you need, and which helps ensure you don't forget anything. That's basically what a Premiere project (ppj filename extension) does.

There are some things you should know about when working with projects. To start with, like most software packages, Premiere processes changes in RAM. If you don't have enough RAM, Premiere will use the hard disk drive as an additional work area. Also, like most software packages, Premiere creates temporary files. You can specify the disk where the temp files will be saved – the **Scratch Disk**. To specify a Scratch Disk, choose Edit > Preferences > Scratch Disks and Device Control. This gives you various options:

- **Captured Movies**
  Select a volume where Premiere should store your files (either video, audio or both).

- **Video Previews**
  Premiere contains a handy option to preview your movie before rendering it. If you make a preview and spot a mistake you can adjust the video and render when you are certain everything is as it should be.

  In this case, select a volume where Premiere will store the preview files. One thing to remember is to occasionally delete preview files, since they take up space on your drive. This can be even more important if you are working across a network.

- **Audio Previews**
  Select a volume where Premiere should store the audio preview files.

An important part of the project is the Project window, since it is here we'll need to import our captured footage. In this window you can create a series of folders – or **bins** as they are known in Premiere, for storing our information. Bins will be covered in detail in **Chapter 5**.

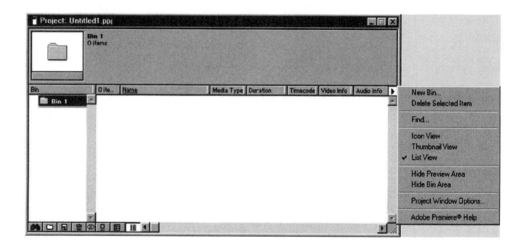

Importing media

Now we'll look at how the files are imported into the Project window and which files can be used in Premiere.

- **Importing Standards**
  Premiere can import the following video formats: AVI (Type 2), MOV and Open DML (on a Windows PC). However, these clips may not exceed 4000 x 4000 pixels.

  Premiere can import the following audio formats: AVI, MOV, AIFF, WAV, MP3, and for a Mac only, the Macintosh Sound Format and Sound Designer I and II.

  Premiere can import the following still-image and sequence formats: AI, AI sequence (Adobe Illustrator), PSD, PSD sequence (Adobe Photoshop), GIF, animated GIF, JPEG, PICT, PICT sequence, Filmstrip, TGA, TGA sequence, TIFF, TIFF

  Sequence, BMP and BMP sequence. On a Windows PC it can also import PCX and FLC/FLI. On a Mac it can import PICS Animations.

● **Importing one or more clips**
This can be for clips that contain video, audio or both. They can be imported in various ways: you can import a single clip, multiple clips or an entire folder of clips.

To import a single clip go to File > Import > File and browse to the file you want to import. To import multiple clips, again go to File > Import > File, browse to your files, select one file then select another by holding down the CONTROL (CONTROL+SHIFT on a Mac) and clicking on another one of the files you want to import. Once you have selected all the files you need, press Open. The shortcut for both these importing methods is CTRL+I (or COMMAND+I on a Mac).

To import an entire folder go to File > Import > Folder, select the desired folder and click OK (Windows) or Select Foldername (Mac). The selected folder will appear as a new bin in your Project window. The shortcut is CTRL+SHIFT+I (COMMAND+SHIFT+I on a Mac).

To view a clip before you actually import it, open it without importing by right-clicking (control-clicking on a Mac) on the file and selecting Open from the drop down menu that appears. You can also import a still image by going to File > Import > File.

● **Importing Adobe Photoshop Files**
Photoshop files (PSD files) can be imported when they are made in Photoshop 3.0 or later. If the Photoshop file uses an alpha mask/channel this will be preserved when using the file in Premiere. Sometimes you might get some problems when importing a Photoshop file, for example if there is a Photoshop file with multiple layers and some of these layers have an alpha channel, you'd need to flatten all layers and give the one layer an alpha channel.

● **Importing Adobe Illustrator Files**
An Adobe Illustrator file (AI file) can be imported into Premiere as it stands, as the image will automatically be rasterized for use in Premiere. You can import Illustrator files up to a size of 2000 x 2000 pixels.

● **Importing a sequence**

The easiest way to import a sequence is by creating one folder that contains all your imagery. Give your files a filename suffix, for example: `MyFile001.pct`, `MyFile002.pct`, `MyFile003.pct`, and so on. Go to File > Import > File and select the first filename (`MyFile001.pct`). Check the Numbered Stills box at the bottom of the Import window and click Open:

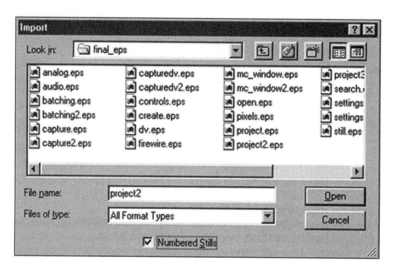

● **Importing Flash or Director content**

When you are working with Macromedia Flash or Director there are also various ways to export your material and make it available for Premiere. One of the easiest ways is to export the material as an AVI or MOV file. With Flash you can export a file as an AI (Illustrator file) and you can import AI files as we've seen above.

Tutorial – Building a music station

It would be difficult to work on a tutorial that involves capturing video because of the varying capture cards and set-ups all of you have. Instead, we'll work on a more general theme that involves importing various media.

To begin with, let's get into the guise of a video editor for a fictional music channel called Music Station. There's a video from a group called "A Group" who've made a track called "Our First Track" (pretty simple so far!). However, there was a problem with the delivery, and the sound has been lost! It's our job to import the video into a project, insert our Music Station logo, and put the artist name in there, as well as the track title and name of the album. Last but not least, we will need to import the lost sound.

This may not be the most realistic example, but it will show us how to import and use various media files. We'll import a Photoshop (PSD) file that contains a mask, a MOV file (given to us by the artist's music company), and a WAV file that we've made by capturing the audio from the artist's CD. The Photoshop file contains all the Music Station elements in one (the logo and the block that contains the text with the artist name, track name, and album name).

This next screenshot is a quick setup of how our Photoshop file might look. In the top right corner there's the Music Station logo, and in the bottom left there's an information box (artist, track, album). In the Channels panel, you can see there's a mask for the rest of the space in this file:

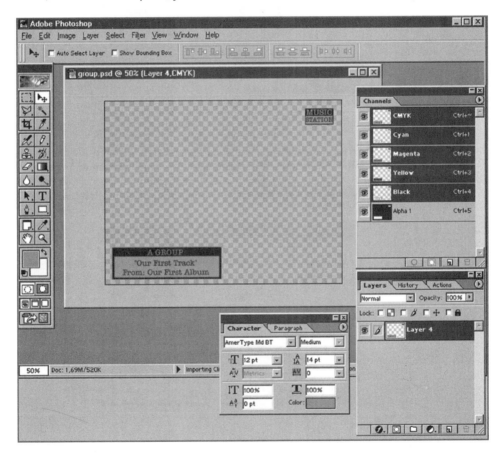

If you give a Photoshop file a mask, (or other image files that are able to save masks), it can be used in Premiere.

1. Now I have all the assets (the video and sound files were already delivered), I can start Premiere. I'll be asked to load my settings for the project, via the Load Project Settings screen.

Depending on geography, you might choose different settings for different regions, I want the videoclip to have PAL settings, and I'll need the optimal settings for sound, in my case DV – PAL, Standard 48Khz.

2. Once I've clicked the OK button, an empty project will open up. I've renamed the bin, giving it a relevant title – A Group (the name of our fictitious group):

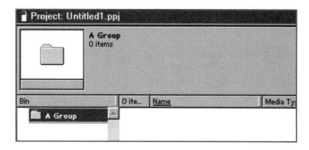

3. File > Import > File selects the Photoshop file I created; Premiere will then let me know that it is in the PSD format. It is possible to use many layers in an imported PSD file, and Premiere wants to know which layer I want to use. In my case, in the drop-down Choose a layer menu, I've chosen Layer 4, because that's the layer with the logo and box:

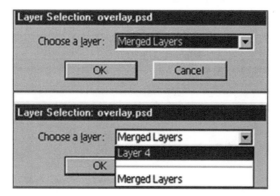

4.   Once I've clicked OK, the file is imported into the A Group folder:

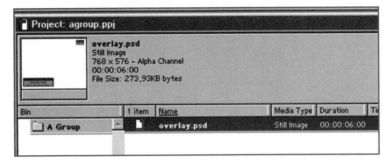

From this window, we can tell that: the file is called `overlay.psd`; it's a still PAL image, sized 768 x 576; it has an Alpha Channel; it lasts six seconds and the filesize is 273,93 KB.

5.   Next I'll import the other assets. I've placed them both in a folder called assets on my system. This means that instead of importing them separately, I just imported the complete folder.

> *This is a good technique for future reference when you have many files that need importing.*

6.   To import a folder, I clicked on File > Import > Folder (CTRL+SHIFT+I). A pop-up box popped up, asking me to select a folder. I did this and clicked the OK button to import this folder into A Group:

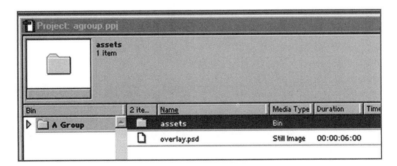

Here, assets has now been imported into A Group. Now, by double-clicking the folder assets, I can look at the structure of the project window, as I would in the standard Windows Explorer.

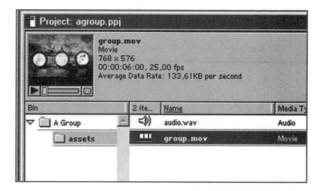

Now I have imported all the materials I need, I'll place them into our timeline window.

7.   I dragged the audio file from the project window into the first audio channel – Audio 1.

8.   Then I did the same with the video file, but dragged this into the Video 1 channel.

9.   Now all I have to do is drag the Photoshop file onto channel Video 2. Because I selected layer 4 (the layer containing the mask) when importing this file, Premiere notices this and automatically sets the alpha mask to true.

My final timeline looked like this:

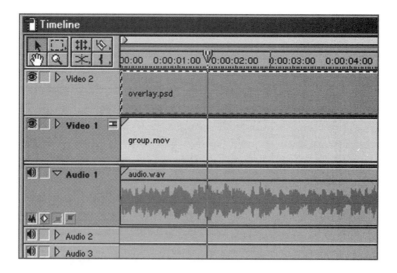

When I exported these files, this was the end-result:

This point, this tutorial wasn't meant to show you how to animate the imported files, it was just intended to give you an example of how to import various media-files (still image, sound, movie) in various ways (import file, import folder). We will be covering how to **really** work with imported files in the following chapters.

Summary

This chapter has outlined the possibilities you have when capturing and importing media into Adobe Premiere, and we've covered the differences between analog and digital media.

We have taken a general look at how to connect that analog or digital source to the PC. For more specific information, don't forget you can always refer to the manual supplied with your capture card for more information.

Now you should have a good idea about the devices and how to connect, as well as how to capture images **or** audio from the source and what to bear in mind (filesize, timecoding). Analog capturing, digital capturing, audio capturing and batch capturing are all facets of the capturing process. Don't forget how the movie capture process cannot happen without the Movie Capture window also described in this chapter.

This chapter has shown how you are able to connect your camera, camcorder or VCR to your computer and capture clips from the source. In the next chapter, we'll start looking at how you can use Premiere to make the most of your raw footage.

Working with Clips

Now that you've captured your footage, it's time to put it together in some sort of order. Most editors find it useful to organize their footage before beginning the editing process. Like the time spent logging the footage, this is another opportunity to get familiar with the material available to you. Knowing the source material back to front will not only help speed up the editing process, it can also prove to be invaluable when it's necessary to find a clip that you may need to use for something it wasn't initially intended for. If you need a cutaway shot to cover something unusable, it's good to know where to go for one rather than having to scan through all the available clips.

The term **clip** is used as a generic name for any media element that will be used in a project. Originally referring to the process of physically clipping out a section of film, it now applies to the segments of video that will be used — as well as audio segments, still images, graphic elements, and color mattes amongst others.

Premiere uses the familiar **bin** model for the organization and management of clips. Bins can be nested in a **tree-like** directory structure, or they can be opened in their own window. Bins can even be exported for use in other projects.

Working with the Project window

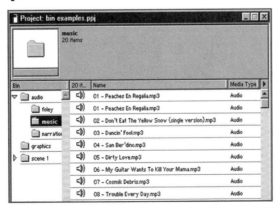

The Project window is where the bins are organized – by default it opens with two panes showing the bins on the left, and the contents of the currently selected bin on the right. It also has a handy preview window at the top left, allowing you to quickly preview the selected clip. The Project window will always have a representation of every element in the project.

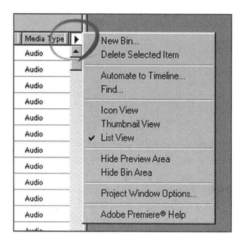

Like other aspects of Premiere, working with the Project and Bin windows can become highly customized. Near the top right of the Project window, you'll find Adobe's standard small triangular Window Options button. This opens several options enabling you to change the display set-up. Options also available allow you to: toggle the view mode of the project window; show or hide the leftmost bin area, show or hide the preview area, and access the project window options.

These options are also available by **context clicking** (right-click in Windows, option+click on a Mac) in the Project window. As well as this, there is a row of buttons at the lower left of the Project window that duplicate most of these functions. As we explore the available options, keep in mind that the Bin windows function is essentially the same as the Project window with the exception of the leftmost 'bin' pane.

The most commonly used functions of the Project window are also available through the seven buttons located in the lower left of the window.

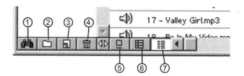

- **1** is the Find button. The find utility lets you search any two data fields for specific content, and will select a clip in the project that matches those criteria. If more than one clip matches the search terms, you can hit the Find Next button to advance through the list.

- **2** is the New Bin button. As you might expect, it creates a new bin.

- **3** opens a Create dialog box, which will prompt you in creating a new title, an offline file (useful as a placeholder for a clip you haven't created or captured yet), a new color matte, black video, bars and tone, or a universal counting leader.

- **4** as the icon implies, will delete whatever clip or clips are currently selected.

- Buttons **5**, **6** and **7** toggle between the Project window view modes.

When we open the Project window options dialog, we have the opportunity to select the current view mode, and determine what information is shown based on that view mode. There are three basic modes to choose from:

- List view

- Icon view

- Thumbnail view

The different views lend themselves to different styles of working, as well as different styles of project.

List View gives you the most amount of information about a clip; its file name, media type, duration, timecode, reel, how many times it's been used in the project, and much more, depending on the options you've specified in the Project window options:

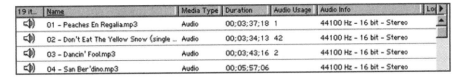

You can easily select the sort order of the clips by clicking on the heading you want to sort by. List View can almost present an information overload, but it is very useful if you need to find a shot from, say, reel 5, that is at least 10 seconds long, and hasn't been used yet in the project.

In comparison to List View, Icon View gives you the least amount of detailed information about a clip, but it does show you a nice big image of the clip – you can specify one of 4 sizes in the Project window options. By default this image is the **In point**. Sometimes this isn't a good representation of the clip's contents, a frame from the middle might be more indicative of what the clip is about.

In this case you can select what frame you see (also called the **Poster Frame**) by opening the clip in the Clip or Source Window and setting the clip marker 0 on the desired frame. We'll cover the exact procedure for setting the markers later in this chapter. The Poster Frame can also be set using the preview console at the top left of the Bin or Project window. To the right of the clip position slider is a button that will set the currently visible frame as the Poster Frame.

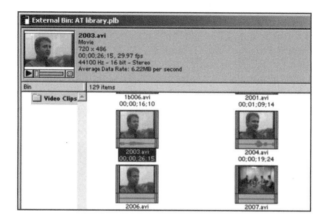

In the Project window options for Icon View, you can specify whether the icons are arranged neatly, or placed randomly about the screen. If you want them evenly lined up, right click in the Project window or click on the Window Options button and select Clean Up View. This will cause all the icons to line up, though the clips can still be moved around as before if you want a more organic feel to the bin.

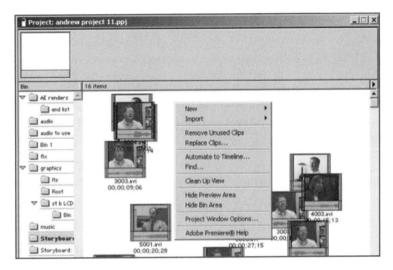

Thumbnail View is something of a hybrid of List View and Icon View. It has the same four possible sizes of poster frame that are found in Icon View, but instead of multiple columns of icons it shows one icon followed by a field with the name of the clip, media type and duration, then up to four additional user defined text fields.

It's Bin Such a Long Time...

Bins can be an essential tool in creating a smooth workflow in editing. A few minutes spent at the beginning of a project organizing clips can save hours of wasted time hunting for clips later.

To create a bin you can use the New Bin button at the lower left corner of the project window. Under the menu go to File > New > Bin, or the keyboard shortcut of CONTROL(COMMAND) + / , and at the prompt, name the bin. To rename a bin, double click on it in the Bin pane of the Project window, or context click on it.

You'll generally always want to create separate bins for different media types – start with bins for audio, video and graphics. You can then further subdivide these bins. For example, the audio bin might contain separate bins for music, voice over, or sound effects.

You can rearrange the nesting of bins by simply dragging and dropping the bins where you want them.

To place a bin within another bin, drag it over the destination bin so that a black box highlights it.

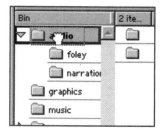

To move it to the root directory of the project, drag it outside the other bins so that the black box highlight appears around the whole leftmost pane.

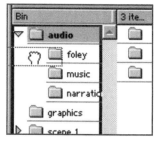

There are no hard and fast rules for this, and every project will be somewhat different. You can even change your mind partway through a project and start organizing things differently. Just remember that good organization of your media assets can help you edit much faster, and can actually give you greater creative freedom.

Storyboards – not just for producers and directors

While the Timeline is the most powerful way to manage and manipulate a project, the Storyboard is an extremely useful tool for beginning an edit. It's a very good visual metaphor for arranging clips in a sequence. Just as a storyboard can make the process of pre-planning and shooting more efficient, it's a good way to start assembling clips for an edit. Once the clips are assembled, they can be sent to the timeline for further editing, or there is even a provision for printing a Storyboard to video if you want to get a rough cut to tape quickly.

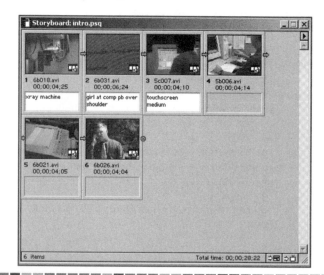

The new Storyboard feature in Premiere 6 bears a superficial resemblance to a bin in Icon View mode, but the functionality is quite different. Like a bin you can import clips directly to the storyboard, but if you import a folder it simply imports all the files within that folder rather than creating a new bin with that folder's name, as would happen in the bin window or project window.

Storyboard Reminder

We have covered storyboards recently in this book, but just to re-cap, a storyboard is essentially an illustrated version of the script, where every major visual element of the movie is represented as an image with a description of the action. It is a kind of "pre-visualization" process, letting the people involved with the project get an idea of what the finished product should look like before shooting even starts.

A storyboard can be as simple or as elaborate as you like. Many large budget productions use very detailed drawings in color, but simple stick figure drawings can be just as effective.

You can create a Storyboard from the menu under File > New > Storyboard, or with the keyboard shortcut SHIFT+ALT+CONTROL+N (SHIFT+OPTION+COMMAND+N a Mac).

You can either drag clips from bins into the Storyboard or import clips directly. By default, the clips are imported to the Storyboard with the in and out points at the extreme limits of the clip, or if they were batch captured or dragged from another bin – they will be in the same places they were set.

The clips in a storyboard are not arranged as they are in a bin. Instead, they can be dragged around and rearranged just like a real storyboard. When a clip is added to the Storyboard it is given a number, which represents the sequence in which it will occur.

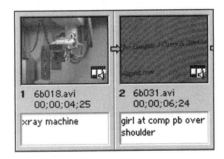

Additionally there is a small arrow icon which points to the next clip in the sequence. Here, by context clicking and selecting Storyboard Window Options, you can choose from four icon sizes to view the clips. In the lower right corner of the icon there will be a symbol indicating whether the clip consists of audio, video, or both. Each clip in a Storyboard has a text field below the icon where you can add notes or a comment to the clip. It can even be printed out if desired.

Unlike bins, which are saved with the project unless you specifically export them, the Storyboard is stored independently from the project, so it needs to be saved as early, and as often as possible – just as you would with the project file. When you create a Storyboard, a link to it is created in the currently selected bin – for the sake of good file management it's a good idea to move this into a bin specifically designated for Storyboards. If you use the Automate to Timeline feature of the Storyboard (bottom right icon), Premiere will automatically create a new bin of the same name with references to all the clips in the Storyboard.

When you logged and captured your clips, you left some padding on either end to allow plenty of room for error in your edits. Depending on how you're going to be working with the clips, it might make sense to trim the clips by tightening up the in and out points before proceeding. When beginning an edit with the Storyboard, it's particularly useful to review and adjust a clip's in and out points since it can get you very close to a rough edit.

Finding Frames

Additionally, sometimes it makes sense to capture something as one long clip even though it will need to be broken up later. In this case duplicate clips can be created to subdivide the master clip as necessary.

If you have the Monitor window set to Dual view (by clicking the pictured icon at the top of this window), a clip's in and out points can be set in either the Clip window or the Source window.

As is common in Premiere, there is always more than one way to do things, and everyone develops their own unique working methods.

I find it easiest to work with video clips in the Source window, and audio-only clips in the Clip window. Setting in and out points is simply a matter of opening the clip, navigating to the desired frame and using the I and O keys to mark in and out points.

To find the frame you want, you can use the location bar or, if you know it, type in the desired timecode to get to the general area.

A really great feature of Premiere is that you don't need to click in a field, or activate anything to type in a timecode. If you are in a window that deals with timecode such as the Timeline, the Source window or Program window or a Clip window, all you have to do is start typing on the number keypad. Premiere will automatically interpret this as timecode – you don't even need to worry about separating the numbers. Typing in 54321 followed by the ENTER key will instantly take you to 5;43;21. So this is 5 minutes, 43 seconds and 21 frames.

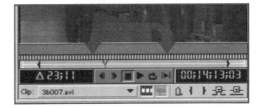

You can also let Premiere take care of math for you; if you want to jump ahead 2 minutes, 11 seconds and 18 frames just type in 21118 preceded by a + sign. If you know you want to jump ahead 83 frames, instead of having to figure out that you need to advance 2 seconds and 23 frames, all you need to do is type in +83, and Premiere will figure out what you mean.

Once you're in the general neighborhood, use the jog tread or the arrow keys on the keyboard to find the specific frame desired. The arrow keys will move the current time one frame in the corresponding direction, pressing SHIFT with the arrow key will cause it to move 5 frames.

If the clip was in a bin, a new duplicate of the clip will need to be added to the bin for the new **in** and **out** points to take effect. To do this, simply drag the clip into the bin window or, if the editing was done in the Source window, you can use the keyboard shortcut of SHIFT+CONTROL (COMMAND) + /. At the prompt, give the duplicate clip a name. If the clip was in a Storyboard, the in and out points will be updated automatically.

If you are making multiple duplicate subclips of a large master clip, just continue by adding in and out points and creating a duplicate in a bin or Storyboard.

During the trimming process, it's often beneficial to put markers in the clip to function as references or cues later on in the editing process. You might have a visual reminder that you might want a music cue or sound effect to sync to. You might need to denote an unusable section of video in a clip that you need to keep the audio away from. If you are editing to narration, you might need to mark specific points to match visuals to:

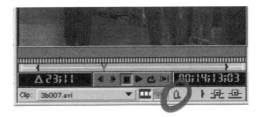

Each clip can contain up to 10 numbered markers, and 999 unnumbered markers. To set and manage markers you can use either the Marker menu button (which is available in both the Clip and Source windows), the Marker Entries in the Clip menu, or by using keyboard shortcuts.

Since there are quite a few keyboard shortcuts available for marker functions these can vary between operating systems, what window you are in, or if you are on the timeline – it's a good idea to keep the Adobe **Quick Reference Shortcut card** handy. If it's become obscured by coffee rings and scribbled timecode references, you can print out the relevant sections from the online help feature.

In the Source window, markers will appear at the top of the window next to the Monitor window mode switches.

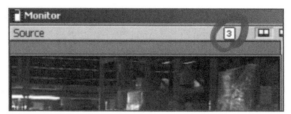

In a Video Clip window, they will appear as a small icon at the top center of the frame:

In an Audio Clip window, they show up with a vertical bar bisecting the waveform;

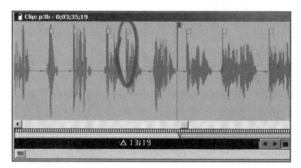

Getting Stills from Your Video

While working with clips you may need to export still frames – possibly as a still for use in the project, a background for a graphic, or for use as a promotional still for print or the web. If your project is for **NTSC** or **PAL** video for broadcast or tape, it will be interlaced (covered in Chapter 1).

The slightest amount of motion in a frame will cause a still image consisting of both fields to appear jagged and aliased on a computer monitor. The same still played on a video monitor will appear to vibrate. The more motion there is in a clip, the more pronounced this effect is:

Premiere has the ability to deinterlace a clip, but the best way to do this with a still is to use a photo-editing program such as Photoshop. Such a program is pretty much a necessity for video production – **Photoshop LE** is included on the Premiere disc and has most of the basic capabilities.

Generally a photo editing application will give you the option of which field you want to discard and whether you want to replace the missing information with duplicates of the other scan lines, or by interpolation of the existing information. Generally **interpolation** will produce the best results, but sometimes experimentation is called for to see what you think looks the best.

Another issue that affects stills for web or print is the aspect ratio of the image. While NTSC and PAL video has a 4:3 aspect ratio, it uses rectangular pixels rather than the square ones that a computer uses to process images. In the case of **NTSC** the pixel aspect ratio is **0.9** and **PAL**'s is **1.067.**

This effect can sometimes be overlooked when the subject is organic, but it becomes really obvious when dealing with precise shapes – such as a perfect circle:

Image 1 shows how the graphic would appear on a video screen, image 2 is the same graphic as it would look after being exported from an NTSC project, and image 3 represents a PAL project.

For NTSC stills, this means they need to be resampled to about 88% of their original width while leaving the height the same. PAL stills need to be resampled to about 94% of their height, leaving the width the same.

Works well with others

When dealing with clips other than video, such as audio and graphic files, Premiere has the ability to launch the program that created them, or that is used to edit them, using the Edit > Edit Original command. If, for example, you had a bitmap still image and you wanted to retouch it to remove unwanted detail, selecting the clip either in a bin window or in the timeline, and hitting CONTROL(COMMAND) + E will launch your photo editing application. Make whatever changes are desired and save the file over itself. When you return to Premiere the changes will be automatically incorporated.

Summary

In this chapter we've done the following:

- Seen the ins and outs of the Project window

- Organized clips in bins

- Seen how to outline a movie in the Storyboard window

- Learnt how to quickly locate specific frames via a variety of methods

- Briefly discussed obtaining still images from your movie

In the next chapter, we're going to move on to start having fun with playing with our clips, by performing some editing.

06 Basic Editing

In this chapter we'll look at the various techniques available to start assembling an edit. We'll examine the basics of editing to narration (or music) and cutting together a dialog scene. With the accompanying source files is a tutorial project with video files, and as we discuss each topic, you can follow along with the included footage. For the basic techniques, you'll see that there are always several ways of doing something and, wherever possible, we'll try and use as many of them as we can.

Once we're done with the project, you might want to experiment some more with the footage to see how many different ways you can put it together, and see how different your editing affects the tone of the piece.

> *Also remember that if you have your own footage or project to work on through the book, you can experiment with applying all these techniques to your own material from the outset. Sometimes though it's best to have a solid frame of reference so I'll work all the examples in the next two chapters around the provided files first.*

As a basis for the tutorial, I've written a simple little piece about cars, a subject near and dear to my heart, and it's easy to shoot a lot of free footage of cars (my alternate topic Paraguayan folk dancing was just going to be too complicated to shoot!)

For the filming, I had a narrator friend provide me with a voiceover track. I also talked some other friends into acting out a dialog scene for me, and I shot a whole lot of b-roll footage of cars doing their thing. I also created some shots with scanned images and some shots with motion effects.

I've included the scripts and shot lists in the downdload I find it useful to have this when I'm editing, because it is a reference to where things will need to be, and gives a useful overview of the project.

I don't have a master script as such – I only had a small window to work with my narrator so I had to dash her script off before I knew exactly what I wanted to do with the dialog scene.

I also had to change my original dialog scene, so was forced to quickly rewrite it around the people and locations I would be able to use. While this is kind of a slapdash way to do things, it's also a good example of what you will be likely to encounter as an editor. Along the way we'll be encountering several of these reality checks that you'll often come across in your DV career.

> You'll remember these kinds of pre-production and shooting-day
> issues were discussed in **Chapter 2**. Always make sure you have a
> back-up plan so that if need be you can rework your scenes as
> circumstances dictate!

Opening the File

1. In the tutorial folder in the source files, you'll find a directory called Chapter6_tutorial. Copy this entire directory to the media drive on your system and open the project folder.

2. Start Premiere and load the chapter6-1.ppj project.

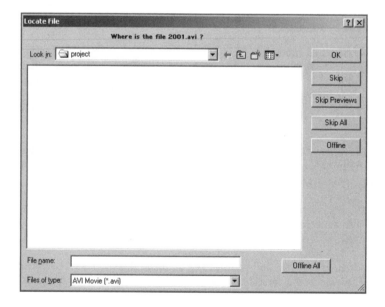

If the drive letter or file path of your media drive is different than mine, Premiere will ask that you locate various files.

3. Navigate to the directory and double-click the file it's asking for. It'll only ask this for one file in each directory, once you show it where that one is; it'll find the rest automatically.

Non Linear Editing

Now, where should we start? Well, that's why they call it **Non-Linear Editing**. It's not critical where you start, you'll soon develop your own style that will vary from project to project. For this tutorial we'll use my methods, but they are by no means the only way to do things.

I'll be looking at the basic techniques for accomplishing certain tasks – the order you approach them in and the details of how you accomplish them are not so important. As long as you know the different ways you can put a clip on the timeline, it's up to you to decide which way is best.

The Blank Canvas

The sight of an empty project can be quite intimidating – a blank canvas always is to any artist. Just like a painter might start by mixing his colors, or a sculptor arranging his tools, the very first thing I do is thoroughly read the script and any production notes or storyboards available. This will give me a good concept of where the story is going, and what the driving element is going to be.

> *It is here, at the very start of the edit, that much of your hard pre-production and planning work comes into fruition. And if you ever find yourself on the first day of an edit staring at a stack of footage with no idea where it's all going to go, you'll see how important this always is.*

In general, most video is edited around the audio tracks; dialog must have linear continuity, narration needs to be cohesive, and music has a rhythm that needs to be taken into account.

In this case it's the narration that will set the pace for the project, so, since I don't have a storyboard, I'll mark up the script with notes of where I want visuals to go.

I usually break the narration into separate clips for each of the major sections so it'll be easier to adjust timing, but for this project we'll go ahead and split it up paragraph by paragraph. For points within each clip that we want to cue off, we'll add markers.

Setting the Scene

1. To do this, open the file `narration.mp3` (which you'll find in the audio bin within the project) in its own clip window.

2. If the Open Movies in Clip Window option from the Preferences dialog is unchecked (which I highly recommend), you can do this by holding the ALT key for a Windows machine or the OPTION key for Mac, then double-click on the clip.

3. Create a new bin called narration within the audio bin, this is where we'll store our sub-clips.

4. For each numbered section in the narration script, find the beginning and end of the section, and set an In point and an Out point with the I and O keys. Use the mouse to get close, and then scrub back and forth with the cursor/arrow keys to find exact points. This isn't always critical, but it can help keep your edits tight, and avoid extraneous noise.

5. If I make a cue notation on the script with an asterisk (*), I put an unnumbered marker at that point as well using the shortcut; CTRL+ ALT + = for a windows machine, or COMMAND + OPTION + = for a Mac. Or you can select it by Clip > Set Clip Marker > Unnumbered.

6. Once you've set In and Out points and markers, drag the clip into the narration bin. This will create a new **sub-clip**, and you'll be prompted to give it a name. Although not very imaginative, I find numerical names very useful. 01 through 09 in this case. Repeat this process for each of the 9 clips. You can look in the bin example narration clips and see how I've done it.

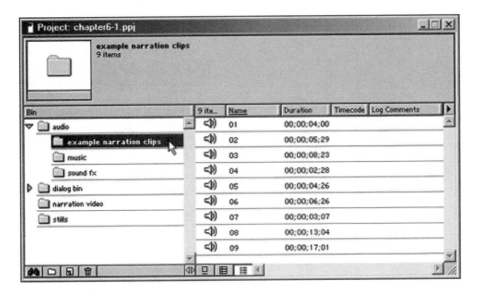

Now that our narration is split up, we should figure out what we intend to do with our other main element – the dialog scene. We don't really have any specifications as to where it is supposed to go in relationship to the narration, so we get to use some editorial discretion here.

7. It would work well as an opening segment, so let's lead off with it. Since that first shot of the scene, the establishing shot of Lorie going from the truck to the house is so long, let's put the first line of the narration (sub-clip 01) under that shot, go ahead with the dialog scene and then the rest of the narration.

8. Logically you'd think we would start off with dialog, right? This is *non-linear* editing: let's start in the middle with the narration and save the dialog for last, since it's more fun!

Now that we're ready to start putting clips on the timeline we should commit to using either **Single-Track Editing** mode or **A/B Editing** mode as our workspace. For this tutorial we'll be working in A/B mode, since it is easier to visualize overlaps, and it's actually my preferred method of working. However, use whatever is best for you.

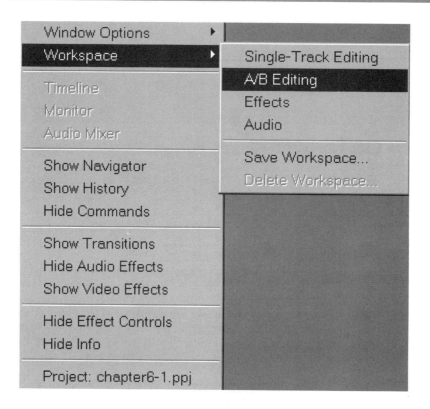

> We'll also be working in **drop-frame timecode** *for this project, as the footage was originally shot in DV (although it's been converted to QuickTime format for the tutorial).*

For our narration section, our first objective will be to space the segments we created to our liking.

Piecing Together the Narration

1.   Position the edit line at 4;00;02 by clicking in the timeline, or by typing 40000 and ENTER on the numeric keypad. Since we're in drop-frame, the last 0 will automatically be rounded up to a 2.

There are several reasons for not just starting the timeline at 0;00;00. In the days of linear editing, you had to leave some space at the beginning of a tape in case you wanted to add something. Once you made an edit, if you wanted to insert something before it, you had to redo every thing on the tape. Non-linear editing gives you the option to group select all your clips and move them about without ruining your continuity, however it is still good practice to leave some space to save you having to re-render your timeline again and again.

> *Another consideration for leaving a gap at the beginning of the timeline is if your project is destined for videotape. If you intend to make a tape master for duplication; you need to have bars and tone for calibration as well as a slate displaying the pertinent information of the project at the head of the tape.*

2. In this case, since we already know we will be adding clips before this, we'll go ahead and start at 4 minutes in.

3. Let's open the narration bin you've created (or the example narration clips bin I've provided), and select clips 02 through 09. Since we'll be dealing with a long chunk of clips, we'll want the timeline zoomed out quite a bit.

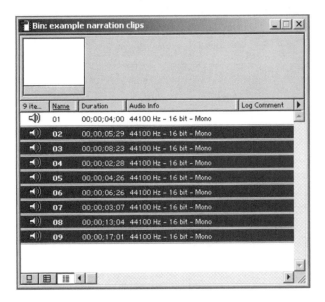

When you manually drag a clip to the timeline, your cursor will be *holding* the clip at its midpoint. If you're trying to position the clip accurately, you will need to have a pretty wide field of view so that you can see both ends of the clip. To do this, zoom out by using the – key and zoom back into the timeline using the + key. The timeline view will be centered on the edit line.

> *The + and - keys are active in any window without taking the focus off of that window, so you can be working in a Bin window, the Monitor window, or even the Effects window, and zoom in or out to examine the timeline without interrupting your workflow, or having to click away from the window you're working in.*

4. So, zoom out to the 4 second view level (indicated in the lower left corner of the timeline), and drag the selected clips (02-09) down to track Audio 1. As the front edge of the group of clips approaches the edit line you'll see it snap to the edit line; just drop the clips there.

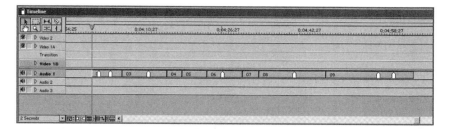

5. We'll edit these clips from the timeline, so zoom in to the 2 seconds level. Make sure that Audio 1 is selected – if it isn't, click on it at the left of the timeline – so that we can easily navigate between edit points. We'll start by adding a 15 frame gap between each clip, and adjust that to our liking.

6. Start by pressing M until the Track Select Tool is active.

7. Press SHIFT + CTRL + RIGHT CURSOR key (Windows) or SHIFT + COMMAND + RIGHT CURSOR key (Mac) to advance to the next edit. If the edit line goes anywhere but the next edit, double-check Audio 1 is selected.

8. Type in +15 from the numeric keypad to advance an additional 15 frames.

9. Click on clip 02 so that all the following clips are selected and drag it until it snaps to the edit line. To preview this edit, type -400 to go back 4 seconds and hit the ~ key to play. We'll go ahead and use this 15 frame spacing for all of the clips except between 04 and 05, let's put 1:15 between them.

Once you've performed these edits, we'll add pictures to the narration. If you want to cheat, you can open up the project file chapter6-2.ppj and start from there. If you want to keep working with your own edits, now is the time to save the project with a new file name.

All of the video clips we'll be using for the narration can be found in the narration video bin. You'll notice that there are numbers missing in the sequence of clips. I shot quite a bit of footage for this section and logged all the clips I thought I'd use.

Putting Pictures to Words

We'll cut together the narration clips using the Source and Monitor window.

1. Make sure your Monitor window is set to Dual View by either **1)** pressing the Dual View button at the top of the monitor window, or **2)** selecting Dual View from the Monitor Window Options button.

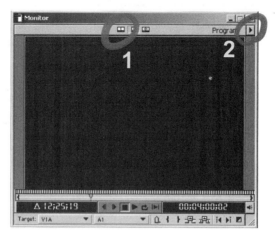

2. Open the narration video bin, select all the clips, and hit SHIFT + CTRL + L (Windows) or SHIFT + COMMAND + L (Mac), to open them in the Source window.

3. We want to start with the beginning of the narration, so click in the Program window and type in 40 000 then ENTER from the numeric keypad.

4. Hit the ESCAPE key to toggle over to the Source window. There you'll see a drop-down menu with a list of clips available for editing in the Source window. These can also be selected using the CTRL+ + (that's CTRL and PLUS) and CTRL + - keys – Mac users substitute COMMAND for CTRL.

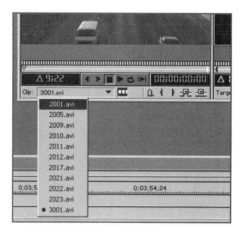

Looking over to the narration video bin window, we see a description of each shot in the log comments. Many of these even refer to specific dialog. We'll use these notes to match our clips to our narrative content.

Big and Slow

1. Referencing our script, for the section beginning "Big and slow", our first shot is 2005.mov – the shot of the Jeeps. Use CTRL and + or - to navigate to it, or select it from the drop-down list.

2. Let's start it with a close-up of the tyre, after the shaky cam. So we'll use the I key to set the In point at about 9:43:15. We'll want about 5 seconds of it, so type in +500 from the numeric keypad and hit O to set the Out point there.

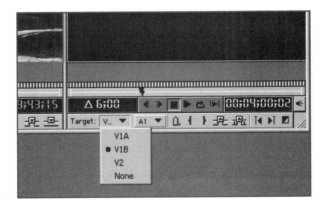

3. Hit Escape to toggle over to the Program window, verify that we are still at 4;00;02, and select the Video 1B track. Just like the clip selection in the Source window, you can select this either from the drop-down menu, or with the Ctrl and + or - keys.

4. Now just hit the . (full stop or period) key to send the clip to the timeline. If the timeline In and Out points have been set, you'll get a warning; The source and destination durations do not match. You'll have the option to; Change the speed, Trim the clip or Cancel the edit. In this instance we would cancel the edit and hit the G key to clear the In and Out points from the timeline. Pressing the Period key again will correctly perform the edit.

> The Period key performs an **overlay edit** – it will put a clip on the timeline without disturbing the total length of the program. The Comma key performs an **insert edit** – it will split the timeline at the edit line and shift all subsequent clips down the timeline to make room for the new clip, lengthening the program by the duration of the clip. The nice thing about using the . and , key strokes for edits, is that they are active from the Source window, the Program window, or the Timeline window. Without taking your hands from the keyboard, you can perform whatever edit is set up in the Monitor window.

We need to match the next two clips to cue markers in the narration, so we'll do a *drag and drop* with them after we've set their In and Out points.

Small and Fast

1. Next we have 2021.mov for Small and Fast. Let's start it at 1:00:35:17 as we're pulling back from the logo. We'll set the Out point at 1:00:41:17 for a 6 second duration. Since we're going to drag this clip to the timeline, zoom in to the ? second level. Grab the clip by clicking in the middle of the Source window, and drag it to Video 1A. As you near the first marker we placed in clip 02 at the line Small and Fast, you'll feel the clip snap to the marker.

2. Our next clip will be 3001.mov – the time-lapse shot of oncoming traffic. It needs to go to Video 1B at the second marker in clip 02. It looks as though we have the first two clips blocking both of Video 1's tracks, so we need to clean them up.

3. Using the Selection tool (hit V on the keyboard), drag the end of 2005 to snap to the beginning of 2021, and do the same for 2021 to the second marker.

4.   While we're in the timeline, click on clip 02, hit the DOWN CURSOR *key* to go to the end of the clip, and hit CTRL+ LEFT CURSOR *key* to go back to the second marker.

5.   Now, we'll select 3001 in the Source window, and use the PERIOD key to send it to Video 1B - make sure Video 1B is still selected, if not; toggle to the Program window and select it, either with CTRL and + and - or from the drop-down.

> You'll notice that we've been alternating between Video 1A and Video 1B for each clip. Since we're putting together a **cuts-only edit,** at this point there's no real reason to worry about alternating tracks. But we might want to come back later and add some transitions. In **A/B editing,** clips must be on opposite tracks in order to add a transition effect. We could deal with this later, but it's generally a good practice to alternate tracks as a general principle to save time down the road. If you know for sure you want straight cuts, don't bother – but if you think you might want (or need) a transition, take the time now.

This also means setting the Out point of clips on Video 1A so that they don't overlap with the start of clips on Video 1B. Generally, the easiest way is to manually drag the end of the clip as we did with 2005 and 2021. Although it makes for a neater timeline, adjusting clips on 1B is not necessary – Video 1A always takes priority over 1B on playback.

Transport Things

Our next edit is 2011, the shot of a car with a big box in the trunk. That will match up with the line "transport things".

1.   Let's set our In point just before the car comes into frame, at 14:24:18. Drag the clip onto Video 1A and snap it to the marker in 03.

2.   Next, let's use 2023, 2009 and 2010 to line up with narration clips 04, 05 and 06. The selected tracks should still be Video 1B and Audio 1, go ahead and select them if they aren't.

3.   Position the edit line at the top of narration clip 04 using the SHIFT + CTRL + LEFT CURSOR *key* or RIGHT CURSOR key. Again, it doesn't matter whether you are in the Monitor window or the Timeline window, this will cycle edits in either window.

4.   For 2023 we'll start it after the telephone pole on the right is out of frame at 1:01:36:00. Don't worry about an Out point for now, just verify Video 1B is active and drop it to the timeline with the . (PERIOD) key.

5. For 2009, we'll start it at the beginning of the pull back at 12;25;16, Hit ESCAPE to go to the Program window and change the destination track to Video 1A, either with CTRL and + or -. Advance the edit line to the start of 05, and use the PERIOD key to overlay the clip on the timeline.

6. We will go ahead and specify an Out point for our next edit, 2010, since it is such a long clip. Select it in the Source window and set an In point at 13;30;09. Advance 5 seconds by typing +500 on the numeric keypad, and make that the Out point.

7. ESCAPE to toggle to the Program window, select Video 1B as the destination track, advance the edit line to 06, and send the clip to the timeline.

> At first, using the keyboard to navigate clips, select tracks, and make edits can seem more cumbersome then simply dragging and dropping. With practice, however, it can be much faster than editing with the mouse. By the end of this chapter, you'll not only be editing, but you'll be doing it efficiently and quickly!

Using Our Stills

For our remaining edits we'll continue alternating tracks.

1. 2001 will start with the close up of the white car at 2;32;23, so set its Out point at +5 seconds since it's a longish clip, and match it to the marker in 06 ("*rent them").

   For clip 07 we'll use the still, named swapmeet.jpg, which is cleverly concealed in the stills bin. Stills don't open in the Source window, since there's no need to set an In and Out point; only a **duration** is needed.

2. Select the file in the bin and hit CTRL/COMMAND + R to specify a duration. We'll make this one 4 seconds.

3. Now, drag the clip from the bin to Video 1B at the start of narration clip 07.

4. For 08, we'll use clip 2010 again, but start it later in the shot, at 13;41;22, where the black car is fully on the screen, and give it an Out point 8 seconds later. Drop it on Video 1A at the beginning of 08.

> *As we discussed earlier, if Premiere gives the old The source and destination durations do not match warning anytime during this process; just cancel the edit, hit G to clear the timeline In and Out points, and perform the edit again.*

5. Another still image – `thriftynickle.jpg` – will go on 1B at the marker in narration clip 08 – and yet *a used jalopy (see the narration script).

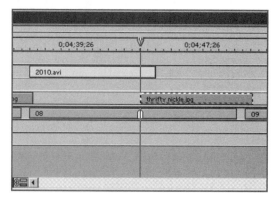

Occasionally, at certain zoom levels, you'll find that a clip doesn't snap accurately to a marker. To quickly compensate for this you can zoom in or out or; select the clip that contains the marker. Use the UP CURSOR key, or DOWN CURSOR key, to go to the end of the clip closest to the marker and CTRL + LEFT CURSOR key or RIGHT CURSOR key to navigate to the marker. This will place the edit line on the marker, and the clip you are manipulating will snap to that.

Polishing a Cadillac

1. For narration clip 09, we'll use 2017 to cover the beginning through the words "daily life". Let's start it at 23;40;19 at the beginning of the pull back shot and give it a duration of 12 seconds.

2. At the first marker, "and all too often", we'll use 2022, the twilight junkyard shot. Start it at 1;01;10;01 at the beginning of the pull back and make it about 4 seconds long.

3. For the final shot of the narration, we'll use 2012 – my friend Doug polishing his pride and joy; a 1989 Cadillac Fleetwood Brougham.

    We'll get a little trickier with this edit, because I want to synchronize a visual to the narration. We're going to place markers on the video clip and the narration clip, then perform a **Backtime** edit. In other words, we have a point in the video that needs to sync up with a point on the timeline, so we'll match those two points, and let the In point of the clip fall where it may.

4. Scrub through the clip and find the point where Doug breathes on the chrome of the mirror to fog it and then polish it. Right at 17;20;07, as he starts leaning back, drop a marker. Back up a second (-100 on the keypad) and make that the In point. That won't be our final In point, but it will keep us from bumping into things.

5. Open up the narration clip 09 from the timeline in a Clip window (ALT + double-click or OPTION + double-click). Set a marker (* or ALT + CTRL + =) at the beginning of the phrase "how you feel".

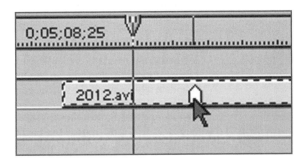

6. Grab the clip 2012 from the Source window and drag it to Video 1A past the end of 09 – it doesn't matter where, as long as it's to the right of where it'll end up.

Now for one of Premiere's "snap to" specials.

7. Zoom in close, to 8 frames. Place your cursor over the marker on 2012 so that the cursor turns green.

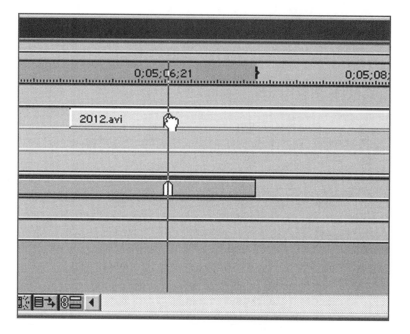

8. Click on the clip at that point and drag the clip to the left.

The snap line will lock into the marker we placed on the audio clip, perfectly synchronizing the two events that we had selected.

9. Now, we just use the Selection Tool, to stretch the beginning of 2012 to snap to the previous marker on narration clip 09, and our backtime edit is complete.

We've gotten all our clips in place for a rough cut to the narration, but we still have a lot of sloppy overlaps. When these are on Video 1A, our edits won't look right – the clip on Video 1B won't be visible until the clip on Video 1A runs out – so we need to manually clean up all those Out points.

10. Just like we did before, use the selection tool (V) to grab the end of each overlapping clip, and drag it to snap to the beginning of the next clip. You don't necessarily need to do this for Video 1B, but it makes for a cleaner timeline.

11. If you'd like to save your version of the project, do that now. We'll open a new version of the project, chapter6-3.ppj, so that we can be sure we are on the same page.

We've put together a rough cut of images for the narration but we don't know how well the whole thing flows yet. Let's put the edit line at 4;00;00 and play through what we have.

That works pretty well! There are just a few places that need some tweaking, and we'll be ready to cut our dialog together.

Fine Tuning Our Automobiles

The first thing that bothers me is the very first line; "Big and slow, or small and fast". The first line is so short that the Jeeps are crowding the Beemer too much. To fix this we'll split up that first line.

1. Open narration 02 in a Clip window and place a marker at 5;13, right between "slow" and "or". Close the Clip window and zoom in to the 1 frame level on the timeline.

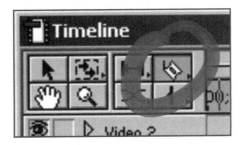

2. Press C to toggle through the Razor Tools until the Single Razor is selected. Next, click on the right edge of the marker. This will split the clip at the marker as indicated by a new 02 designation to the right of the split.

If the clip splits on the frame to the left of the marker, just hit CTRL/COMMAND + Z to undo, position your cursor to the right a bit and try again. That's why we zoomed in so close – so it would be simple to snap to a single frame.

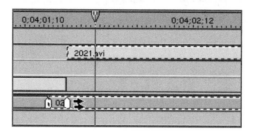

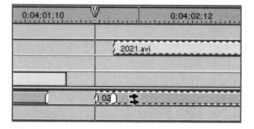

3. Once you've split the clip, position the edit line at the beginning of the new clip and advance it 10 frames. Use the M key to toggle through the Track Select Tools until you have the Multi-track Select Tool active.

4. Click on the audio clip just to the right of 2005 – this will select everything in the timeline after that clip – and drag until the beginning of the second 02 clip snaps to the edit line, and stretch the Jeeps out to meet the beginning of 2021.

That flows better. The audio edit sounds a little strange, but we'll cover that up with a music track before we're done. In Chapter 8, you'll learn how to cover that up even better, but for now it'll do fine.

The next issue I have is with the line "Ferry our children around" in clip 03. This is another good example of a real-world editing dilemma. I'd originally intended to get a shot of a soccer coach with a horde of kids in a mini-van, but I never found one. So, the choice is to either leave it, keeping the time-lapse shot as the visual – which works okay – or get rid of it. First rule of editing: If in doubt, chuck it out. Let's lose it.

5. Open clip 03 in a Clip window and place markers where we want to make our cuts. Since we have another marker nearby, we'll use numbered markers to eliminate confusion. Find the exact frame of "to" and back up 1 frame. Use ALT + CTRL + 1 to place marker number 1 there.

6. Find the frame before "and to transport" and place marker number 2 there. By placing the marker at the very top of the phrase; we can use the narrator's natural timing for the new edit, and not have to jockey the clips around. Very rarely will this not work with simple voice edits.

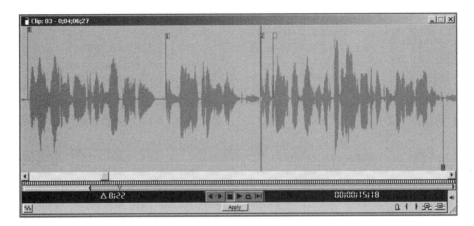

7. Using the same process we used on narration clip 02, Razor clip 03 at marker 1 and again at marker 2. Right-click (context-click for Mac) on the segment we just created, and select Ripple Delete from the drop-down menu. This will delete that section of the clip and slide everything that follows up to meet the previous clip. It will also shorten 3001, so that its edit stays the same in relation to 2011.

> *As with the previous edit, you **will** learn some more advanced audio techniques to make this edit seamless, but it will do for now.*

8. The next thing that bothers me is the space between narration clips 04 and 05. It's a bit too long, so let's use the Multi-track Select Tool (M) and click on Clip 05 to select everything after that. Press the UP CURSOR key to position the edit line at the beginning of the selected clips, and type -15 to move it back 15 frames. Drag the selected clips to snap to the edit line and play through the edit now to see how it flows.

Adjusting the Images

I like the audio spacing now, but the images just don't quite look right. Let's lead the narration a bit with the shot of the hotel sign.

We don't want to start it any sooner because the camera is way too shaky before the current In point, so let's slide the whole clip to the left to somewhere around the mid-point between the audio clips.

You thought I was going to ask for a specific number of frames didn't you? A lot of times that's a good way to work, but the very visual nature of non-linear editing also lends itself to seat-of-the-pants moves like this.

1. Use the Select Tool and drag the end of 2009 out to the next clip, then that tweak is finished.

    The shot of the rental cars starts a little early; I'd like to see the sign a little sooner and for longer, so we know for sure what we were looking at. We don't want to change where the clip starts and ends in relation to the timeline, just in relation to itself, so we're going to perform what is called a **slip edit**.

2. Press the P key to cycle through the Edit Tool options until the Slip Tool is selected.

    Clicking on the clip in the timeline will cause the Monitor window to show two thumbnails – the in and out frames of the clip – and at the bottom of these thumbnails will be an indicator of the amount of offset for the slip.

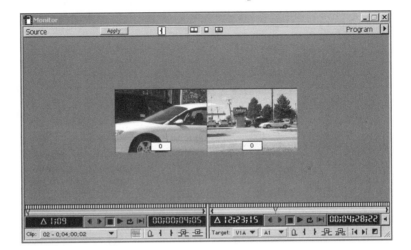

The functionality of this tool is somewhat counter-intuitive. Sliding the tool to the left, causing the offset to read negative values, makes the clip start later. Moving it to the right, increasing the offset value, causes the clip to start earlier. Just remember, "left is later" (referencing the negative values). It seems backward, but once you get used to it, it becomes second nature.

3. For slip edits, the accuracy of the tool depends on the level of zoom, so zoom in to the 1 Frame level. Click on 2001 and slip it to the left (later) so that the offset is –60 frames, and the clip starts 2 seconds later.

   The final thing I want to change is the shot of the junkyard. It runs into the last line too quickly, and loses some impact. To fix this, we want to lengthen clip 2017 and move the last line of narration and the shot of Doug with his Cadillac down a bit.

   To do this we'll need to first split the narration clip.

4. Switch back to the Select tool (V) and jump to the edit between 2022 and 2012 which is also the marker that indicates the beginning of the last line of narration. Under the Timeline menu, select the Razor at Edit Line option. Now our narration clip is split and we can move it independently of the first part of the clip.

I would now like to introduce you to your new best friend – the **Trim Edit window**.

5.   With the edit line still at the edit between 2017 and 2022 hit CTRL + T (COMMAND + T for a Mac) to activate the Trim Edit window, and CTRL + TAB to get over to it.

If you hold your cursor near the center of the window, you will see it change to indicate that both clips will be affected.

If you hold it near the center of one of the clips, it will change to indicate that only that clip will be altered.

In this instance, we want to increase the Out point of 2022 by 20 frames.

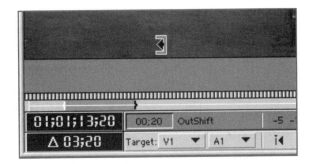

6. Click left of center on the left most clip, and drag to the right until the OutShift display reads 00;20 frames.

Pressing play (~) while in the Trim Edit window will preview the selected edit with 5 seconds of pre and post roll.

If you are working with the Trim Edit window and accidentally get things completely jammed up, the small x at the lower right of the Trim Edit window will cancel out all edits made in the session with the window.

Our timing is good now, but the end of the previous line still has the breath leading into the last line on it.

7. Open this first section of the clip in a Clip window and set a new Out point before the breath. Click Apply, and the clip on the timeline will be updated.

It's important to understand how Premiere handles editing a clip from the timeline in a Clip window, or the Source window. Premiere always resolves any changes made to the clip to its original starting point on the timeline.

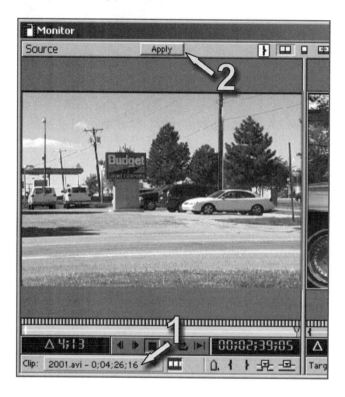

You'll notice that in a Clip window, the lower left corner will show the name of the clip, and the timecode at which it appears on the timeline. The same information is displayed in the Source window where the clip name is normally displayed (**1**). Once you change the In or Out point of the clip, an Apply button will appear (**2**). Pressing this will update the clip instance on the timeline to reflect the changes you have made. Remember; the clip's timeline In point will not change. Whatever you do to change the duration of the clip, it will still start at the same place it did before.

The Dialog Section

Now that we have our narration section dialed in nicely, let's put the dialog together.

I shot the dialog scene with help from my friends Stephen and Lorie. They are not professional actors – in fact, up till now they had both managed to avoid so much as a school play.

We shot this very basically, a few lines at a time from a couple of angles. I logged and loaded the usable takes, and have included as much footage in the downloads as space will allow so you can experiment with this as much as you like.

For now, we'll cut it together the way I see it (a true director's cut). We'll get experience at cutting together a multi-angle dialog scene, and we'll also have a little fun with a bit of a fast cut action sequence à la Guy Ritchie, and a Sam Raimi style shot!

For the dialog segment, we'll use one of Premiere's **storyboards** to arrange our clips in the proper order and create a rough cut of them. To start, let's create a new storyboard from the menu File > New > Storyboard. We'll save it in the storyboard folder as dialog storyboard.psq. You'll notice I have a storyboard in there already, called dialog storyboard example.psq. Go ahead and open it for reference, because that's where we're going to want to end up with your storyboard.

I've also sorted the shots into three bins inside the dialog bin; wide shots, Stephen's reverse angles, Lorie's reverse angles, and miscellaneous shots in the dialog bin itself. Each clip's log comments references the dialog that it covers, so we'll use that to search for shots.

If you have the facility to print out the script (it's a Word file named dialog script.doc in the documentation folder, also as a text file), it will be helpful to have as a reference while you're editing.

The Storyboard

1. We know we want to start with the establishing shot of Lorie going into the house, so grab clip 1024 from the dialog bin and drop it in the storyboard. Let's be conventional and start the dialog with a wide shot. I like 1004, up to "I picked up..." so toss that in.

2. For the next line we'll cut to Lorie in 1010, and then Stephen's query in 1014. Back to the wide shot with 1004 again for Lorie's response. After "The wedding planner..." the wind makes the audio unusable, so we'll cut back to Lorie in 1010 again.

3. Back to the two-shot for Stephen's line, this time the best performance is in 1002. At this point, your Storyboard should look like the screengrab:

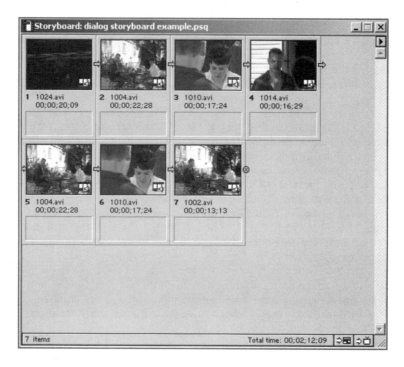

As you've no doubt noticed, we're not worrying about each clip's In and Out points yet. We just want to assemble the master clips for each section and then we'll trim each one to fit.

> As you're going along here, it might be helpful to be marking your hard copy of the script, for reference when we set the In and Out points. I usually scribble some brackets around each cut point we've picked, and jot down the clip number.

4. We'll finish Stephen's line with a close-up from 1015, go to 1011 for Lorie's reply, and finish with Stephen again from 1015.

Rather than trying to get reaction shots from the guys, I just worried about getting good coverage of each line so we could just cut it together.

5. We'll cut back to a wide shot again with 1005, and then focus on Stephen with 1016. Wide again with 1007, as Lorie begins to question Stephen's ability to balance the needs of a healthy relationship against the demands of deranged friends. We'll get close and personal with 1012 as Lorie drives the point home.

6. Yikes! Let's use 1007 to try and reduce the force of the withering glare that was directed at yours truly here, and then back to 1017 so Stephen can make a last valiant attempt to avoid a mind-numbingly awful experience.

7. Success! Lorie was a little too defeatist in 1008, but if we just use 1013 it makes her seem to capitulate too readily. So... we'll use one word, "alright", from the wide shot and cut to Lorie for the more upbeat permission.

8. Let's make sure your Storyboard has the same 18 clips in the same order as my example. If anything is different, shuffle the clips around, add them, or remove them as necessary.

Now, let's set the rough In and Out points for each of the clips. To do this, we'll open each clip in the Source window and set In and Out points like we normally would. Changes will automatically be updated in the Storyboard window.

Since we have multiple instances of some clips I will refer to them with their storyboard designation of 1 through 18 for this process.

9.   Open up clip number 1, and start it at the very top, running it to where Lorie walks behind the frame of the door. Referring to our script we see that clip 2 starts just before "How was work..." and ends after "The usual".

Rather than number each one, I'll leave it to you to go through and set each clip's basic margins, based on the notes you made on the script, as we put the clips in the storyboard. Of course, you could just cheat, because I'm going to get you to open another stage of the project, so I know with some degree of certainty that you're looking at what I think you're looking at.

10.   Now, save your work and load the project chapter6-4.ppj.

We're now going to use a handy feature new to version 6 of Premiere called Automate to Timeline, where we can drop our clips into the project.

Automate to Timeline

1.   Click or TAB into either the Timeline window or the Program window, and type in 20000 to place the edit line at 2;00;02 (drop frame, remember).

2.   Go back to the Storyboard window (use my storyboard for this so we'll be on the same bit) and either press the Automate to Timeline button at the bottom right of the Storyboard window, or select it from the Project menu.

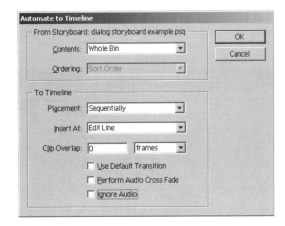

3. In the Automate to Timeline window, verify that the options are; Contents set to Whole Bin, Placement set to Sequentially, Insert At set to Edit Line, Clip Overlap set to 0 Frames, Use Default Transition is unchecked, Perform Audio Cross Fade is unchecked and Ignore Audio should also be unchecked.

4. Click OK and voila, you have a rough cut to the timeline! And notice that we didn't disturb our edited narration segment at 4;00;02.

Checking in at the Garage

We're still nowhere near "ready for prime-time" yet. We need to make a minor audio adjustment, and we need to really tighten these edits up.

First off, the dialog audio is only on the left channel – the right channel is the camera mic. We need to get rid of it so things don't sound goofy.

1. To do this, we'll zoom back so we can see all of the dialog clips. Press the M key to cycle through to the Marquee Selection Tool.

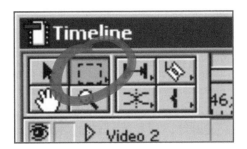

2. Select all of the audio portions of our dialog clips – *audio only*, no video. Then from the menu bar, select Clip > Audio Options > Duplicate Left. This will put the better left channel audio on both tracks.

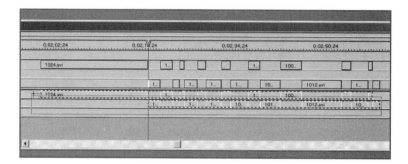

3. We don't need audio for the establishing shot at all, so select 1024 with the Regular Selection Tool (V) and from the menu bar, select Clip > Unlink Audio and Video. The clip will change from green – that signifies synched audio and video – to the individual yellow for video or teal for audio.

Premiere will also drop a marker in the middle of both audio and video clips so that if you need to re-synch them later, it will be simple to do. In this case, we don't even want the audio, so select it and delete it.

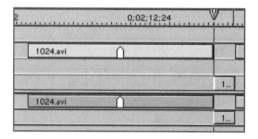

This long establishing shot needs to be tightened up too. I like starting with the closed car door, and I like ending with the out of focus house door. We don't want to speed it up so that it looks like Keystone Kops, so we'll find a way to make it move along quicker *without* changing its duration. We've already talked about using the first line of narration under it, which will help, but we'll also put a music bed down, to give it a little more energy.

The other thing we can do is a **split edit** with Stephen's first line of dialog. By starting his voice while we are still seeing the previous visual, we can *push* the feel of the edit.

4. Start by opening 1004 in the Source window and putting a marker where we want the visual to cut. Let's put it right between Stephen and Lorie's lines, at 38;35;15.

5. Zoom in to the 2 frame level and using the Normal Selection Tool, hold down CTRL + ALT and position the cursor over the beginning of 1004. You'll see the cursor icon change to indicate the *split* edit mode. This will allow us to temporarily modify the video track without affecting the audio track.

6. Drag the video portion of the clip to snap to the marker. Select the Multi-track Selection Tool (M) and click on the video portion of 1004 to drag all the subsequent clips up to close the gap. Notice that our narration section is moved by the same amount. No harm there, since we will eventually be combining it with the end of the dialog segment anyway.

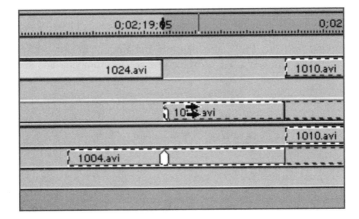

7. To tighten the rest of the dialog edits up, we'll go back to the Trim Edit window. Go to our first edit – between 1004 and 1010 – and hit CTRL/COMMAND + T to launch the Trim Edit window, and CTRL + TAB to go to it. From here on, we won't need to leave the Trim Edit window until we're done tweaking the dialog edits.

The Trim Edit Window

Everything we need to do at this point can be done from this window. We can adjust each edit point, either modifying the clips individually or at the same time. Modifying each clip by itself produces what is referred to as a **ripple edit** – all the subsequent clips move forward or back in the timeline in relation to the changes we make.

Dragging in between the two clips to modify them together performs what's called a **rolling edit**. In a rolling edit, only the interface point between the clips is adjusted, all subsequent clips remain in place. If we drag the edit to the left, we will remove frames from the end of the previous clip, while adding the same number of frames to the beginning of the following clip.

The edits can also be done *numerically* by typing in a value from the keypad. Or you can nudge them one frame at a time with the arrow keys, or five frames at a time using the SHIFT key with the ARROW keys. Like the Monitor window, the focus of the Trim Edit window is determined with the ESCAPE key to select the preceding clip, the following clip, or both clips to perform a rolling edit. You can navigate through the edits with the CTRL + LEFT CURSOR or RIGHT CURSOR keys.

Each edit can be previewed by hitting play (~), and the OutShift and InShift displays will continue to show the amount of change from the original edit points – meaning you can tweak the edit to a high standard, without getting hopelessly off track. And, if you do get it too snarled up, there's always the Cancel Edit button.

Just keep in mind as you are previewing edits which edit you're supposed to be looking at. When you are working with very short edits like this, the amount of pre- and post-roll will often cover several edits. It's easy to lose track of which one you're modifying and should be watching.

> *One thing to remember when you're cutting dialog and nothing seems to be working; close your eyes. Listen to the rhythm of the voices – if they don't sound natural, the visual won't look right either!*

After you've had a chance to experiment with tweaking the edits for the **dialog** section, open up the chapter6-5.ppj project, and we'll put the little action sequence together, melt the two segments together, and put the finishing touches on the rough cut of our little movie.

Finishing Touches

After Lorie gives Stephen her blessing to go off-road drag racing, we want to use a series of very quick cuts to show that Stephen isn't about to give her a chance to change her mind!

1. Create a new storyboard and save it as action sequence storyboard.psq. For reference, mine is called; action sequence storyboard example.psq.

2.	Into this storyboard we want to place most of the remaining clips from the root level of the dialog bin. In order, they are: 1019, 1021, 1022, 1020, and 1023. With the exception of 1023 (where we'll let the truck get a fair way down the road), these will each be about half a second long. We'll use the Automate To Timeline function again to place them at the end of the current dialog segment, and touch them up like we did with the dialog edits.

	These shots really need to pop – we need to give Stephen just a breath to react to his unexpected freedom, then the whole sequence should come across like a single motion.

	In the next installment of our project chapter6-6.ppj, I have my interpretation of the action sequence in place, and we're ready to finish up the rough cut.

3.	At the beginning, I want to add the first line of narration right where Lorie starts to swing the car door closed. Scrub the timeline to that point, about 2;05;18 is where I see it, then open clip 01 in a clip window, set the In and Out points at the beginning and end of the line, and drop the clip on Audio 1 at the edit line.

4.	The car door opens a little too quickly also. Let's drag the start of that shot back about 1 second.

	It's still just laying there, still lacking something. It needs.... cheesy music!

5.	Open the song *Get Happy* from the music bin. We don't need all the introductory nonsense at the beginning, we want to jump right to the heart of its cheesy goodness. Set the In point at 10;04, and drop it on Audio 3 at the beginning of the first clip.

6.	We also want it to fade out when the dialog starts, so drag the end to about the middle of the second dialog clip.

7.	Expand the Audio 3 track to show the waveform and level rubberband.

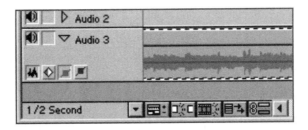

8.	Using the Standard Select Tool, place your cursor over the red rubberband, just before the downbeat before 1004. The cursor will turn into a pointing finger. Clicking on the red line will add a **node** to it.

9. Holding the Shift key as you click, will bring up a tool tip that will show you the exact level the node is placed at. In this case, we want the node to be at 100% to start the fade.

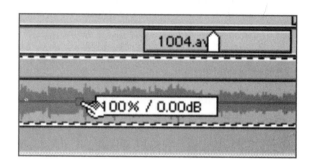

10. There is already a node at the end – every audio clip has a node at the beginning and at the end. We want to drag this one down to 0% to end the fade.

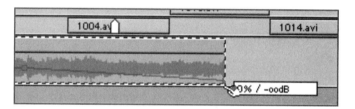

11. It's still a little too loud overall so go to the menu bar, and under Clip > Audio Options > Audio Gain, set the Gain Value to 50%. This will affect the basic volume level of the entire clip, and any changes we make with the rubberband tool will add or subtract from this level.

    That gets the intro moving along a little better now.

    To heighten the tension, and show that Stephen is indeed facing a very real threat, we'll use a cutaway shot of a super-fast push in to the dreaded tape itself. This is clip 3002 in the dialog bin.

12. Let's start it just after Lorie says "don't you remember" at about 2;26;00 on the timeline. We'll use the clip from the top, so we can just drag it straight from the bin to the timeline. Rather than cutting into the video we already have there, we'll just drop it on Video 2 and drag its end to match the start of 1002.

    Hmmm... again it's just laying there – It still needs something... another cheesy sound effect!

13. In the sound effects bin, there is the aptly named zoom.mp3. Drop that on Audio 3 at the beginning of our zoom and now we've got something.

14. I knew I'd want something to push the quick cuts at the end over the top so I had Stephen give me a reading of "thankshoneyloveyabye" all rushed together as one word. It's clip 1018 in the ra stephen bin. Open it up in a Clip window and set it's In and Out just at the edges of the dialog.

15. Hop to the Program window and select a destination track of None for video, and Audio 3 for the audio. Let's drop it in the timeline right as the fork comes to rest at about 2;59;28. Also, under the menu bar, click Clip > Audio Options > Duplicate Left channel, as we did with the rest of the dialog. There, that adds a bit to the general mayhem of this sequence.

As you might guess, it's time to go back to the well for more cheesy music. In the music bin is a song called make it stop okay.mp3 (I swear I'm not making the names of these songs up). We're going to do another **backtime edit** with this song so that we can match the last snare drum hit before the slide whistle to the fade of Stephen's brake lights.

16. Open the song in a clip window and drop a marker at 3:10 with the drum hit.

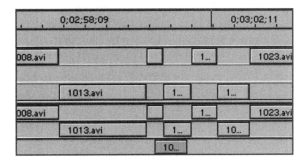

Now we need to put it on the timeline, but we seem to have a bit of a dilemma. We want the song to start with the action sequence, but with the voice over, all of our tracks are full. We *could* add an audio track, but because of our layout, we are limited on space. However, if our clips weren't alternating tracks, we'd have plenty of room.

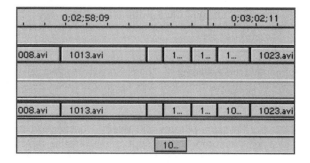

17. Since we know for sure that we'll always want this sequence to just be *cuts*, let's put all of the last 6 clips on the same set of tracks.

18. Now we can drop the music on Audio 2 and snap our cue point to the beginning of 1023. It's a bit loud too, so we'll set its overall gain to 50% like the first music clip.

    Stephen got what he wanted, so we need to give Lorie the last word. We'll do another audio overlay just like Stephen's mumbled farewell, this time from the clip 1026 in the dialog bin.

19. Set the In and Out to bracket the line, "Don't come home with a pink truck!" and do an overlay edit to Audio 3 (make sure Video is set to None for this one too), right at the point where Stephen pulls fully into the frame at about 3;05;00. Just like all of the others on camera audio, we need to duplicate the left channel on this one too.

    Shortly after that point, you can hear myself and Lorie discussing the merits of that take on the camera mic, so let's do another **split edit** and shorten *just* the audio track.

20. While holding CTRL + ALT, drag the end of the audio track only of 1023 until it snaps to the end of 1026.

    Now we just need to bring in the narration segment.

21. To do this we need to temporarily shorten the music to the end of 1023. Next, we need to move the video track of 1023 to Video 1B so that it's on the same track as the first clip of the narration sequence. Just as holding ALT + CTRL while sizing a synched clip allows you to affect only the audio or video portion, it also allows you to move the audio and video independently of each other, either to a different track or to a different point in time.

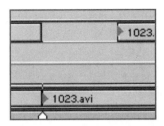

In the event that the tracks get out of synch a small red triangle will appear at the beginning of the clip. From there it's a simple matter to snap the clips back to each other.

22. To move 1023, hold ALT + CTRL and drag the video clip to Video 1B. Now that it's on the same track as the clip immediately following it, you can select the empty space between them, just as you would any clip. By selecting from the menu bar Timeline > Ripple Delete, the narration will take its place at the end of the dialog segment.

23. Now we can stretch the music track out to the end of the narration section, and that's it! We've got a rough cut together.

Summary

In just a few dozen pages, we've learned the basics of editing with Premiere – and it is an editing package after all. But, as with all the chapters in this book, we've also took the occasional pit stop to discuss best practice and talk about the real challenges you'll face as an editor or filmmaker.

We've looked at:

- Editing audio and video in sync

- Pacing our video alongside narration

- Techniques and shortcuts in Premiere

- Tidying up our cuts with some of Premiere's features

In the next chapter we'll look at transitions and discover how to add yet more finesse to our little movie with the minimum of effort!

3. Back to the two-shot for Stephen's line, this time the best performance is in 1002. At this point, your Storyboard should look like the screengrab:

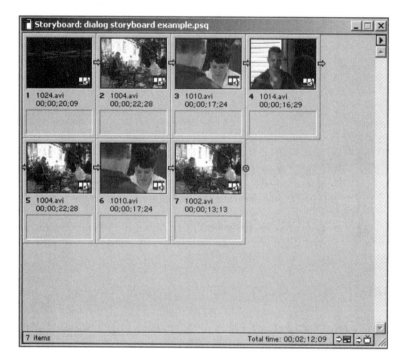

As you've no doubt noticed, we're not worrying about each clip's In and Out points yet. We just want to assemble the master clips for each section and then we'll trim each one to fit.

> *As you're going along here, it might be helpful to be marking your hard copy of the script, for reference when we set the In and Out points. I usually scribble some brackets around each cut point we've picked, and jot down the clip number.*

4. We'll finish Stephen's line with a close-up from 1015, go to 1011 for Lorie's reply, and finish with Stephen again from 1015.

Rather than trying to get reaction shots from the guys, I just worried about getting good coverage of each line so we could just cut it together.

Transitions are, as the name implies, a method of changing from one scene to another. In this chapter, we'll look at the various types of transition and how to use them most effectively and appropriately in Premiere.

The simplest of all transitions is a cut – an abrupt and instantaneous change from one image to the next – but you didn't need a degree in film studies to guess that! In fact, these are simply named after the process of physically cutting a piece of film at the desired edit point.

More advanced transitions include dissolves, wipes, pushes, and picture in picture effects such as zooms and 3D moves. We'll cover all of these later on once we start playing in Premiere.

Transition Traditions

Where and when to use transitional elements is a highly debated issue. As a general rule, dramatic presentations tend to be more cuts oriented, while other types of programs such as promos or commercials might be suited to the visual flair of more exciting transitions.

Sometimes a dissolve (fade between shots) or other transition is used to cover an edit that would otherwise be a **jump cut** – for example, if you were editing an interview and wanted to edit two parts together, there would be an ugly jerk in the picture, an awkward jump from one sentence to the next where the interviewees head and mouth would suddenly change! It used to be that these cuts would be covered over by overlaying some background footage or a cutaway shot, but these days, even in high-end news-journalism, it is now acceptable to place a quick dissolve over such a cut to soften it.

Cuts tend to imply continuous action, whereas a dissolve or a wipe often indicates the passage of time, or a change in location.

A lifetime of TV and movie watching has conditioned us to not even notice a smooth cut. On the other hand, blending images with a dissolve or the motion of a wipe or effect move, can draw attention away from the action on screen. Sometimes this is the desired effect, and sometimes it's detriment to a the narrative flow.

There aren't any hard and fast rules, just commonly accepted conventions. Old editors have an adage though: "If it don't work as a cut, it ain't gonna work as a dissolve neither!" and while grammatically incorrect, this is good advice. As much as possible, try to fine tune edits so that they flow naturally as a cut before using any other type of transition. If it's a cosmetic cover-up you need, see if you have something you can use as a cutaway shot – it might not even directly relate to the action on screen – maybe you can use the opportunity to foreshadow a coming event. While a wipe or dissolve or other effect might help to obscure a bad edit, if the underlying rhythm of the edit isn't smooth, it will still seem strange on a subliminal level.

Let's think about all this on a more practical level.

Learning to Notice Transitions

This is just a quick exercise to get you started noticing cuts and transitions. You won't need to turn your computer on for this one, although a trip to the video store might be in order!

1. Pick a video or DVD of your choice; something you've watched to death would be ideal.

2. Choose a fairly important scene or sequence and sit down with a notepad. Pay attention to which transitions are used: and also when and how they are used. Take note of any which interest you.

3. Now turn on the TV and watch a few commercials, following the same procedure with your notebook.

4. Repeat this for as many different kinds of program as you care to. This is your research, and just looking at how different transitions are used in different situations and in different genres, will teach you loads about how and why they work.

5. Once you've spent a little while analyzing the scenes, start thinking about why those transitions were used. You'll probably have noticed a lot of trends:

   - Action scenes tend never to use dissolves – they're too slow and distracting.

   - Dramas of any kind tend never to venture beyond the cut or dissolve. Page turns and wipes are usually confined to commercials and promos.

   - Lastly, if you saw one, you'll have noticed that dream sequences are the playground of the transition-obsessed editor.

Transitions can be used to underline, highlight, or reinforce the emotions or events being conveyed in your scenes, so it's important to understand from the outset how pivotal they are.

Transitioning in Premiere

With 75 transitions at our fingertips in Premiere, the temptation to go crazy can be overwhelming. The only way to really get a feel for transitions is to freely experiment with them, and overusing them on an experimental basis will help get past the impulse to make every edit a 3D-picture in picture-fly out with shadows and trails.

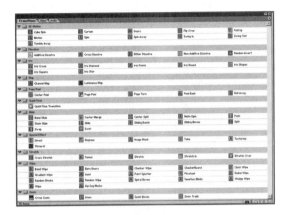

In addition to an abundance of built-in transitions, Premiere also has many effects filters that can be used as transition effects. Additionally, many capture cards come bundled with supplemental proprietary transitions, and there are many third-party plug-ins available. For our purposes here, we'll just familiarize ourselves with the transitions native to Premiere, and we'll focus on the most commonly used ones in order to get comfortable with how transitions are applied and customized.

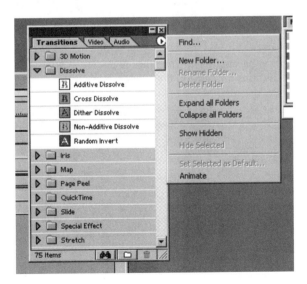

To begin with, all of your transitions are managed from the Transitions palette (if it's hidden you can show it from the Window menu), which has the usual options button – the triangle within a circle at the top-right corner. You can search for a transition by name, create new folders to organize the transitions to match your workflow, and hide seldom used transitions. You can specify a default transition and duration that can be applied from a keyboard shortcut (CTRL+D), and indicate whether it should start at the cut, end at the cut, or center on the cut. You can even animate the icons in the palette window – but this is a huge waste of computer resources, not to mention a good way to induce a splitting headache.

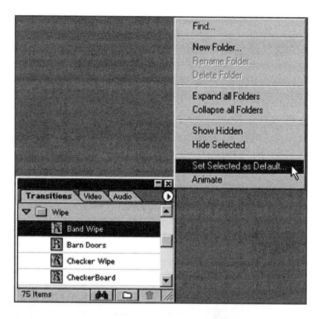

Transitions can only be applied to the track Video 1, although there are techniques that can simulate most transitions for clips on the super tracks, Video 2 and above.

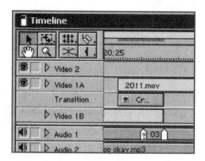

Using a transition also requires that you have an appropriate amount of footage available – if you're currently cutting on the last usable frame of a shot and you want to add a 30 frame dissolve, it's going to have to start 30 frames earlier than the cut or it's going to look mighty strange.

Types of Transition in Depth

Cuts aside, transitions can be divided into three major categories:

Dissolves

We've mentioned these already. A dissolve is where one image gradually fades into another. Cross Dissolves are the most common – the opacity of the preceding clip is reduced to 0 to reveal the next clip. Other types of dissolves such as Additive make calculations based on the total luminance or color values in the pixels of the transitioning clips. Besides simply fading one clip into another, a common technique for dissolves is to *touch black* – where the first clip dissolves to black, and the following clip comes immediately up from black. The same type of technique can be used with a slightly tinted white matte rather than black to simulate the flash frame artifact created when starting and stopping a film camera. And, of course, every movie begins with a dissolve up from black, and most end by fading out to black as well.

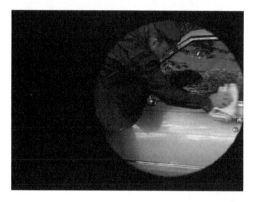

Wipes

Wipes are transitions where one image is literally *wiped* off the screen to reveal the next picture. Wipes come in a limitless variety of shapes: diagonal, vertical, horizontal, box wipes – you can even create your own wipe pattern by using the Gradient Wipe function.

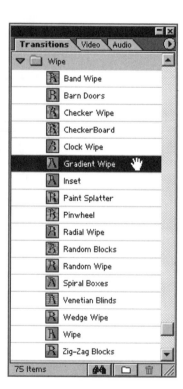

A sub-category of wipes is the Iris transition. Rather than starting at one edge of the picture and moving to another edge to reveal the next clip, an Iris effect starts or ends with a point *within* the picture, like the circular wipe featured in the screengrab earlier.

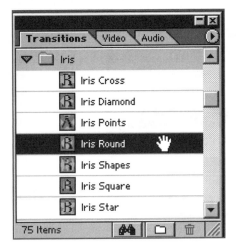

Digital Video Effects

The third category of effects is often referred to as DVEs, or Digital Video Effects. Unlike a wipe where all of the pixels of both images remain in the same place during a transition, a DVE actually applies geometric transformations to the image data.

Compare for example a horizontal wipe to a slide transition. In each instance the new image comes on from the left, but the slide actually moves the entire frame into view over the underlying image rather than just gradually revealing it. Page peels, zooms, 3D moves – anything where the video image actually moves around the screen – are all example of DV effects.

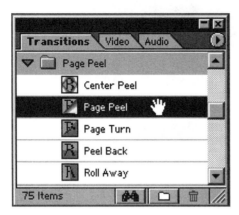
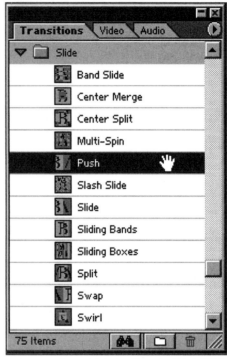

Desktop video technology also gives us the ability to create transitions that defy classification. Filter and motion effects can be keyframe-animated to generate complex multi-layer transitional elements that would be difficult or impossible any other way.

Let's apply some of the more tasteful effects to our work in progress and see how we can enhance the production values. Then let's slap on some that are so hideously tacky they would have been rejected for use on Batman.

Making the Transition

1. To make sure we're on the same bit, go ahead and open chapter7-1.ppj from the projects menu.

First off, let's put a simple 30 frame dissolve at the beginning to fade up from black. Since the cross dissolve is the most commonly used transition next to the cut, let's go ahead and make it the default transition.

2. In the Transitions palette, open the Dissolve folder and select Cross Dissolve. Click on the Options button and select Set Selected as Default...

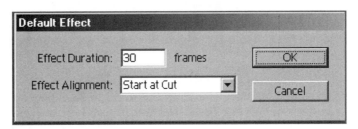

3. In the following dialog box set the duration to 30 frames. This will give the dissolve a default duration of 1 second whenever it's applied (unless it is applied to an existing overlap in which case it will automatically become the length of the overlap). For the Effect Alignment option select Start at Cut. The other options are Center at Cut, or End at Cut. Every edit will be different, so it's not critical what you choose here. I prefer Start at Cut since that's the way it seems to fall most of the times, so that's what we'll use for the tutorial.

4. Now that that's out of the way, grab the Cross Dissolve icon and drag it to the Transition track so that it snaps to the beginning of the first clip 1024.mov. Since we set the default it's already 30 frames long, which is what we want. Since we're fading up from black, we can just dissolve the empty timeline (which is automatically black) to the clip.

5. With a non real-time-enabled system, we'll need to render the transition to see what it looks like. To do this we would set the Timeline Work Area to cover the transition and select Timeline > Render Work Area. Another option to preview the transition is hold the ALT key and scrub the timeline over the transition. This won't show you the pacing of the transition, but it will let you verify that the two images blend well together, and that the transition is going in the proper direction – from track Video 1A to 1B or vice versa.

You'll notice right away that ours isn't! Since our clip is on 1A it should be going from B to A, but it defaults to A to B if the transition isn't being applied to overlapping clips. By previewing the transition, you can see that it abruptly starts with a flash frame of the clip, fades to black, and then snaps back to the clip again.

6. To fix this, right-click the transition on the timeline and select Transition Settings. Here you'll see a control panel for the transition:

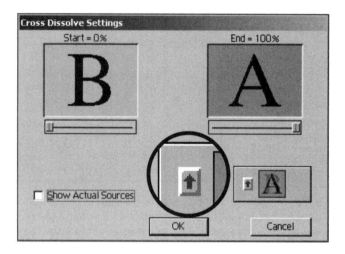

For a Cross Dissolve, this panel is very simple – it consists of a Start and End Percentage, an option to show the actual source in the Start and End control windows, and at the lower right is an animation indicating the direction of the transition with an arrow to the left to modify the direction.

7. In this case, we want to click on the arrow so that it is pointing up, and the animation shows the B dissolving to A. Click OK to apply this change to the timeline. This directional control is also visible when you zoom in closely to the timeline.

You might also be wondering what the Start and End percentages might be good for. For most transitions, you'll simply start at 0% and end at 100%, but occasionally you might want to dissolve a clip halfway in and hold it there momentarily for a superimposed look, then continue the transition. This could be done on Video 2 with the opacity controls (more about these shortly), but it can also be done with 3 dissolves – 1 from 0% to 50%, one from 50% to 50% for the length of the hold, then a final one from 50% to 0%. The same technique can also be used for picture-in-picture and split-screen effects.

That takes care of that abrupt beginning. I like the pacing of the dialog section as cuts, so let's jump ahead to the narration segment.

The first two edits of the narration segment are already pretty short, so we'll leave those as cuts. Let's put a transition between the Beemer and the time-lapse shot – 2021 and 3001.

When I'm using transitions other than dissolves, I like to try and fit the transition to the images. For this edit we have a car that's at a kind of Dutch angle to the lower left, followed by cars moving from top to bottom.

8. Let's use a DVE that reflects the motion of the cars in 3001. Position the edit line at the top of 3001 and add 1 second. Drag the end of 2021 to snap so that there is a one second overlap.

9. From the Slide folder in the Transitions palette, drag the Slash Slide transition to the transition track between 2021 and 3001. Now, right-click on the transition on the timeline as before to edit its settings. At the lower left of the Settings window is the animated icon surrounded by 7 white triangles and one red one (1).

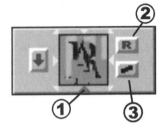

10. Transitions that have a directional option use this to specify the direction of the effect – as indicated by the red arrow. We want this effect to go from top to bottom to match the motion of the cars in the second clip, so select the bottom triangle. If you check the Show Actual Sources option, you can use the slider under the Start or End thumbnail to preview the effect – just don't forget to set it back where it should be. If you slide the Start slider you'll see the time-lapse shot appear to fall in strips over the Beemer.

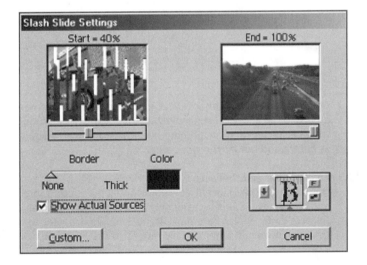

11. It would look immensely cooler if the speeding cars seemed to push the Beemer off the screen in strips, so we need to reverse the effect somehow. To the right of the preview animation, you'll see a button labeled F for Forward. Click on it, and it will change to R for Reverse (see 2 on the earlier diagram). Much better looking.

12. There are too many strips though, so let's click on the Custom button at the bottom-left and reduce those to 8, so the width of the slices is closer to the width of the lanes. The final adjustment we'll make is to the odd-looking button below the Forward/Reverse switch (3). This controls the amount of anti-aliasing applied to the transition. It's absolutely critical with any effect that has a diagonal component but it's not a bad idea to just set it to maximum quality on everything. Clicking it toggles through three levels of anti-aliasing as indicated by diagonally stacked boxes. The maximum setting will give the best-looking results, and won't really increase render times appreciably.

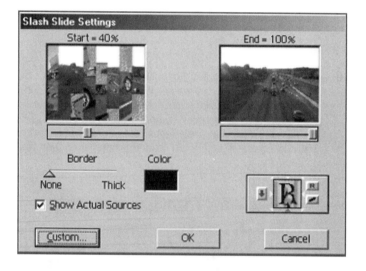

At this point we can either render the transition, or keep working and render them in groups, or all at once. I generally just ALT+SCRUB to make sure that it generally looks like what I expected, and then render everything at once. If you just can't wait to see it, do as before and render the work area.

13. For the next edit, between 3001 and 2011, we'll just use a simple dissolve. This one should end on the current edit point, so let's position the edit line there, and back it up 20 frames. Drag the beginning of 2011 back to snap to the edit line and hit CONTROL+D to apply the default transition. Since we set that to be a Cross Dissolve, that's what we get; automatically resized to the 20 frame overlap.

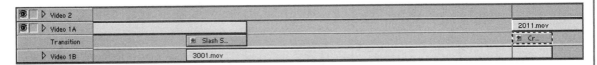

				2011.mov
Video 2				
Video 1A				
Transition		Slash S...		Cr...
Video 1B		3001.mov		

14. For the following edit – 2011 to 2033, we'll use another DVE effect, this one called Cross Zoom which can be found in the Zoom folder:

15. We want this transition to center on the cut, so let's drag the start of 2023 back 15 frames, and drag the end of 2011 15 frames later. Drag the Cross Zoom transition over this overlap, and open it up for editing.

16. You'll notice that it doesn't have any of the options by the animation display that the Slash Slide had, nothing but the directional control, which all transitions have. Look in the Start and End thumbnails though, and you'll see a tiny white dot. This sets a centerpoint for the zoom effect.

17. Let's position the Start centerpoint right in the middle of the steering wheel. You can slide the Start amount up a bit for more precision in placement; just don't forget to put it back. You can actually see the animation change to reflect the positioning of the center points. Put the End centerpoint in the middle of the truck's passenger window, and it'll sort of look like we zoomed into the car and out of the truck. The truck is actually at the wrong angle for this to look at all believable, but I'll leave that for you to reshoot if it bothers you too much!

We'll just do a regular Cross Dissolve for the next edit. We'll make this one a 1 second dissolve, and center it at the cut too.

18. We talked earlier about using transitions as filters, so that's what we'll do with the next clip, 2010. We'll still lead into and out of it with a cut but we'll use a Barn Doors wipe to simulate a "letterboxed" widescreen effect. This not only not the only way to accomplish this, but if you just need it quickly for effect it's a handy alternative.

19. Drag the Barn Doors wipe from the Wipes folder to the beginning of 2010, and drag it out to cover the entire clip. Open it up for editing, and we'll make it A to B and set the directional parameters to be vertical. Set the anti-aliasing where you want it and set the Start and End points both to 75%. This keeps the wipe in the same place for the duration of the transition, and since the A track is empty we get a black letterbox effect. If nothing else, this does illustrate the fact that with a little creativity, transitions are good for more than just transitioning things.

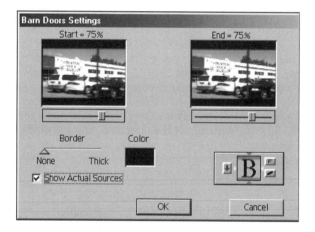

Since we just used a transition as a filter, it's only fair that we now use a filter as a transition, or as part of one at least. One common transition effect is actually performed at the time of shooting – a shift into or out of focus to lead into or out of a scene. Despite my meticulous pre-production work, I didn't think to do this when I shot the next clip, 2001.mov. Premiere has several blur filters that somewhat simulate this effect. It's not quite the same as a focus shift in actual camera optics but it looks nice, and there are plug-ins available that do it more accurately for the purists. For our purposes, we'll use the Fast Blur filter. It does render significantly faster than the Gaussian Blur and looks nearly as good.

20. In the same window as the Transitions palette, there should be a Video tab. This contains all of the video effects filters, and is laid out similarly to the Transitions palette. The filters will be addressed in detail in Chapter 10, but for now we'll jump ahead just a bit and play with one of them. This is *non-linear* editing after all, right?

Before we proceed, we need to determine where we want the blur effect to start. We're going to use keyframes to manipulate the intensity of the effect over time, but we don't want to apply the filter until the actual point where we want it to start rising from 0. If we were to apply the filter to the whole clip, but keyframe it so that it only blurred the last few seconds, the whole clip would still have to be rendered. If, instead, we split the clip a few seconds from the end and only applied the filter to the new second half, only that clip would need to be rendered.

I decided to start the effect during the word "place" in the narration. This didn't fall on any even number like most of the others have, so I'll walk you through how I have it and you can see what it looks like.

20. Start at the top of audio clip 07 and go back 24 frames. Zoom in tight and use the clip Razor tool to split 2001 here. Go forward 39 frames (1;09) and drag the out point of this new subclip to this point. Go back 24 frames from here, and drag the beginning of the swapmeet still to this point.

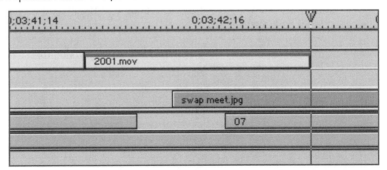

22. To apply the blur effect to the new subclip of 2001 drag the Fast Blur filter from the Blur folder onto the clip.

23. If your Effect Controls window is not active, select it from the Window menu.

We won't get too technical with the effect controls yet, but we'll set a couple of simple keyframes to make it look like a *rack focus* effect.

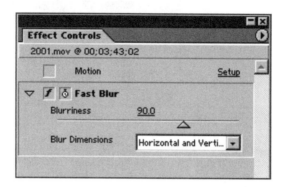

24. Expand the Fast Blur entry in the Effect Controls window and you'll see a slider to set the amount of blur and a drop down to select whether the blur dimensions affect the horizontal, the vertical, or both. In this case we want it to apply to Horizontal and Vertical.

25. Place the edit line at the top of the clip, set the amount of Blurriness to 0, and click in the box next to the name so that a stopwatch appears. This signifies that a keyframe has been set at this point. Keeping this clip selected, move the edit line to the start of the swapmeet still. Set the Blurriness amount to 90 and create a new keyframe. Just to be thorough, we'll move the edit line to the end of the clip and create another keyframe of 90 for the blurriness. This isn't always necessary, but it's a good habit to get into when working with keyframes. Leave nothing to chance, or you'll occasionally have a keyframed value unexpectedly ramp back to a previous value.

26. ALT+SCRUB to verify that our effect is indeed there and does what we want it to, then we'll add a cross dissolve to the overlap of this edit, and we have a nice little simulated focus shift dissolve.

Another example of the transitions and filters working together is the Motion transition in the 3D Motion folder.

Every video and graphic clip in Premiere can have a Motion filter applied to it that offers very powerful capabilities in animating, among other things, the position, size and rotation of the clip. These parameters can also be exported as a motion file. The Motion transition uses these motion files to apply the animation as a transition effect.

This edit, between the swapmeet still and 2010, is also based entirely on feel so there are some odd numbers involved in the timing of the edit.

27. We'll start the edit 12 frames back from the end of Narration clip 07 – drag the beginning of 2010 back to snap to that point. Jump forward 1;27 and pull the end of swapmeet to there. Drop the Motion transition on this overlap and open it for editing. Click on the Custom button and load in the file `fallaway.pmt` from the motion paths folder of the tutorial project. Now we've got a nice little "fly out" DVE effect!

28. For the next edit, let's follow the motion of the cars off of the right of the screen and apply a Push transition from the Slide folder. We'll select the directional arrow on the left of the animation icon so that the newspaper graphic appears to follow the cars onto the screen. That's not too awfully tacky is it?

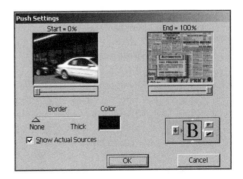

29. You'll have noticed that many of these transitions have the option of a colored border. For some reason, these don't do anything for me so I seldom use them. Don't let that stop you from experimenting with them; you might well come up with some good creative uses for them.

30. Whenever I have a graphic like the newspaper ad, I have to be physically restrained from using a page turn transition. Since it's just us ... let's go for it! In the aptly named Page Peel folder you'll find the Page Turn transition. Page Peel and Page Turn are essentially the same effect – Peel puts a white backing on the clip and Turn shows a mirror image of the clip, as if it were translucent. Since this is supposed to be a newspaper with printing on both sides we'll use the Page Turn transition so the back will look a little busier.

31. We'll center this one at the cut as well. Drag the two participating clips' edges 15 frames in the opposite directions, and drop the Page Turn transition on the overlap. The only editing we need to do to this one is to set the directional control so that the turn starts from the lower right corner:

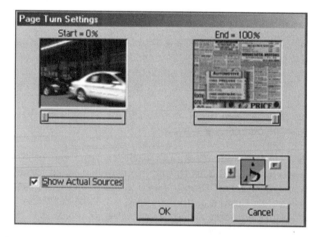

A subtle sound effect with a transition can really help enhance it. It can also be incredibly annoying. This technique should be used only with the greatest of discretion. Since we're already so far over the top on this little project, we don't even have to stop and think.

32. Since we've got a page turning sound effect (it's in the sound fx bin and it's called pageturn.mp3) let's just drop it right on there. About 5 frames in from the start of the transition should feel right. It's not a bad idea to build up a good library of whooshes, swishes, whirrs, clicks, and other similar miscellaneous sound effects. It's easy to overdo these, but they're really cool when they work.

Another powerful transition available in Premiere is the Gradient Wipe. This is a wipe that uses a grayscale gradient image to determine the wipe's direction and speed. Black indicates the start of the wipe, and white indicates the end. This is easily visualized with a simple horizontal wipe. What is harder to visualize are the complex wipe patterns available with advanced gradient images.

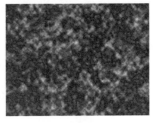

What I wanted for the transition between 2017 and 2022 was a wipe that suggested erosion and decay, so I created a gradient for it in Photoshop using multiple iterations of the Difference Clouds filter. We'll start this edit at the same place, we'll just draw 2017 out to overlap 2 seconds of 2022.

33. Drag in the Gradient Wipe transition from the Wipes folder. Premiere will show you a dialog box where you can click Select Image to load the file `rustycar.pct` from the wipes folder in the tutorial directory. We don't want any softness for this one, but that can be a nice organic effect for a transition.

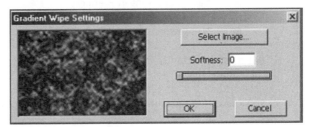

34. Hit OK to accept the edits, and we have an interesting wipe. Gradient wipes are challenging to create, but they offer an infinite number of wipe patterns. You can use Photoshop or your favorite image editor to create them – or there are a number of them available from third party developers.

35. To get into our final clip of Doug polishing his car, we'll use a 30 frame dissolve that ends on the current edit point. I'm sure you can by now manage this on your own!

This just leaves us with the question of how to close the project. Obviously a traditional old fade-to-black is completely unacceptable. This project demands a little more creativity than that! What could be better than a good old-fashioned cartoon style Iris wipe? Let's start the wipe just as soon as the push-in of the camera stops.

36. Scrub to this point, and drag the Iris Wipe transition from the folder to the Transitions track to snap to the edit line. Since there is no overlap, it assumes the default duration of 30 frames. We want it longer than that, so select it, and hit CONTROL+R for duration and set the duration to 3 seconds. Now just drag the out point of 2012 back to match the end of the transition.

37. The only editing we'll need to do on this one is to set the End centerpoint somewhere to the right of center about halfway up. We want it to appear to close on his hand as he's polishing the car. This might take some experimentation to correctly position the centerpoint, since at the end of the transition all you can see is black. Use ALT+scrub on the timeline to dial it in.

Congratulations! Our little masterpiece now has that much more production value going for it.

Summary

Transitions are a great way to add impact to a project, and can be a fun creative exercise. In this chapter we've covered:

- How best to use transitions

- Different types of transition

- Basic transitions in Premiere

- Using effects and filters to enhance our transitions

But most importantly we learned that, no matter how breathtakingly original our transitions are, the minute they interfere with the story, they're a bad, bad thing. Do some more silly little fun projects like this so you won't be tempted to show off on the really important ones. On those, you'll have the restraint to use transitions subtly, cleanly, and tastefully.

08 Sound

It can't be overstressed just how important good sound is to your productions. You could possibly get away with shaky camera shots, the odd bit of poor quality video, or even a little bad editing, but if there's one thing that will really mark out your work as being amateur, it's inaudible, or poorly edited sound. Like editing in general, you tend to only notice it if it's bad, so you need to pay plenty of attention to the **sound design** of your production.

By the end of this chapter, you should be able to edit sound in a range of different ways, create overlapping **sound** cuts, and sync and un-sync your audio and video. You should also be able to use Premiere's Audio Mixer and understand how to layer sound to create an interesting **soundscape**. We'll also cover Premiere's audio effects, and how they can be used to create effects, and improve the quality of your recorded sound.

Ultimately, the quality of your sound is going to depend on how well it was recorded. There are a few things you can do to boost the quality of poor audio, or to disguise background noise during editing, but at the end of the day, you're pretty much stuck with what you've recorded.

Therefore, it makes sense to devote a little attention to getting good sound in the first place. If possible, always make sure one person on your shoot is completely dedicated to sound, and give them the appropriate time and equipment to do their job properly.

When recording sound, always make sure you're using a good set of headphones. If you're using more than one mike at the same time on a shoot, you could do with a mixer box so you can set the relative levels coming from each microphone.

Most camcorders allow you to plug in additional microphones, but if you want the camera to move freely, you might consider bringing along a separate DAT (digital audio tape), or minidisk recorder so you can record the sound independently. If you do this, you'll need to sync the sound up again in the edit. This is the purpose of the famous clapperboard.

Using a clapperboard with the scene and 'take' number written on it at the beginning of the scene, whilst reading out the scene and take number, gives you an audio and visual reference which makes life a lot easier when you come to sync the scene. As long as you match the clapping sound of the board with the visual image of it snapping shut, everything else in your shot will be in sync.

Audio in Premiere

Premiere has probably the best handling of sound of any editor in its price range. As well as some very good general tools aimed at audio editors, there are many audio effects. Some of these can be used to clean up and improve sound; others are there to process it, providing echoes, choruses, and other weird and wonderful effects.

If the effects included with the package are not enough for you, you can expand them by adding any third party *DirectX* audio plug-ins. These are available from many sources, but one of the largest choices comes from Sonic Foundry – a company famous for producing audio software. From this and other companies, you can get plug-ins to do everything from creating amplitude modulation to cutting out pops and crackles, and restoring vinyl recordings.

Once DirectX plug-ins are installed on your system, they should be directly accessible to Premiere through the Direct X effect. The only disadvantage with DirectX effects is that they can't be animated by placing keyframes. They're either on or off, so you can't, for example, increase or decrease an effect over time without a lot of tedious messing about with volume controls.

Audio tracks are more or less unlimited (you can have up to 100 which should be enough for anyone!), so you can have multiple effects playing at the same time.

There is also a new audio mixer allowing you to adjust the volume and stereo panning of any audio track either globally throughout the project, or live so you can interactively fade sounds in and out as you watch the video - recording the effects directly onto the timeline.

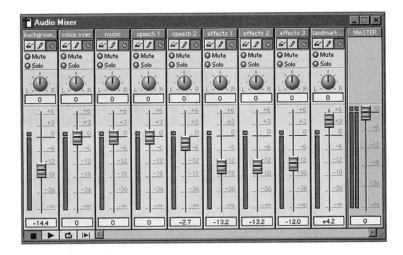

There is one thing to watch out for when editing sound in Premiere, however. The sound you hear when playing your work back from the timeline isn't always the same as you'll hear when the final piece is rendered. If you're using lots of effects and lots of audio tracks, the computer can't always process them all in real time. If it tries, and fails, you begin to hear pops and crackles that won't appear when you render your finished piece. There's also a setting in the rendering dialogue for **logarithmic audio fades** which, if engaged, smoothes out the volume changes in your production, making them sound more natural. However you don't by default hear them like that while you're editing.

The solution to both these problems is found in the Project > Project Settings > Audio dialog – which lets you set up the amount of audio tracks which need to appear before Premiere starts creating preview files, and whether logarithmic fades are heard when playing back the timeline.

Cutting an interview

When you're cutting an interview, the sound always comes first. If you get the sound correct then everything else should follow. Here we'll learn some important lessons about cutting sound, creating cross-fades, and using the volume controls.

1. For this exercise, use some footage of someone talking. Using File > Import > File, import the file. I used an interview as my footage – if you have some similar footage that would be ideal.

Our interview has been shot and captured as one long piece of footage. Putting it onto the timeline reveals an unorganized rambling interview full of repetitions and unwanted information. This is going to take some work.

2. By clicking the Play button at the base of the Monitor window, we can look at our clip and begin to weed out the unwanted parts. Nothing we do here will harm the footage on disk, so we can be as ruthless as we like.

3. Switch to the Razor Tool at the top left of the timeline. This will let us slice up the clip.

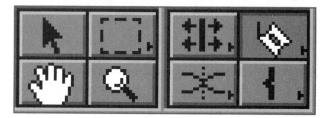

4. Scroll through the timeline, listening to the audio and find the place where you want to make your first cut. This is usually just before the dialog begins. With the playback head over the correct point, click on it with the Razor. The clip is split (although, since we haven't moved the parts to separate them, we can't see the cut as we play it back).

5. We don't need to place the playback head – clicking the timeline at any point with the Razor tool active will slice it, but using the playback head to locate your cut point is good practice as it allows you to be very precise about your cuts.

6. Now locate the point at which you want to go back to the interview – this is the end of the piece you wish to remove. In the case of my clip, the subject is talking rapidly meaning it's quite difficult to find the right point.

However, using the controls under the Monitor, we can advance or go back one frame at a time.

In addition, the playhead in the control bar just underneath the image on the Monitor window can be carefully dragged to slowly move the footage back and forth whilst listening to the slowed down audio. This should allow you to place the cut more accurately.

7. Another trick is to make the waveform visible. This can give you visual clues about when the sound starts and stops. Click the down-arrow next to the appropriate audio track to expand it.

If you still can't see the audio waveform, try zooming in, or right-clicking (SHIFT+click on a Mac) on the waveform to display the Timeline Window Options. Here, you can set the Draw audio when zoom is.... list to display audio waveforms at whatever magnification you like.

8. When you're happy, click with the Razor to make your cut. Now switch back to the Arrow tool and select the section you've just isolated (the part of the clip you want to remove), right-click and select Ripple Delete. This removes the unwanted footage, and shuffles everything else up to close the gap.

9. You can now carry on and cut the whole clip in the same way. Once I was finished with my interview, the result was a monolog in which the sound track makes sense as well as being short and to the point. However it's not perfect - because parts have been cut out of it, the video jumps.

10. It's now time to cover the joins. I shot a range of short **cutaways**, which I loaded, into the Project window as separate files. Traditionally, these are images that illustrate the interview.

> Sometimes these cutaway shots take the form of **noddies** – shots taken after the interview was filmed of the interviewer nodding attentively at the interviewee – used to fill the parts where a clip jumps at its cut.

11. Taking the first cutaway, drop it onto another video track – probably Video 2 (or any track above the interview track) so that it covers the cut. We then drag to trim it to size - a couple of seconds is fine. The audio for the clip appears in audio track 3, but we don't want it, so we just click on the speaker icon at the left of the track to turn that track off entirely. Playing it back, the audio cut is barely noticeable.

> It's worth noting that nowadays, some interviewers are using a different technique to cover cuts. When the interview is particularly intense, or you want to focus attention on the subject, it's quite reasonable to leave out the cut-aways, and instead, place very short mixes (less than half a second) between pieces of speech.

Creating Cross Fade

This requires a little more work - especially in ensuring the audio works well over the join, but it can be effective. Here we've set up a mix - and then zoomed in to the timeline and used the audio rubberbands to create a very brief cross fade.

Learning to cross fade is important in all kinds of audio editing. A basic cross fade can be created automatically in Premiere.

1. First overlap the two clips that need to be cross-faded. Now go to the tool palette at the top left of the timeline and select the Cross Fade Tool.

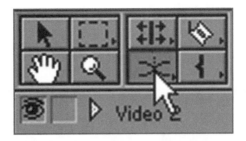

2. Finally click on the two clips in turn. A fade is automatically inserted.

On this version, the cross fade is slightly different. The speaker has had to be cut at a very brief gap in the dialogue, so when the fade was inserted the interviewee ended up talking over themselves. To solve this, I faded the first voice out, and brought the second one in while the first shot was still on screen. It's a small compromise, but seems to work.

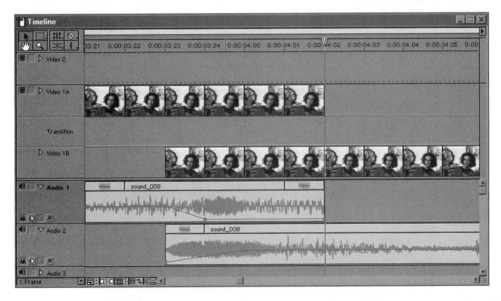

The interview is taking shape now, but it still needs work. Here's a moment when the cut was especially fine. A good job has been done in getting between words, but listening back to it, the result is not good. The interviewee appears to gabble constantly without a breath.

3. The solution is to insert a **pause**. We introduce a gap in the interview - just less than a second - by dragging the second clip slightly away from the first. Here the clip is right in the middle of the interview, so we have to use the Range Select tool to grab all the clips after the gap, and drag them out.

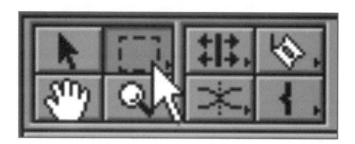

A good idea here is to drag the clips quite a way out, then switch back to the Selection Tool, to finely tune the size of the gap. You can then select the gap between this clip and the rest of your footage, and right click to ripple delete it. This method is a little fussy, but you'll get used to it.

Now, there is a gap - the interviewee sounds less rushed, but the gap is very obvious. The problem is that there is **dead air** between the two clips. **Dead air** is absolute silence - something that you never get in real life and always to be avoided – especially when dealing with sound. We need to fill the gap with the ambient sound of the room the interview was recorded in.

Usually, professional sound recordists will make sure they get a section of silence on tape at any location they work. This gives the editor some ambient sound to slip in if gaps are produced. In this case, I haven't specifically recorded silence; so have to go hunting for it within the interview.

4. Having found a second of silence, use the razor tool to cut around it on the timeline, then either use Edit > Copy or right-click and select Copy. You can now move the playback head, and paste the copy of the silence in between the two pieces of voice. The gap is filled, and the interview sounds much more natural.

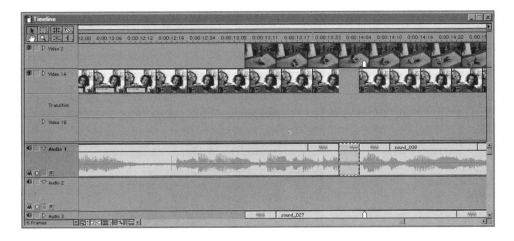

Finally, if you want to be really fussy about your clip you can use a technique often used in radio. It's known as "de-umming", and it's exactly what it sounds like. The idea is that we go through the interview finding points where the interviewee hesitates, is unsure what they're going to say, or repeats words - we then remove the mistakes one at a time, with the razor.

This can only really be done when the interviewee is off-screen (i.e. during a cut-away) but it does make them sound a lot more positive and eloquent.

The process is just the same as we used to chop out the sections of the interview we didn't want, only we have to work much more finely. The result can be worth the effort, but if you're not careful you can end up making the interview sound too choppy, so be careful. All in all, the more you use the razor and the cross fade tools, the better and faster you'll become at audio editing, and the tighter your productions will sound.

More advanced audio editing

With some basic understanding of cutting audio, we'll now take things a step further and look at some of the advanced techniques used to create more interesting edits. In the following example, I've assumed that I need to create an audio track for a montage in a reminiscence video using a selection of vintage photographs. If you can find and scan in some old looking sepia tone or black and white photographs, that will match the exercise well.

Ok, I've got my rough cut and here it is. The video montage has been cut together already - I just need to add the sound. This sequence is a photographic montage, and will require me to create an interesting soundscape to liven up the images because, whilst they tell an interesting story, they're not terribly interesting when viewed in silence, so in order to bring that story to life, I've decided to re-create the sounds of the time.

1. Firstly, I've imported my sound effects in to the Project window. Library CDs of sound effects and backgrounds can be purchased quite cheaply, and several Internet sites offer free downloads of audio 'clip-art' (although the quality of these can vary).

> *If you plan to sell, or exhibit your video work publicly, copyright is something you need to be very aware of - especially if you're using sound or music from professional sources.*

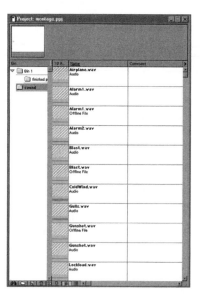

2. My first job is to lay in a background track. I've got quite a nondescript piece of ambient exterior noise. A little wind and a few birds singing. I've dragged this on to the Audio 1 track.

3. The sound is a little loud, so I right-click on it, select Audio Options and bring up the Audio Gain window.

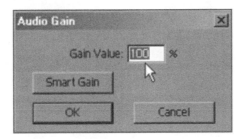

Here, I can take the Audio Gain down to reduce the overall volume of the clip to 50%. I copy the music so it's long enough to cover the entire montage.

4. While we're here, it's worth noticing the Smart Gain button. This will automatically scan the clip, and bring its volume up so that the loudest part of the clip is at maximum volume. If you have a clip recorded at very low sound levels, Smart Gain can often bump it up to the level of all the rest of your sound.

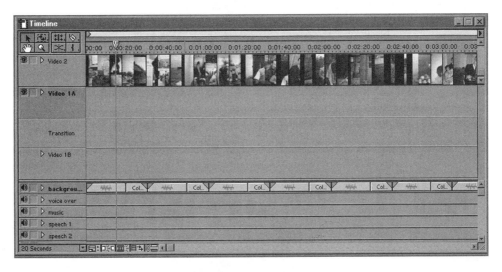

Now I notice a problem in the way the timeline is set up. I've only got three audio tracks. This is plenty for most situations, but here, I'm going to be doing a lot of work, so it's wise to have a few more.

5. I right click on a blank audio track in the timeline and select Add Audio Track. However, I want to add several tracks, so I right click on a blank audio track and select Track Options. I can now select Add and automatically add any number of new audio or video tracks in one go (up to 100 of each). For the purposes of this exercise I add 6 new tracks.

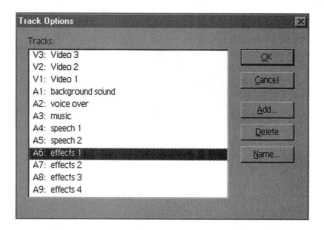

It's also good practice to keep in mind what each track is for. If you mix and match your audio throughout a complex production, you can quickly lose track of what sound is where. It also makes mixing more difficult.

6. By right clicking and selecting Track Options again, I get a list of the audio and video tracks.

7. By selecting each one in turn, I can give it a descriptive name. Here I've set up the documentary sound track in a more orderly way. There are two speech tracks, one for narration, one for music, one for background sound, and four more for the spot effects I'll be using in the montage.

8. The problem now is that I can't see them! I right click on the timeline and select Timeline Window Options. Now I can reduce the icon size for the video tracks to the minimum so they take up less room.

With everything prepared, I can start to add in more sound effects. Different editors have their own preferred way of working, but it's a good idea to start with a few audio landmarks. In this case, they will be sounds like air-raid sirens, gunfire and explosions - sounds that we can easily decide where to place.

9. I can play through the video montage, watching the images, and deciding where each important landmark sound will be placed. Each time I find the right position, I hit the asterisk (*) key or go to Timeline > Set Timeline Marker and insert a marker. This places a marker on the timeline.

By doing this 'live' as the video plays, I can easily set up the pattern of the sound, and work with the rhythm of the edited video.

> *It's worth noting here that you can do the same work in reverse when you're editing images to match sound. Say you've got a music video to cut. Laying down the music first, then playing through and setting markers on the beat lets you place your video easily in time with the music.*

10. Now I can start to insert spot effects. As an effect is dragged onto the timeline, it will snap to the position of the nearest marker. Because of the markers I don't need to tediously line up every sound to the video.

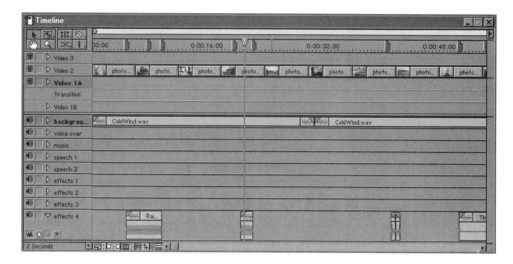

Of course, if I'm not happy with the sound when I play back the piece, I can still fine-tune it. Here, I zoomed into the timeline to move the sound of gunfire so that it began a fraction of a second before the associated image appeared on screen.

11. With the landmarks in place, I can move to a different track and start filling in the background sounds. These are less crucial in terms of where they're placed, but just add to the ambience of the piece, building on and aiding the landmark sounds.

The soundscape is looking quite polished now - but it's also a lot more complex. If I hadn't prepared and named our tracks, I'd be losing track of which sounds were which about now.

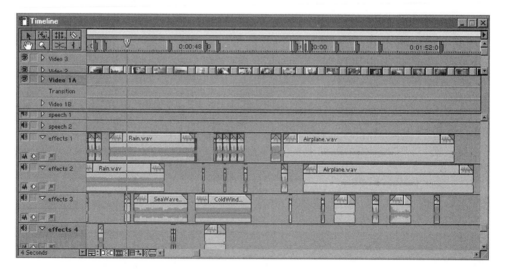

Note that for repetitive sounds - especially ones where effects have been added, it's usually easier to cut and paste on the timeline to duplicate them than to keep going back to the Project *window and dragging, trimming and altering the sound.*

With all the sounds in place, the montage is certainly loud, but it's not well balanced. Most of the important sounds are drowned out, and everything is fighting to be heard. I need to set the volume of each track.

12. I opened Windows > Audio Mixer to display the Audio Mixer. The window presented to me displays a **slider** and **pan-knob** for each audio track.

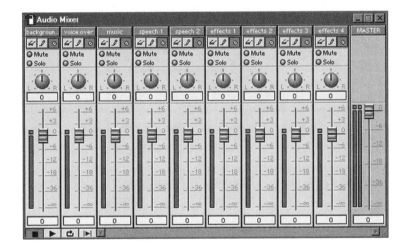

Here you can set the stereo position, and volume of every track individually. Additionally, you can do it while listening to the production play back. I've set the **landmark** track to a high volume so that all the important sounds are clearer, and reduced the background sounds slightly.

It is possible to record the settings of the audio mixer live, (see the next tutorial) but in this case I'm just setting their volumes (and stereo position) globally for the whole piece. As I've used dedicated tracks for my montage sequence this won't affect the rest of the production.

13. I still need to do a couple of small volume adjustments to individual effects. I've zoomed in on one particular effect - an air-raid siren. To start with, the volume is constant throughout. The line runs through the centre of the clip indicating the volume is level.

The siren should gradually fade in; become suddenly much louder, and then trail off, disappearing into the background noise. Clicking the **marker** at the left of the volume line and dragging it down to the bottom creates the silent start and you can see the line rising as the effect fades in.

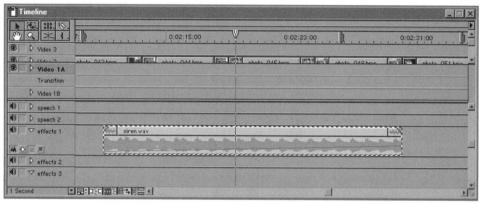

14. I next clicked about half way along the red line. This creates another point that can be manipulated.

15. Leaving that point where it is, I then clicked again a second further on - this time moving the new point up to the top of the clip. This creates a sharp increase in volume. Finally, dragging the end point of the line down to the bottom fades the clip out.

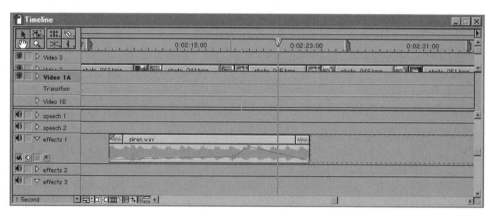

Note that as you drag points around, the monitor gives you a visual cue displaying the frame the point is on. You can use this to line up fine audio edits. If you create a point, which you later decide you don't need, just drag it down beyond the bottom of the clip, and release the mouse. The control point will vanish.

If you want to preserve the slope part of your audio edit, but move the whole volume up or down, you can select the Fade Adjustment Tool by clicking and holding the Crossfade Tool and selecting the middle icon from the new options box that will pop-up.

By clicking the blue button at the left of the audio track, you can display the blue stereo pan line and edit the stereo position of your sound in exactly the same way.

Split Sound Edits

Going back to the documentary we started work on in the first tutorial, we can start to work with the relationship between audio and video tracks. **Split Edits** are a method of cutting where either the sound from the next clip appears before the first has finished (known as a **J cut**), or the sound from the first clip continues over the video of the second shot (an **L cut**).

Here, we have a scene in which we want our interviewee to finish her sentence over the next shot. The overlap is just a couple of seconds, but it will blend the two shots together and give the piece a certain continuity.

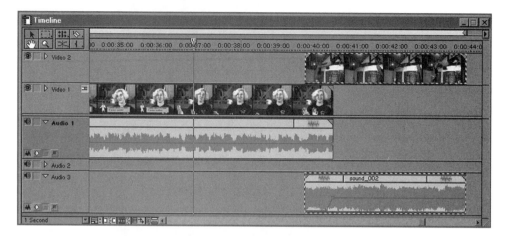

1. The simplest way to do this is just to drag the two clips onto separate tracks. The second clip is placed on the top track, and the shots are overlapped. All we need to do now is use the rubberband volume control to fade in the sound of the second clip after the sound from the first has ended, and the cut is done.

   This method can get a little messy. However, there is a way to do split edits using a single track. In this case, we're making the audio precede the video by a second or two. This creates anticipation in the viewer - making them imagine the next shot before it appears.

2. First we click the icon at the top of the monitor to open Dual View.

   You should now have two versions of your monitor open.

3. We drag our first shot from the project window into the left hand source monitor. We then scroll through to find the point at which we want the audio to end. Right clicking, we select Set Clip Marker and choose Audio Out.

   Now when we drag the shot to the timeline, it appears with its audio still in sync, but finishing just slightly early.

4. We can do the same process with the second clip, only this time marking the video in point to be slightly later than the audio in point.

The two shots should now fit together to form our **J-cut**. Split editing has only just been introduced to Premiere in Version 6, so it's not that advanced. Future releases should see some more interactive methods for producing these complex cuts.

Music, Narration, Mixing and Syncing

With our documentary taking shape, it's time to work on **syncing up** the sound and vision in some of our shots, and adding the music & narration, which will link it all together. We'll use the Audio Mixer to create a live mix doing some linking and unlinking of sound and vision.

Capturing Audio

Premiere isn't the best package in the world for recording voice-overs, but you can do the job. Once you've done this, you can begin to place the narration throughout the production.

Our first step is to record the narration. Unfortunately, Premiere doesn't yet allow you to record a voice-over whilst watching your edit on the timeline. This means you'll have to time, and plan your narration more carefully before you record it.

You can however, capture audio in Premiere. The package doesn't have its own capture software, but relies on loading up an external utility to do the job. In windows, it's usually **sndrec32** - the standard Windows sound recorder, that Premiere asks you to find for it (its generally in your Windows/system32 directory). On the Mac, you're offered a menu depending on your audio hardware.

1. Select File > Capture > Audio Capture, find the utility and load it. You can then record your audio using a mike plugged into your sound card. Nowadays with the size of hard drives increasing, there's no reason not to capture all your audio at the maximum quality - usually 44mhz, 16bit stereo.

2. With the audio recorded and imported into Premiere, it can be placed onto our audio track. We've made sure to set up a track used only for the narration so it's clear what it is, and where it's supposed to be. Using the razor tool, we divide up the narration so that each part of it can be placed appropriately on the timeline.

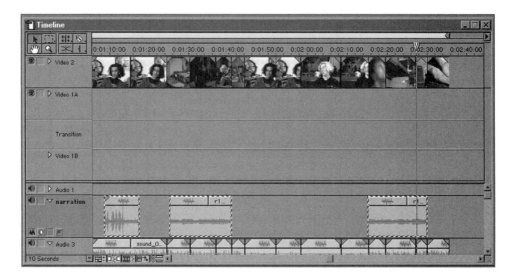

Now, since we haven't finished our edit, we want to make sure that the audio for each piece of narration stays with the appropriate video for that particular shot. Right now, when we move the video, or change an edit, the sound stays right where it is, and everything goes out of sync.

3. Click and hold the Cross Fade Tool at the top left of the timeline. When the selection of other tools pops up, pick the Link Tool. This will allow us to stick clips to each other.

4. Now we click the audio clip containing the portion of narration we want to stick. When we now hover the mouse over a video clip, the link icon appears. We click the appropriate section of video.

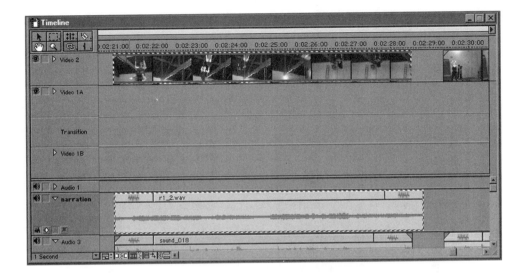

The two are now linked. When we move one, the other moves so their relative positions are retained. If we try to resize either the audio or the video, the other is lengthened or shortened too. You can only link one audio clip to one video clip. You can't link audio clips to each other, or to more than one video clip, and you can't link more than one video clip to a single audio clip. It's a purely monogamous relationship.

Switching back to the selection tool, we can now do some **un-linking**. Here, we have a piece of video in which the background sound is not only irrelevant, it gets in the way. While we were recording our **cut-aways**, somebody was talking in the background. We want to get rid of the audio portion, but when we try to delete it, the video track vanishes too.

5.   We right click, and select Unlink Audio and Video. The two are now completely separate; we can select the audio, and hit DELETE *on the keyboard.*

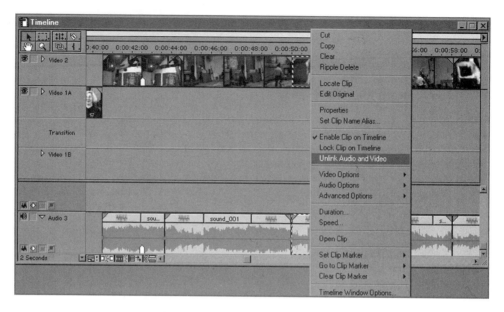

6. Of course, we don't have to delete the audio. Unlinking is also very useful when we want to move the audio and video about separately. One especially common reason for unlinking is to create overlaps. I unlinked the audio and video, and then dragged to shorten the audio clip without moving it.

7. When we now **re-link** the two clips we have a shot in which the video extends beyond the audio in both directions into the previous and next shot, but which remains in sync while the video's playing.

SmartSound

With the narration in place, it's time to add some music. A rather intriguing little utility called **SmartSound** is included with Premiere 6. This isn't a substitute for especially composed music, or a replacement for stock music CDs. However, it can put together an instant piece of music with an appropriate mood and exactly the right length for your production in seconds. It is basically a small library of musical loops and styles, each of which SmartSound can combine and loop in such a way as to intelligently produce a piece of the correct length and in whatever style you need.

You'll find the package on the second Premiere disk.

1. Go to File > New > SmartSound, and the front page of the package appears - it's organised as a wizard. This will ask you a series of simple questions from which it will generate your music. Tick the relevant check boxes to match your decision.

2.   First we choose a general style. Then from the list presented, we pick the type of music we're after. After a little experimentation, you'll get to know the 30 or so different basic themes in SmartSound's range.

3.   Finally, check the Custom radio button and type in the exact length we want our music to end up. Then decide whether we want it to be loop, or to have a definite beginning and end, decide this by checking the Loopable tick-box or leaving it blank.

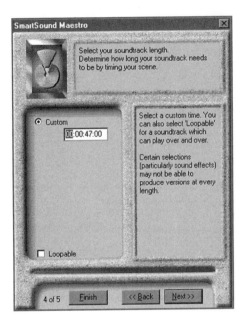

4.   The program now generates a series of interpretations of its material, each of which you can listen to before choosing one for your production. Highlight any example and use the QuickTime-style controls at the bottom of the box to sample it.

5.   The finished piece is then saved to disk and appears automatically in the Project window to be imported just like any other media file into your show.

If you decide that SmartSound is useful for your productions, and need to expand its range, you can order extra CD's to expand the program's musical range from the SmartSound website: www.smartsound.com/music

Premiere's audio effects

Premiere ships with a range of effects designed to improve and alter the qualities of your audio. There are 21 in all - more than almost any other editing package in Premiere's range. Some of them are designed to reduce noise, some are there to create effects and some are just for fun!

The effects are grouped into eight folders:

- **Bandpass**
- **Channel**
- **DirectX**
- **Dynamics**
- **EQ**
- **Effect**
- **Reverb**
- **Delay**

Bandpass

Highpass allows you to cut out low sounds entirely. The cut-off frequency is the frequency below which sounds are removed. The Mix slider defines the way the original sound is mixed with the effect.

If you have sound in which low noises are a problem, but in which high noises need to be preserved, this effect might help if used with a low mix value. However, there are usually better effects for this type of situation – we'll come to these soon.

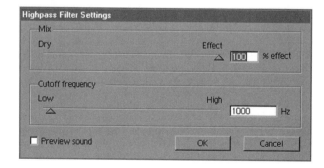

Lowpass lets you cut off high sounds. The effect works in exactly the same way as the Highpass **effect**, but removes any sound **above** the cut-off frequency.

Probably the only time you'll need Lowpass or Highpass effects is to filter out electronic sounds that are either unpleasant or potentially damaging to your equipment.

A Notch/Hum filter is used to completely remove single frequency sounds from your audio. Specifically, this effect was designed to take out the kinds of noise produced by the hum of mains electricity cables. These sounds are constant and low, generally at 50 or 60hz.

If you have another single frequency noise to remove, the Notch/Hum effect is a possibility, but you need to know the exact frequency of the sound for it to have any effect.

Channel

Auto Pan is one of the 'fun' effects. It automatically sends the selected sound back and forth between the stereo speakers. The sound will keep moving like this for as long as the clip keeps playing.

Auto Pan has two adjusters; Rate controls the speed at which the sound moves, and Depth controls how far it moves.

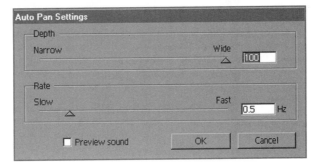

If you set the rate to be very slow with a sound effect of footsteps, the feet will appear to walk from left to right and back again. Set it fast, using a wind sound, and you'll appear to be at the centre of a manic storm.

Set the depth low, and the sound will seem to quiver about the centre point between the two speakers. Set it high, and the sound will sweep from the extreme edge of one speaker to the extreme edge of the other.

Fill Left and Fill Right take the whole sound clip and throws it right to the furthest end of the stereo field. Go for Fill Left, and your effect will be heard just in the left speaker, and vice-versa.

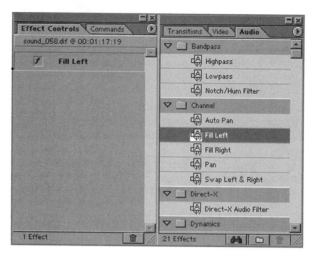

The Fill effect is a pretty blunt instrument. You don't have any control over it at all, and you can't keyframe it. All in all, unless you want this very specific effect, you're usually better off with the Pan effect as it's much more flexible.

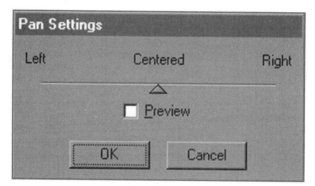

The Pan effect lets you set the exact stereo position of your audio clip at any time. Its control is simple enough, if you click Setup it lets you hear a preview for the position of your sound as you play around with the slider.

The stereo position of your sound can also be changed interactively using the Mixer, or by dragging the blue rubberband on the audio clip on the timeline (if this can't be seen, turn it on with the blue Display Pan Rubberbands button at the left of the audio track).

All clips will appear to be completely centrally balanced when you bring them into Premiere - even if they've been recorded or edited previously with varying stereo positions. This can be a little confusing, but try to think of it in the same way as you do with video clips - you may look at an image and know that it's black and white, but Premiere doesn't. In the same way, the package can't tell where someone was standing in your stereo field when you recorded them!

Swap Left & Right flips over the stereo landscape of the sound. Anything that was to the left is moved to the right, and vice-versa.

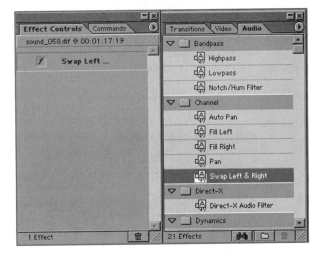

This effect is most often used where the audio leads have accidentally got swapped over sometime during recording or transfer of the sound. This is a common mistake. Providing you spot it, you can instantly correct it.

Direct X

Direct X Audio Filter appears to be just one filter - if don't have any other sound software on your system, it won't have any use. However, if you buy or download extra Direct X audio plug-ins such as those available from **Sonic Foundry**, or those supplied with some other audio and video packages, you'll be able to use them directly from this filter. Unfortunately you won't be able to keyframe them for animation.

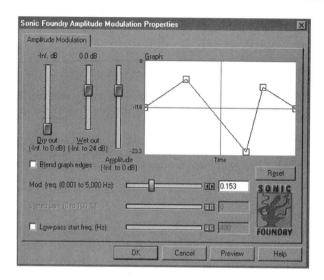

Dynamics

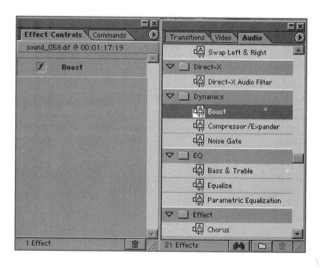

Boost amplifies quiet sounds in your clip whilst keeping louder noises just as they are. If you've got a voice clip where an actor moves between whispering and shouting, applying the Boost effect should bring the overall volume of all the speech roughly into line so that it can all be heard whilst retaining the actor's emphasis.

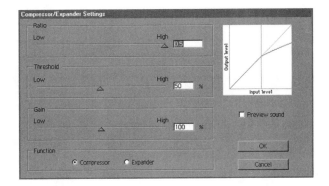

Boost isn't a very subtle effect. If you want more control over the effect, try the Compressor/Expander effect.

Compressor/ Expander lets you control the dynamic range of your audio clip. Think of this as being like turning the contrast up or down on a video image. The higher the dynamic range, the greater the difference between the very loudest and the softest sounds in the clip. The lower the dynamic range, the closer the volumes are to each other.

This is a much more versatile version of the Boost effect, offering four controls:

- Ratio - defines how strongly the effect is applied, as quiet sounds get louder.

- Threshold - The volume point at which the effect begins or ends - depending on whether the function is set to expander or compressor. Threshold is represented by the vertical green line on the graph.

- Gain - represented by the red line on the graph - the gain increases the overall output.

- Function - controls whether the effect is used to increase (expand) or decrease (compress) the dynamic range in the clip.

Noise Gate scans the audio file for quiet points, removing all sound at those moments. You can set the duration of the fade between loud and quiet points, and use the Threshold slider to define the volume at which sound starts being cut out. These adjustments are best made whilst previewing the effect.

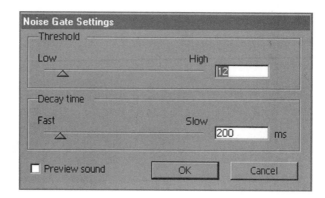

The most common use of the noise gate is to isolate sound effects from background noise, or to focus your audience only on what is important in your clip rather than on the whole thing. You'll usually only use it when you have another audio track carrying background noise because the effect tends to create areas of dead sound, or complete silence, which are to be avoided in any production.

EQ

Bass & Treble is pretty self-explanatory. This is a simple version of the graphic equaliser, which just lets you make rough adjustments to the relative volumes of the low and high frequency sounds. Boosting the bass will give your audio a fuller, more resonant sound. Boosting the treble will tend to make it sharper and potentially more tinny.

Equalize is a standard graphic equalizer. Few editing packages have a graphic equalizer as standard, but Premiere does, and goes further with an even more finely tuned Parametric Equalization effect. The graphic equalizer allows you to remove or boost sounds over a range of frequencies.

> *If you're trying to use it to improve the quality of recorded voices, it's worth remembering that most speech sounds appear in the middle three sliders. If you boost these, and reduce the outside ones, you should be able to cut out some unwanted noise.*

Parametric Equalization is a much more highly tuned and controllable version of a graphic equalizer. The basic idea is that you can pick out specific frequency ranges and boost or reduce them. The effect offers you up to three parametric equalizers in one go – the settings of which you can see on a graph.

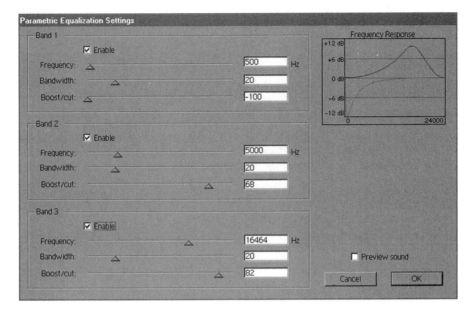

For each equalizer, you have three sliders to set the frequency of the sound you want to boost or cut, to adjust the bandwidth (the range of frequencies you want to affect) and vary the degree to which you want to increase or decrease the volume of sound at these frequencies.

The result of all this is an incredibly useful effect which can improve the quality of many difficult audio recordings. You can apply a parametric equalizer to an audio track containing strong background noise, and, by playing with the frequencies you can locate and remove much of the unwanted sound whist boosting the volume of the sound ranges you want to keep. Poorly recorded dialogue or other sound can be significantly improved.

Effect

Chorus is used to turn a single sound into a chorus. The audio is copied, de-tuned very slightly, and played over the top of the original sound. Depending on your settings, the result is either a stronger, fuller sound, or a completely unintelligible jangle that sounds like it was produced by a sci-fi villain!

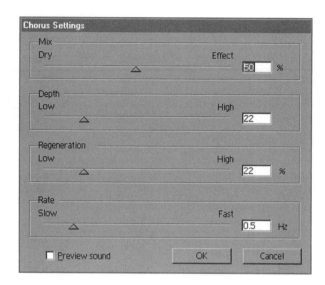

Chorus is controlled by four sliders:

- Mix determines the strength of the effect (by simply mixing the effect with the original sound) - a mix of 50% gives a decent effect without overpowering the original audio.

- Depth controls the amount by which the copied sound varies in pitch from the original. The greater the depth, the more extreme the effect and the deeper the chorus.

- Regeneration determines the strength of the echo compared to the original sound.

- Rate controls the speed at which the pitch of the sound cycles. High values give a warbling, pulsing effect whilst lower settings make the sound appear to 'swoop'.

Flanger flips over the phase of the audio. The effect can be a little like the chorus effect, but often seems to contain more vibration. The effects of the flanger can be quite subtle, or very extreme, adding a metallic touch to audio.

The Mix slider is used to control the strength of the effect. The Depth control sets the delay between the original and flanged sound (the depth of the echo). Rate sets the flanger cycle rate - or the speed at which the sound warbles and swoops.

Multi Effect creates a whole range of echoing and chorus style effects. It gives you greater control than the Echo or Chorus effects, basically because the effect creates a copy of your sound in the same way as Echo or Chorus, but allows you to play around with it, and alter the way it interacts with the original noise.

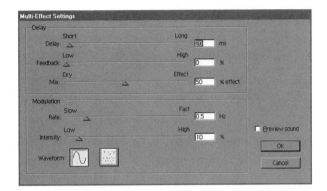

The Delay time slider alters the length of the delay between the original sound and its echo. Feedback controls the how the delayed audio affects the original sound. Mix controls the strength of the effect. If you set it at Dry you'll hear no change. Set it to Wet and the effect is at its most extreme.

Modulation Rate sets the speed at which modulation is applied to the affected audio. This slider has the most powerful effect on your sound, giving it a very pronounced resonance - as though the sound is coming through a harmonica.

Modulation Intensity controls the strength of the modulation.

Below the sliders, two buttons allow you to choose whether the modulation is derived from a sine wave (so that your sound swoops evenly from one pitch to another creating the traditional wah-wah sound) or from a random waveform (creating a more unusual effect which at its extreme can sound like a poorly tuned short-wave radio in a thunderstorm).

Reverb and Delay

Echo creates a simple echo. You can control the volume of the echoed sound as well as the delay between it and the original noise. If you want slightly more control, try the Reverb or Multitap Delay effects (coming up).

When using any of the Echo effects, bear in mind that none of Premiere's effects continue after the clip ends on the timeline. In other words, if you place an echo with a long delay on a short audio clip where the original noise stops right at the end of the clip, the echo will be unrealistically cut off when the playback head passes the end of the clip on the timeline. The only way to avoid this is to extend the clip so the echo can finish naturally.

Multitap Delay creates echoes, but offers a very high degree of control over the way they are produced. Multitap Delay uses musical terminology in its controls and this gives a clue to its primary purpose. It's there to help create the kind of timed, synchronised echoes found in dance music.

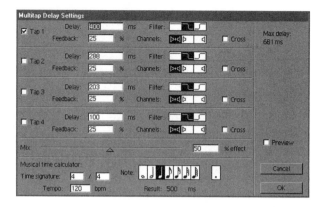

At first glance, Multitap Delay looks a little complex. However, once you realise that it's divided into four separate copies of the same effect, things begin to look a little more manageable. Each tap is a complete effect in itself and can be turned on or off.

Each contains the same controls:

- Delay is the time between the original sound and its echo.

- Feedback is the amount of the delayed audio that's fed back into the original sound.

- Channels (if you've got a stereo audio clip) lets you choose to send the echo to one speaker or the other (or both).

- Cross lets you bounce the echo back to the opposite speaker (if it's a stereo clip).

There's also an overall Mix control for all taps letting you set the strength of the whole effect compared to the original sound.

Musical Time Calculator is a panel that has no effect on the effect itself. It is simply a handy calculator that, if you're setting your sound effect to music, helps you get all the echoes in time.

Simply feed in the speed (in beats per minute - bpm) of your music, the time signature, and the note spacing at which you want your echoes to appear (just click the appropriate note duration, and use the dot for dotted notes). The calculator will then give you a result, which you can type into the delay section of your tap.

Reverb creates an echo, which combines flexibility with simplicity. If you're trying to create the effect of an echoing room, on sound that has been recorded in very sterile sounding studio conditions, Reverb is probably the best way to do it. You can choose an effect for a large, or medium room, then use several sliders to refine your effect:

- Mix - sets the strength of the effect and how it mixes with the original sound.

- Decay - controls the time the echo takes to subside into silence. The longer the delay, the larger the environment sounds.

- Diffusion - softens the original sound. This can create a warmer or more distant sounding effect.

- Brightness - sharpens the sound of the echoes - as though it's being bounced off very hard surfaces. Imagine the difference between the echo within a metal pipe and that inside a concert hall.

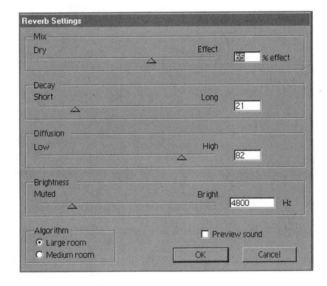

Weird Voices

Some of Premiere's audio effects are there to create interesting musical effects, some are there to improve the quality or depth of your audio recordings, and some are just there for fun.

In this tutorial, we're going to have a bit of fun. We'll use a couple of effects, and animate them over time to produce the effect of a person giving a speech in an auditorium whilst turning into an alien. We'll learn to add effects, to tune them, and to animate them.

1. Our first step is to import the voice. It's best if you use an audio clip of someone talking somewhere quiet, with no background sound. Place the clip onto the timeline, and if not already open, open the Effects window by Window > Workspace > Effects go to the Audio tab to locate our first effect.

2. In the Reverb and Delay folder, find the Reverb effect. Drag the effect and drop it onto our audio clip in the timeline. Instantly, the controls for the effect appear in the Effect Controls window.

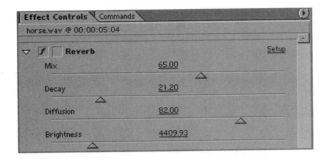

3. We could create the effect here, but we don't want to. By clicking Setup in the same window, we bring up a box which gives us *all* the controls (instead of just the animating ones we get in the Effect Controls window) and we can preview the effect here. Turn on Preview, and then the first part of our speech will play on a loop in the background, while we play around with the controls.

4. If we click the Large room radio button, and slightly increase the decay and the diffusion sliders, we can create an auditorium effect. When you're happy with it, close the window and play back the entire speech to check how it sounds.

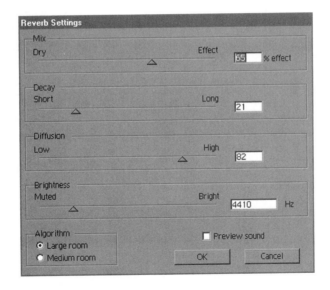

5. Going back to the Effects window, find and add the Chorus effect. This will be our alien voice effect. Again we click Setup to create the effect. This time we increase the Depth, and Rate sliders, and bump the Regeneration slider right up to full. The effect is metallic, and slightly disturbing.

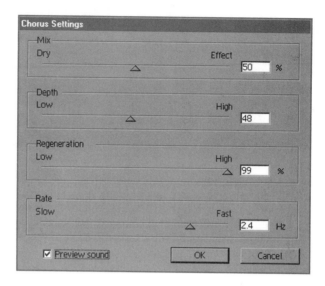

Clicking on the OK button and closing the box, we now need to animate the effect.

6.   In the Effect Controls window, click the small box to the left of the word Chorus. This turns on keyframing by showing a small stopwatch in the space. Now, instead of setting our sliders universally for the whole clip, we'll be setting keyframes individually at whatever point the playback head is positioned on the timeline.

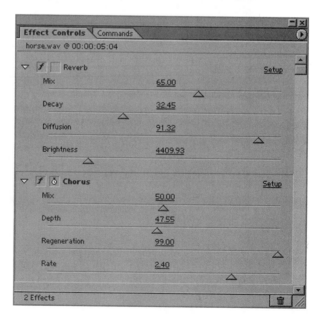

7. Move the playback head to the start of the clip and set the Mix slider to 0. This creates a keyframe at the start of the shot where the voice is completely normal.

It is worth noting here, if you click the white diamond at the left of the audio track, you'll be able to see your keyframes as you place them.

8. Moving about 10 seconds into the clip, we again set the Mix slider to 0. At about 15 seconds in, we bring the slider up to full. Now, when the scene is played, the voice begins normally, stays normal for 10 seconds, then the effect builds over the next 5 seconds until the speaker is completely unrecognizable!

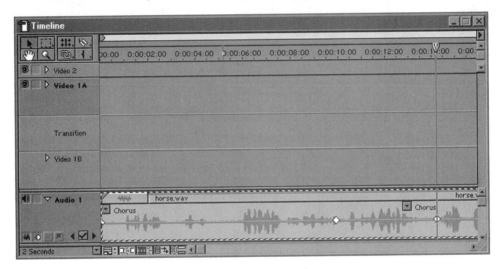

Summary

When shooting, you should always do your best to get a good audio recording first time out. However, it's not always possible; either you're forced to record in a poor sound environment, or you don't have appropriate microphones, or quite simply, sudden sounds appear when you don't want them.

Rarely can you solve these problems completely, so Premiere's array of various effects can be used for very useful repair work, or for taking the audio quality of your footage on to an extremely high level.

In addition to Premiere, there are other packages that offer more complete solutions. You can buy independent packages or DirectX plugins that do the job in a number of ways. I tend to use a popular choice - Sonic Foundry's Sound Forge. With it, I can select a portion of audio containing just the unwanted noise and use various refining effects to keep that noise to a minimum.

Hopefully this chapter has acted as a guide to help you experiment and produce original and interesting sounds. Remember, there are infinite possibilities out there, so start experimenting!

09 Transparency and Compositing

A composite is basically any video scene that requires elements from two or more separate video clips or images to be combined into a single frame. A wipe transition is a composite, a title overlay is a composite, and most special effects shots contain some degree of compositing.

In this chapter we'll learn how to create basic overlays, and how to fade clips in and out. We'll also look at chromakey - where we use a blue screen to superimpose objects (and people) from one shot into another. In addition, we'll go further, and add entirely computer-generated creatures into a real video scene, and build a title montage from a sequence of still images. Compositing may sound fancy when we talk about special effects and bluescreen, but many of the best applications of compositing are when it's used completely invisibly to solve shooting problems, or create shots which would be too expensive or impractical to create in real life, and this will be the last application we'll cover.

A Simple Bluescreen Effect

The starting point for any composite is the ability to create transparency. In order to get two shots to merge together, you'll need to run them both at the same time on different tracks in the timeline, then cut holes into the top image so that parts of the bottom one are seen through it. The skill and ingenuity with which you layer your shots will define how effective and convincing the final composite is.

Premiere contains some very nifty functions for building composites. These include a range of keying tools - which allow you to automatically make parts of a video clip transparent based on their color, or brightness. There are also sets of tools allowing you to make areas of the screen transparent based on what are called mattes. Mattes are black and white images or video clips which, when loaded into the transparency dialog let you replace all the black areas with one video clip, and all the white areas with another. Grey areas produce a blend between the two images.

The result is a very flexible system for creating composites. However, this kind of effect is a whole subject area in itself, and Premiere, although it contains some excellent tools, barely scratches the surface of what's possible. Other packages such as Adobe After Effects, Discreet's Combustion, or Pinnacle's Commotion are entirely dedicated to compositing, and as such contain a far greater range of tools.

For example, in After Effects, you can fly objects around the screen in 3D, create animated masks to cut one object out of a moving video shot, or use motion tracking to make composites from moving camera shots. You can even write scripts to define the way an object will be animated around the screen.

Other packages too can be helpful in compositing. A 3D design package will let you create and animate objects which can then be brought into Premiere and included in your scenes. A program like Macromedia Flash can also create animations suitable for compositing. However, probably the most useful package you can add to Premiere for effects work is an ordinary still image editor - like PhotoShop. With it you can draw mattes, create still images with transparency built into them, and alter frames of video in whatever way you like.

In addition, if you are using Photoshop, there's another trick you can use to create a whole range of effects – as long as you've got the patience. Premiere allows you to export portions of the timeline as a filmstrip file. A filmstrip is simply a long, thin image containing every frame in your video clip in sequence. This can be loaded into Adobe Photoshop, where you can work on each frame as a still image. You can use any of Photoshop's tools to paint, clone, or alter your shot in any way you like. It's time consuming and can be monotonous, since you have to alter every frame of your scene by hand. However, for effects like painting lightning flashes onto a sky, cutting out a figure who wasn't shot against a blue screen, or animating drawn images, it can be a real boon.

> *If you're going to be doing a lot of this kind of work, however, Photoshop really isn't the ideal tool. It may be worth investing in a specialized video painting or* **rotoscoping** *package, like NewTek's Aura.*

Shooting for compositing is a particular skill. You need to know exactly how your finished shot is going to look while you're shooting the elements for it. This means getting the perspective, and particularly the lighting absolutely consistent. It's important to keep the camera still because even the slightest motion will have the effect of separating the two composited images, and destroying the illusion that they're part of the same scene. Finally, if you're planning to superimpose an element of one shot into another scene, you need to know before you shoot the scene exactly how you plan to remove the background of your shot and separate out the objects to be superimposed.

Once you have the basic skills, however, compositing can open up a whole new world to the enterprising videographer. Some really stunning effects can be created with a little effort, and common shooting errors, such as poor exposure or unwanted microphones in shot can be corrected.

Superimposing a Title Screen

The simplest type of compositing is the overlay - where one video image is simply faded over another. In this example, we're going to learn to fade in a title on a black background over a piece of video, and animate its opacity in a much more complex way than you could achieve with a simple dissolve.

1. Our title screen has already been generated using a still image package (Adobe Photoshop). We could also have created it using any of the three titling plug-ins that come with Premiere as standard (see the chapter on titling for details)

2. The footage over which we're fading the title is already on the timeline. We place the title over the top of it, in a higher video track, and stretch it to cover as much time as we like (because the title is a still image, we can alter its length as much as we want.

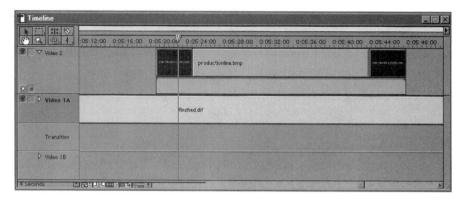

3. Click the triangle beside the label for the title track at the extreme left of the timeline. This opens out the track so we can see the pink strip beneath it. This is where the keyframes appear for animated visual effects, but it's also where you'll find the rubberband that controls the opacity of your clip.

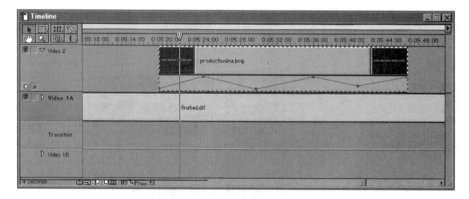

4. If you can't see the **rubberband** (the red line at the top of the pink strip), check to see that the red button at the bottom left of the track is pressed in (so the track is in opacity mode rather than keyframe display mode).

> *Note - make sure the track you're using isn't* Video 1A *or* Video 1B.
> *These tracks don't have an opacity rubberband.*

5. Click the rubberband at any point and drag down. A point appears, which lets you control the opacity of the title image. At the bottom of the strip, the title is invisible, at the top, it's fully opaque. You can place points anywhere on the clip.

6. Here we've created a complex fading sequence where the title fades in about half way, stays there for a few seconds, fades in fully to obscure the video completely, then fades out gently. To see the results, we either hold the ALT key and drag through the timeline, or render a preview of the effect.

Keying Effects

Making a whole clip fade in or out is easy enough. However, most compositing is a little more complicated. In order to combine two or more video images into one, you'll need to be able to make just a part of the top image transparent so that the bottom one shows through. For this you need to create a **key**.

Keys can be based on **color** - so that you make a given color transparent – or on **luminance** – where either the brightest or darkest part of an image is made transparent. Additionally, transparency can be introduced using mattes.

To gain access to Premiere's advanced keying tools, you must right-click/control-click on the image to be made transparent (usually the top shot in the timeline), and pick Video Options > Transparency.

> *Note: You can't make tracks* Video 1A *and* Video 1B *transparent. The idea behind this is that however many tracks you put in, these are considered as the very back of the screen, so there's no point in making them transparent.*

Before we take a look at Premiere's keying options individually, there are a couple of points worth mentioning about the Transparency window.

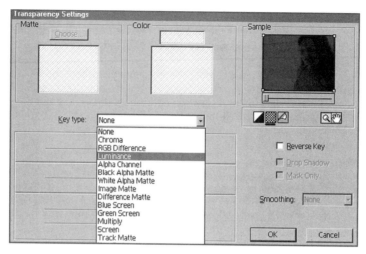

Whichever method of transparency you decide to use, you'll want to see how well it's working. The sample image at the top right of the window lets you check the results of your work. You can zoom into the Sample window by clicking on any portion of it, and zoom out by alt-clicking. You can switch between moving around the image and zooming it by selecting one of the two icons (hand and magnifying glass) at the bottom right of the sample image.

You can also create a basic matte within the sample window. The four corner points of the image can be dragged so that parts of it are obscured. This is useful if you want to have just a portion of the screen obscured by another image – for example a split screen, or superimposing a name caption underneath an interviewee.

Below the image, a time slider lets you shift through your clip to check how your keying works at any point during the shot.

Additionally, there are three buttons at the bottom left of the sample image. These let you choose how you view the composite. The first lets you view your transparent clip against a white or black background (useful if you want to see the contrast at its edges) the second displays the background as a Photoshop-style chequered image (useful for seeing degrees of transparency in semi-transparent objects) and the third shows you the final composite as it would look on the timeline.

Premiere includes 14 different types of key composite, which can be selected from the Key type drop-down menu shown.

Chromakey

The basic color-keying tool. It's very effective, and has a range of options to refine the transparency. Once selected, an image of your shot appears in the Color section of the window. Click on a portion of it to define the color you wish to make transparent, then adjust the sliders to get the best possible key. The controls are:

- Similarity – you don't usually want to just remove one single shade of the color – so increase this slider to increase the range of colors which become transparent.

- Blend – if the results of your chromakey aren't too good, you may want to reduce its opacity a little, blending your image slightly with the background. Here you're simply altering the opacity of the clip.

- Threshold and Cutoff – these two sliders are used together to determine the way shadows and areas of darker color in your transparent color are treated. By bringing the two settings towards the right, shadows are preserved and increased – that way, a shadow on a bluescreen can be preserved as a shadow in your composite. Moving them to the left removes shadows making your blue-screen smoother and cleaner.

Moving the Cutoff slider to the right of the Threshold slider can have undesirable effects, as it inverts the effect of the shadow.

Smoothing

The Smoothing option simply softens the edges between the transparent and opaque portions of the image, smoothing your two composited images together.

RGB Difference

A much simpler version of the Chromakey tool. Here, you select the color you want to key out, and adjust the single Similarity slider to define how much of the image is made transparent. You can't preserve shadows, and you can't get very accurate results on a poor screen. However, if you're working quickly and have a well-lit backdrop (or if you're using a computer-generated image with a perfectly smooth color from which to key) RGB difference is quick and easy.

Luminance

This creates transparency based on the brightness of each pixel in the image. Say you have a video shot in which you've had to overexpose the sky in order to get the scene exposed correctly. This happens all the time - especially when recording indoors where a window is in shot. By placing a sky photograph on a lower video track, then using luminance transparency to key out the brightest part of the video shot, you can seamlessly replace the overexposed sky with your photo creating the impression of a perfectly lit shot.

Luminance keying has two adjusters, Threshold and Cutoff. Put simply, if the Threshold is to the right of the Cutoff, then dark areas are being made transparent, and if the Cutoff is to the right of the Threshold, lighter areas are being removed. The closer together the two sliders are placed, the sharper the definition of the key, and the harsher the blend between transparent and non-transparent areas.

Alpha channel

Some types of image file are capable of storing alpha channels. These are simply maps to define which areas of an image are transparent (and how transparent they are). Alpha channels can be created using Photoshop, and a range of other packages, and are then saved along with some image files (for example GIFs). Their advantage is that they can be created very carefully in advance, and turned on or off at will. This means that you can cut out the objects you're intending to composite in another package, then import them into Premiere without worrying about how you're going to key them.

Alpha keying is suited to still images, but not so suited to motion video where creating your alpha channel in the first place can be a time consuming and difficult job.

Black and White Alpha Mattes

Usually used for superimposing titles which have either a black or white background and a certain type of alpha matte (a pre-multiplied alpha matte) which a few image formats create. Mostly, however, you can get just as good a result using other transparency methods.

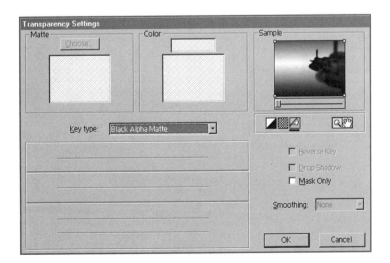

Image Mattes

A very useful matte which allows you to decide exactly which parts of your video clip are made transparent - not by any aspect of the video itself, but by loading in a completely separate black and white image which you've created to define the shape of the transparent areas.

Say you're doing a title sequence, where you have an animated backdrop, and you want to lay your title over it in the shape of burning fire – as though the words are cutting through the backdrop to show fire behind it. You'd place the fire and water onto the timeline, and make the top (fire) clip transparent using an image matte. In the Matte > Choose... section of the window, you'd load in your title as white words on a black background. Premiere would then replace the black areas (the background) transparent so the water showed through, and replace the white areas (the writing) with the fire clip.

Difference Matte

This lets you load in a still image or video clip which it then compares to the transparency clip pixel by pixel. Only those parts of the image which are the same in both images are kept solid. Those that are different are made transparent.

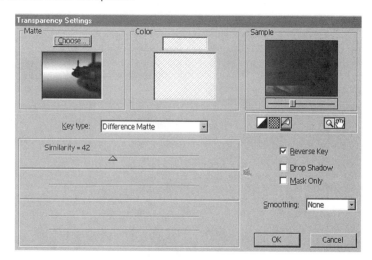

The difference matte is most useful when used in reverse (with the Reverse Key button selected). That way, you can isolate just the part of a video clip which changes during a shot. Say you've got a locked off camera shot, of a street, and you drive a car through it. By loading the shot in, using a reversed difference matte, and bringing in a still frame of the empty street as the matte, you should be able to make everything but the car transparent, and you can then place that moving car into another scene.

That's the theory, but in practice, most video cameras introduce a lot of noise to an image, so unless you have a very well lit simple shot and there's plenty of contrast between the object you want to isolate, and the rest of the scene, Difference mattes can become quite dirty with parts of the original background flickering in and out.

Blue-Screen and Green-Screen

If you're working with blue or green screens which are brightly lit and correctly colored, you can get very good clean results from a blue/green-screen key. You could simply use chromakey here as we did in the example at the very start of the chapter, but blue and green screen mattes can produce better results – especially where you're keying transparent objects like glass or hair, or where you want to preserve shadows on the background.

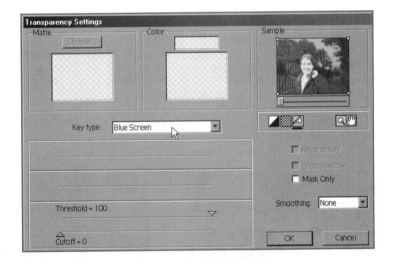

The only two sliders here are Threshold and Cutoff. Start by dragging the Threshold to the left until the screen becomes entirely transparent. This often makes the foreground start to become a little transparent too, but sliding the Cutoff to the right should bring it back, defining the edges of the matte more sharply.

Be careful not to take the Cutoff slider past the Threshold one, or the mask will become inverted the background will be visible, and the foreground will become transparent.

Multiply and Screen

These two transparency settings create ghostly effects by working in the same way as the Multiply and Screen settings in Photoshop. Images are made transparent based on their own luminosity and the luminosity of the image underneath. The result is either a brightening effect in the case of the Screen option, or a darker image in the case of Multiply.

Track Matte

This is similar to the Image matte setting, but allows you to use a moving image to create the composite. It's often used where a black and white matte video has been created by another package with better keying tools than Premiere, or where 3D animations have been produced with matte clips for compositing. This allows you to create very clear and realistic composites.

Track Matte (or Travelling Matte) is the only transparency setting which requires three timeline tracks: The bottom one holds the backdrop into which the composite will be placed, the middle contains the foreground - the clip to be matted in - and the top track contains the matte itself. To create the effect, the track matte transparency is only applied to the middle clip.

Non-Red

If you don't have any luck with the blue or green screen keys, try the Non-Red key. This works in pretty much the same way, but lets you blend out the background color for a softer key. It can also improve the edges of an object where the getting a good key is most difficult.

Creating a Basic Color Key

Color keying is the basis of much compositing work. Here, we're going to use the basic blue-screen tools of Premiere in a well-lit professional studio. The backdrop has been painted evenly, with a light-catching paint, and we should be able to expect very good results.

1.   We drop our background onto the timeline. We're using a still image - in this case it's one generated in a computer. This is an environment our actor could never be placed into in real life, so compositing is the only way to do it.

2.   Next comes the blue-screen shot itself. We place this onto the timeline directly above the background shot. When we do our effect, all the blue in this scene will be replaced by our computer generated image.

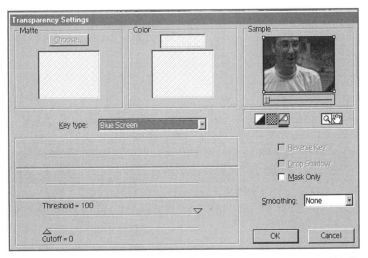

3.   Right-clicking on the top clip, we select Video Options > Transparency. We then choose Blue Screen from the drop-down list. Instantly, we get a pretty good key. Most of the background has vanished, and our actor is in place.

4. It's not perfect, though. We zoom into the sample window, and can see where the shadows aren't well handled (to zoom in, just click on the image - to zoom out, alt-click. To move around, select the hand icon at the bottom right of the image).

5. If we scrub through the shot with the slider beneath the image, we can see there are moments when the key isn't at its best.

Dragging the Cutoff slider to the right darkens our foreground, and increases the shadow. Dragging the Threshold slider to the left increases the pixels it treats as blue - thus eating away at the edges of the foreground image. We experiment to find a happy medium where the image blends most realistically.

Now we know how to quickly put together a realistic blue-screen shot with fairly good studio material, let's have a look at what we do when dealing with slightly poorer source material.

Rescuing a Poor Key

It's rare to get the opportunity to work with perfect blue-screen material. Usually it's either badly lit, or covered in shadows, or the blue-screen itself is unevenly colored. Here we have a particularly poor example, and it's been left up to us in the editing suite to rescue it. What's more, the object we need to key is glass, so we want to maintain its transparency.

1. We can see from the start that this is going to be a job. The blue screen is not only badly lit, it's also poorly framed, so bits of the wall behind it are visible in shot. What's more, it's not even a proper blue screen anyway - it's just a piece of blue cloth that happened to be lying around.

2. We select Transparency, and try out a chromakey matte. The result isn't encouraging. We can see the smudges and marks on the screen as well as the thick black line around our subject. This clearly isn't going to work.

3. The Blue Screen option is better at handling transparency than Chromakey. This gives a better result, but there are still problems. Each keying job is different, and presents different problems. In this case, Non-Red turns out to be the best method.

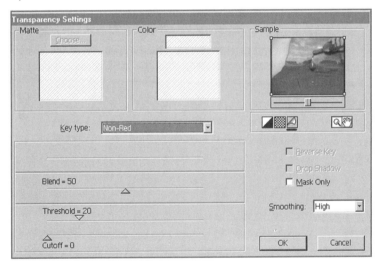

4. Slowly, we reduce the Threshold, and the background begins to fade in. We now bring the Cutoff value up a little way towards the Threshold. This increases the contrast in the shadows, bringing them out - which is good because the dark areas of the glass become denser. However, it's also bad because the shadows on the screen are also emphasized.

5. The glass slowly strengthens, and we have to make a compromise between the re-appearance of parts of the blue background, and the transparency of the glass.

6. Switching the Sample image to a chequered background, and zooming in lets us see exactly what's happening.

7.   To soften the edges of the mask, we turn the Smoothing function on. This blends the edges between the transparent and opaque parts of the image.

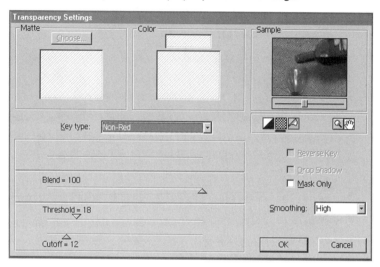

8.   We now increase the Blend setting to full. This doesn't change the image much, but it removes the blue coloring from the glass, making it appear more real.

The key is now as good as we can get it, but we still have the problem of the shot's edges. As you can see, the edge of the backdrop is clearly visible, and we can't allow that in our composite. We need what is known as a garbage matte - a mask which is used to cut out an unwanted portion of the screen.

9. Luckily, the edges are quite a simple shape, and we can easily get rid of them. Move to the sample area of the transparency window, and drag the four points at the corners in slightly towards the center.

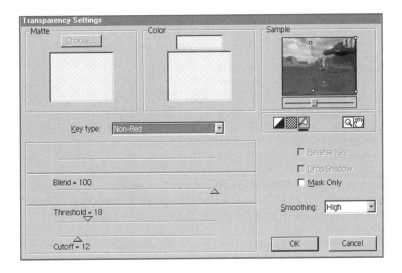

10. These points define a primitive mask which we can use to cut out the borders of our image. It's not a very flexible mask, but for our purposes it's fine – we can just exclude the unwanted edges of the shot. If we wanted a more complex garbage matte, we'd have to generate it as a blue shape in a still image package, then import it, and do two separate keys on our shot.

We've done our best to improve the mask. At the end of the day, you have to work with what you've got, and if the material isn't shot properly to begin with, everything else is compromised. Specialised compositing packages like After Effects can help a little, but your result will only ever be as good as the image you start with. However, we've seen how you can cope with the inevitable problems with shooting conditions you'll encounter in your video career.

Lighting for Compositing

If you're shooting for any kind of compositing work, you need to make sure you do the job properly. As we've seen, Premiere can produce some very good keying results, but it needs a little help from the director. Here are a few tips:

Size matters. The bigger your blue-screen, the harder it will be to light evenly. Film studios often create massive chromakey backgrounds so they can do wide shots. However, they need to use dozens or hundreds of lights to get an acceptable key.

Beware however, of making your screen too small. A small screen means your actor (or whatever you're keying) needs to be placed very close to the screen in order to make the backdrop fill the camera viewfinder. This increases the problem of light spillage, and often allows light reflected from the backdrop to fall onto the keyed object - thus making parts of it prone to becoming transparent.

Use a bright, pure blue (or green) for your screen. Darker colors tend to reproduce less well on camcorders, and you'll have a harder job lighting it correctly. The closer the backdrop is to pure blue, the more easily you'll be able to use blue-screen keying.

A bluescreen backdrop needs to be evenly and thoroughly lit. It needs to be made from a smooth, and even material, and it needs to be kept flat. Spend some time looking at your backdrop to try to detect shadows and lighting changes.

Even if you don't notice them, the chances are that the camera and the chromakey software will, so if you can, use a light meter.

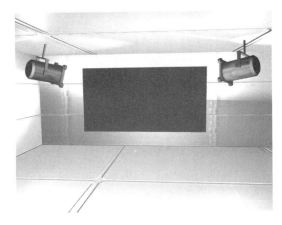

Here's the minimum lighting set-up – two lights are positioned at 45 degrees to the backdrop. They're positioned so that the light just about overlaps so there are no unlit areas and no *hotspots* of bright light.

The lights are often covered with diffusing material to de-focus their beams, and pointed slightly away from the backcloth so that they don't overexpose parts of it.

Once the backdrop is lit to your satisfaction, you can start to light your subject. If you have enough lights and a big enough backdrop, always try to make sure the two lighting set-ups are as separate as possible. If light spills from the backdrop to the foreground you'll get blue light on your subject. If light spills from the foreground to the background, you'll get highlights on the back-cloth creating a wider range of shades in it.

Sometimes it's desirable to have shadows cast on the backdrop. In a weather forecast, for example, it often makes the whole thing more natural looking if the forecaster's hand casts a shadow on the map superimposed behind them. Similarly, in a drama, it helps to make your subject appear a part of the scene if they cast a shadow.

On the other hand, it's not going to look particularly good if you're compositing a model aeroplane into the sky to have a shadow cast onto the empty air. Decide whether you want shadows, and where, and light accordingly.

Remember when lighting your subject that usually, you're lighting it to copy an existing environment. It's not enough to have your subject well lit - they have to be well lit to blend into the environment you're placing them in.

There's no point creating a dark, moody lighting set-up for someone who's going to be placed into a bright sunlit day. And there's no point in doing a flat studio lighting set-up for a character who's about to be placed into a rocky cavern.

Take notes about the lighting set-ups for your backdrop shots, and try to copy them as faithfully as possible.

Try to use a backlight. It often helps to put at least one bright light between the subject and the screen, facing towards the camera. Position it so that the edge of the subject is lifted slightly, and separated from the background.

This helps to give the subject a clear outline which will aid the keying process later on. Hair and fluffy clothes can be particular problems in keying, but if they're illuminated well, it's easier to get a good effect.

When it comes to shooting, there are a few important rules to follow. The most significant is that the camera needs to be mounted on a sturdy tripod. When shooting for compositing, you need to make very sure that the camera remains absolutely still. You can't zoom. You can't pan. You can't tilt. And you can't track. A composite by definition involves blending two shots into a single image. This means that if the camera moves - even by a millimetre - in either shot, the foreground and the background will appear to part company, it will become instantly obvious that they're not part of the same shot, and the illusion will be lost.

Also, make sure that *all* of the automatic camera functions are turned off. Just as moving the camera destroys the illusion of your composite, so any other automatic function will also ruin things.

- Automatic focus – although useful in most circumstances, it will be disastrous if your foreground subject keeps dipping in and out of focus while the objects you composite around them remain rock steady.

- Automatic exposure and color balance are also to be avoided. You don't even notice them most of the time when shooting normal footage. However, if your subject becomes suddenly brighter or darker, or changes color whilst everything else remains unmoved, the effect is going to fail.

Finally, do make sure that your foreground subject doesn't contain any of the same colors you're using for the backdrop. If you're shooting an interviewee against a blue background and they're wearing a blue tie, the tie will disappear, and you'll be left with a wide transparent stripe down the middle of their chest. This doesn't look good on anyone, especially not the camera operator who failed to notice it. Nor does it make things easy for the video editor who has to work with that footage!

We've now got a basic idea of the way compositing works, and we've had a go at a couple of bluescreen composites bringing one element into another shot. Now let's take things a little further by creating a montage of the type you'd see in a title sequence. We'll be using several still images and a video background to produce an intro for a program about the environment...

Compositing with Still Images

1. Using Photoshop we produce our still images. Here we've taken an image which needs to be cut out. We don't want the background, just the fossil against a transparent background. We can use soft-edged transparency without any keying problems because we're saving our images as Photoshop files which Premiere can directly load.

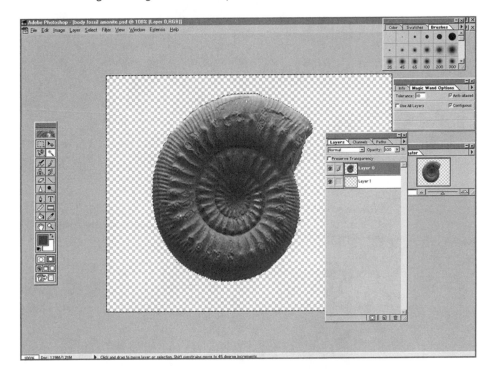

2. We could create all our elements as separate images ready to be combined in Premiere, but we don't. Instead, we make them as layers in a single Photoshop document - that way, we can scale and position each element to compose the scene much more easily. We can turn individual layers off and on to see how our shot is built up.

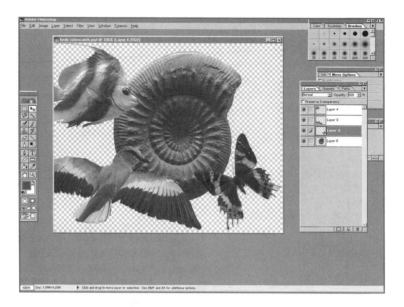

3. When we turn to Premiere, we can load in each Photoshop layer as a separate image. It's a bit of a pain because there are a lot of layers, but we've got the composition of the piece sorted out already.

4. When we double-click on an image to view it, we notice that it already has transparency - we can switch between the RGB view, and the Alpha view (in which we can see how the transparency is stored). We don't need to do anything to composite the shot. However, we do need a few more video tracks. Right click on the timeline, and select Track Options, then add 3 more video tracks.

5. We start by putting in our background. This is a video shot of an ocean. Over the course of our title, we place it on track Video 1A.

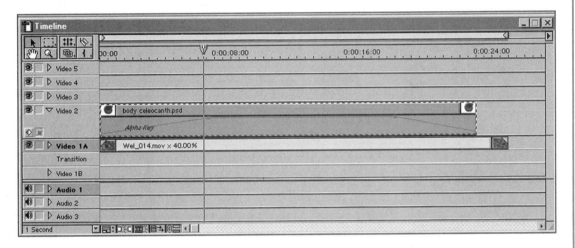

6. Next we start placing our images. We select the first image and drop it onto the timeline on track Video 2. Scrubbing through whilst holding the ALT key lets us see the composite. It looks OK, so we click the triangle to the left of the video track and open the Opacity bar. We now drag the red line at appropriate points so that our image fades in, remains on screen for a few seconds, then fades out (see the first tutorial of this chapter).

7. We place the next shot on top of the first, but make it fade in just before the first creature fades out. For this one, we'll be a little more adventurous. Right click, and go to Video Options > Transparency. Although our shot's already transparent, we can still add another type of key. We choose screen keying, and the creature now appears lightened and translucent.

8. We now place in a few more images, making them appear and disappear throughout the intro. Feel free to experiment with different opacity settings and transparency methods. You can even try using a few image filters to add interest to the shots.

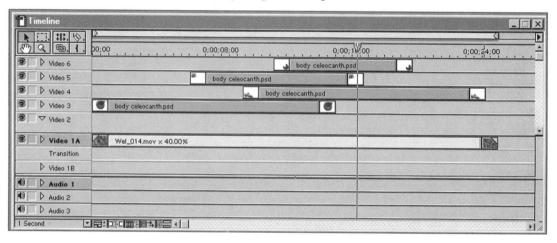

9. Finally, we want to add some interest to our backdrop. Right now it's just an ocean scene - which is nice enough, but not very active. We bring in a fire video – which the director has asked us to include to symbolize damage being done to the environment... or something.

10. We place the fire between the ocean video, and the images we've placed over it. It's been shot against a black backdrop so right now we can't see the back layer. Bringing up the transparency window, we add a Luminance key.

11. We play around with the Threshold and Cutoff settings until the black areas are removed. Now when we render a preview (by dragging the yellow bar at the top of the timeline to cover our shot and hitting return) we can see the fire burning, with the background visible behind it.

12. The only remaining job is to fade the scene out at the end. We drag a cross-dissolve transition from the Effects window onto the transitions track at the end of our shot, and use File > New > Black Video to create a black image. We drop this onto Video 1B, overlapping it with the dissolve, and the sequence is complete.

Now we've used our new-found techniques to composite some still images in Premiere, let's turn our attention to a pretty ambitious moving sequence!

Track Matte - Walking with Dinosaurs

Track mattes or traveling mattes use two separate video clips to composite one image with another. They combine the high degree of control available with image matting with the animation ability you get with color keying. In this example, we're going to show just how convincing a traveling matte can be.

1. Using a 3D package (3D Studio Max) we've created an animated creature. It's been a major job, and the result is a pretty realistic looking animal. It's been textured with appropriate skin colors, lit, and animated to move realistically with an invisible skeleton.

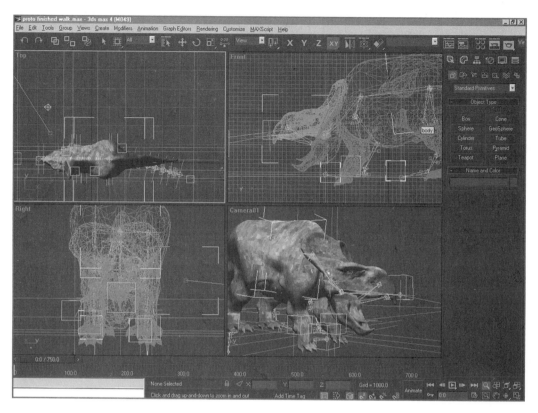

2. We *could* render it out against a blue background, and use chromakeying. This would work OK, but not brilliantly. Our creature has motion blur added to it, so the chromakey would have had trouble dealing with the transparency of the blurred parts of the object.

3. Instead, we render it as two separate video sequences. The first is a simple image of the creature. We've drawn it against a black background, but the color of the background really doesn't matter. The second clip is the same animation, but as a matte. The creature is completely white, the background is black, and the blurred edges are represented in shades of grey.

4. We import this creature and its matte into Premiere, and also bring in the backdrop we're going to be compositing it into. This is a straightforward locked off camera shot of some empty countryside which we drag and drop onto the timeline.

5. Right-clicking on the timeline, we add another video track to accommodate our effect, and place our two creature shots onto the timeline. The matte is placed in the top track, and the creature itself is positioned directly underneath it.

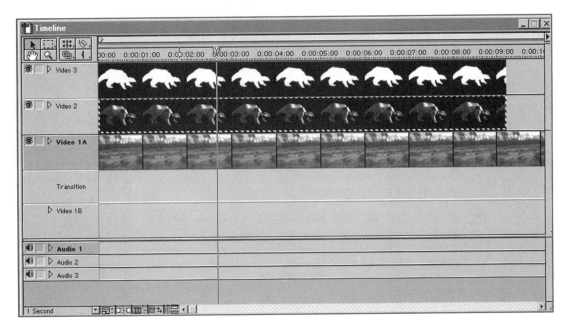

6. We need to make sure that the two shots are lined up perfectly – if they're even a frame out, then the "hole" produced by the matte layer won't be directly over the creature, and we'll get a very unrealistic composite.

7. When we're happy with the positioning, we right-click again and choose Video Options > Transparency. In the Transparency window, we pick Track Matte as our transparency method. There are no other settings to be made here, so we close the box.

8. Dragging the work area (the yellow strip at the top of the timeline) to cover our effect, we hit return to create a preview of our effect. After a minute or so it has rendered, and the creature looks pretty good in its new environment.

9. There are still a couple of things we can do to improve it, however. The first is to add another matte. This is a mask we've created in Photoshop. It's a transparent image made from the original landscape. We've rubbed out the top part of the picture, but left in the foreground bushes. We simply want to lay this over the feet of the creature to make the shot more realistic.

10. When we add yet another video track to the timeline, and drop this image into it, expanding it to cover the length of the effect, we can see the point of our effort. Now, instead of appearing to have been dropped in over the top of our shot, the beast is actually in the landscape, bushes are growing in front of him and behind him, and he really appears to be part of the scene.

11. Because the new layer has been made from a still taken from the old background, it composites with it perfectly without any messing about. Importing it in Photoshop format meant that the transparency was preserved. We could have exported it with a matte and composited it in that way, or used alpha matting if it had been a different type of file.

12. There is still more we can do to improve the shot. The monster's lighting, contrast, and color balance levels are perfect because it's been created in a virtual world. Unfortunately, our landscape has not. To truly blend in, the creature will need to be color corrected to its surroundings.

13. We add a brightness and contrast filter (from the Video Effects window, under Adjust) to the creature, and pull down its contrast so that the absolute black in its shadows is faded to the level of the darkest point in the real world image.

14. Now, we add a color balance filter to give the creature more of a green/blue tint so that it better matches its surroundings.

15. Finally, we drop in a very slight blur. No video camera is perfect, and the shot we have is slightly softened. The creature, on the other hand is so perfectly pin-sharp that it appears too computer generated. The blur filter just softens it enough to blend it into the real world. The result would fool anyone but a paleontologist.

Sometimes, as we've seen, a composite is supposed to be noticed – it's there to make a splash, or create an effect you couldn't otherwise do. But often, however, you need to create a composite which nobody notices. In our last tutorial we want to do two things – correct a mistake, and alter a landscape...

Working with Invisible Masks

1. Our first job is to change a landscape. The scene is for a sci-fi drama. The view of London needs some extra buildings. It's a still camera shot, but the image is a moving video image, and later, an actor appears at the right of the shot, so we can't just work on it as a still

2. That said, there's no reason why small parts of the image can't be still images –. we export a single frame to a photo editing package (Photoshop in this case). Here, we start to make our changes.

3. Using the clone brush, we paint in images of some buildings we've constructed in a 3D application. A little softening with the airbrush gives the impression that they're receding into the clouds.

4. With the scene looking as we want it, we cut around our new additions. We add another layer to the image, and move our shot onto the top layer so that we can create a transparent background. We then use a soft eraser to rub out everything but the buildings and a small area around them.

5. Now we can import this image back into Premiere, and place it on the timeline over our original scene. Most of the shot is moving – the clouds still roll, and the trees sway, and the actor can walk into shot, but the newly added elements still look like they're an integral part of the shot.

This next shot contains a very common problem. This scene was shot next to a window. The camera couldn't handle the difference in lighting between the outside and interior. Hence, when the exposure is correctly balanced for the actors, the window appears as an overexposed white rectangle.

On the other hand when the scene was re-shot using the correct exposure for the window, the actors can't be seen. We're going to use a matte to combine the two shots.

6. First we export a still image to Photoshop. We use this to create a soft edged mask – a black and white image where the window area is completely black, and the rest of the shot is white. We use a soft-edged brush to paint this so that when we composite, the edges of our mask will be invisible.

7. Going back to Premiere, we place our two shots on the timeline - one directly above the other – and open the transparency window. For our Key type, we choose Image Matte.

8. Clicking the Choose… button at the top left of the window, we locate our black and white matte, and load it in. Depending on which version of the scene we've placed in the top track, we may need to click the Reverse Key check box (to avoid ending up with the worst aspects of both scenes).

Looking at the monitor, we find the shots are now combined. The well-exposed window is seamlessly integrated into the well-exposed room shot. Nobody need ever know how difficult it all was!

This technique can be used to remove boom mikes, or unwanted passers-by. Try using it to bring several versions of the same actor into one shot. This kind of matting works well until somebody tries to walk across the shot – as soon as anything tries to cross the line of the mask, it will vanish.

Summary

You've now seen how to implement the most common kinds of compositing effects in Premiere, and also how you can shoot your footage to help them along a bit.

We've covered:

- Basic superimposing with titles

- Keying effects

- Managing keys and enhancing poor ones

- Special lighting tips for bluescreen and chromakey

- Traveling matte effects

- Using invisible masks

In the next chapter, we're going to look at how you can add professional looking effects to your movies.

10 Applying Effects

Video effects are one of the fun parts of editing with Premiere. Sometimes they're used to shock or impress the audience. Sometimes they're there to convey information. Other times, they're far subtler, and the audience may not even notice them at all.

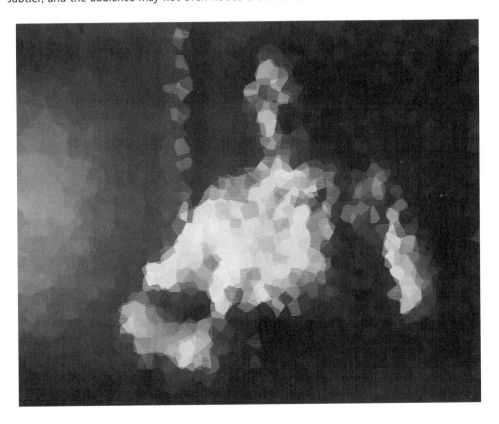

With Premiere's built in effects, you can turn the screen inside out, upside down, and distort it in any number of different ways. You can turn the sky green, or change your shot into an oil painting. You can also correct poor color balance, restore depth to a flat looking image, or bring out colors in your shot to make it more vibrant.

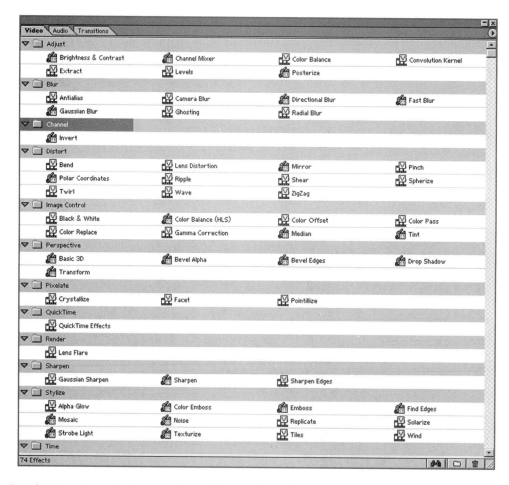

Premiere's main method for creating effects is the effects panel. Premiere contains dozens of effects – each designed to create a specific effect. Some change the color values in an image, while others alter its shape, distort, or warp the image. Still others produce effects like lens flares, textures, and de-focussing effects.

Each effect comes with a range of unique controls designed to allow you to alter the parameters of the effect. These controls can be animated over time to produce moving effects.

In order to use an effect, you simply need to drag and drop it onto a clip, to affect that clip. You can layer as many effects as you like on a single shot, shifting their order as you wish.

> *The order in which clips are positioned is important. If you applied a blur to a shot and then added a lens flare, you'd see a blurred image with a sharp lens flare. If you applied the lens flare first, when you added the blur, it would de-focus everything.*

Don't think that the effects standard Premiere comes with are the only ones available. The program also accepts After Effects style plug-ins. Many companies have produced effects designed to plug into and augment After Effects, but now a lot of these will also now work in Premiere. In addition to this, many Photoshop filters will also work with Premiere.

All you need to do is install them into Premiere's **Plug-ins** folder. As soon as you load the package, they should appear in the effects panel ready to use. You should check before buying, however, as some third party effects have been tuned specifically to After Effects, meaning they either won't work in Premiere, or will have limitations on their function.

The range of available plug-ins is pretty wide, they range from the **Cinelook** plugin – which simulates a range of different film looks from video footage (see the above image) – through to **Realsmart's Blur** plug-ins which create realistic motion blur on computer generated images. Some Photoshop plug-ins offer pretty good painting effects, whilst other After Effects ones are pretty good at warping and distorting images over time.

If you wish to animate your effects, you'll need to have some understanding of **keyframes**. Whenever you change any aspect of a clip at a given point in time, a keyframe is created at that point. In other words, Premiere records the settings of the effect at that frame. You can then move to other points in the effect and alter the settings to create other keyframes. The effect will then be animated so that its settings move smoothly from those of one keyframe to those of the next.

For example, if you:

- Set up a brightness and contrast effect

- Set a keyframe at the start of the clip with the brightness at full - so the clip is completely white

- Move to the middle of the clip and set the brightness to normal

- And finally, set it to full again

The result will be a clip that slowly fades in from white, and then fades out again back to white.

You can set as many keyframes as you like throughout the shot, and can add as many effects as you want to combine effects. The result is a very flexible system which allows a huge range of effects. By combining effects with compositing, you can be very specific about the effects applied to a shot. It is worth remembering though, that applying large numbers of effects can slow down the render time of any footage you have created.

For example, if you put two copies of the same clip running parallel in different tracks on the timeline, then use a matte to make a part of the top clip transparent, you can then apply effects to the bottom clip. They will appear to affect only those parts of the screen you want to apply them to.

Premiere contains a great range of effects tools, but in addition, there are dedicated effects packages available that offer you the same kinds of effects as Premiere. These include After Effects, Combustion, and Commotion.

Using Effects

There are 74 video effects in Premiere. To go through them all here would be time-consuming, so we've put them in the Effects appendix at the back of the book. In the appendix are all the effects with screenshots showing what they do and explanations of how they work. Go and have a flick through and see which ones you like.

Meanwhile, here we'll show you how to apply some of those effects. The principles behind applying effects are similar, no matter which ones you're using. We'll select a couple here to play with so you get the idea.

The first is easy enough – we've got a scene, which is supposedly being received on a TV monitor through a lot of interference:

Before you continue, you need to make sure the right windows are showing. To do this, go to Window > Show Effect Controls and Window > Show Video Effects. Under the Video tab, click on the right-facing arrow to open one of the folders, in this case the first on view, the Adjust folder. Now you should see a choice of differing effects.

To apply an effect to a clip, either: highlight the clip, then drag an effect from the opened folder in to the Effect Controls folder; or simply drag the effect from the effects folder and drop it straight on to the clip.

1.   Our original shot is very clean and sharp. We want it to look a lot worse, so effects are the way to do it. We place the clip onto the timeline, and use Window > Workspace > Effects to put the workspace into effects mode.

2.   Time to apply our first effect. From the Effects browser, select the Video tab, open the Image Control folder, and choose Color Offset. Then drag the effect onto our clip, and drop it there.

3.   The Effect Control window displays some of the controls of the effect, but to get access to the full controls, click the Setup button next to the effect's label.

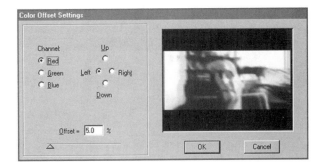

This effect allows us to separate the red and green parts of the image. The result is that the shot now looks as though the monitor is not working properly. This is not the original intention of the effect – the effect is actually there to create 3D images, however, the effect is just what we need.

Now we want to add another effect, but we don't want it to affect our entire clip (otherwise it would become unwatchable).

4. Click on the Razor Tool on the top left of the timeline, and cut the shot into about eight or nine sections. Our first effect will remain over the whole scene, but any new ones we add will be confined to the section we place them in.

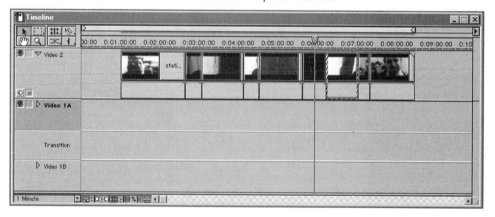

5. From the Transform folder in the Effects browser, choose the Horizontal Hold effect and drop it into one or two of the shorter sections. Setting the Horizontal Hold on each clip to a different level, we'll get a range of flickering effects that appear and disappear throughout our scene.

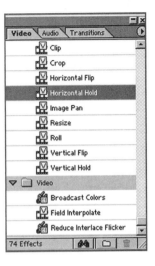

If you want to leave the effect in place, but just de-activate it temporarily, click in the Enable Effect box to the left of the effect's label. This is useful if you have a lot of effects, which are slowing down previews.

> It's worth noting that if you place an effect you're not happy with, you can remove it at any time by selecting its name in the Effect Controls window, then clicking the recycle bin at the bottom right of the window.

Animating Effects

We've learned how effects are placed onto the timeline, and done a some limited animation with them by slicing up the video clip and putting different effects on different parts of it. We've also learned how to make the adjustments that control the effect.

Now it's time to animate those controls to produce a more impressive effect. We're going to create our own custom dissolve, where, instead of simply fading from one shot to the next, the shot appears to ripple into the next scene as though a stone has been thrown into a pond.

1. Drag each scene onto tracks Video 1A and Video 1B of the timeline, overlapping them by about half a second.

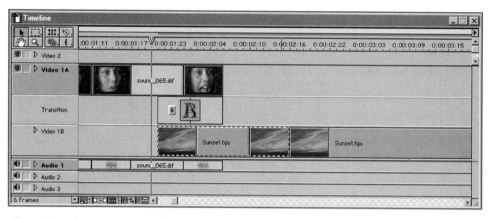

2. Now drag a Cross Dissolve from the Transitions panel onto the Transition track to cover the join. Preview this effect, and you can see we have a simple dissolve.

3. Switch to the Razor Tool (at the top left of the timeline), and slice the first clip about two seconds before the dissolve.

4. Now cut the shot on Video 1B about two seconds after the transition. We do this because we only want to affect the clips during the transition itself.

5. From the Distort Folder, pick up the ZigZag effect, then drag and drop it onto the end of Track 1A – the part we just sliced off. For the moment, click OK in the controls box which appears.

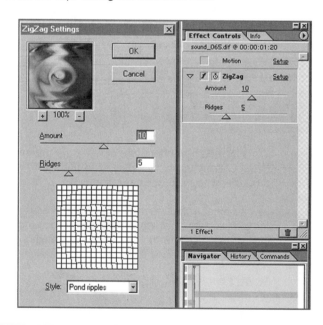

6. Before we can animate our effect, we need to click the box to the immediate left of the effect title in the Effect Controls window:

A stopwatch icon appears to indicate that we're now in animation mode. Any changes now made to our effect will happen just at the frame where the playback head is positioned, rather than over the entire clip.

7. We move the playback head on the timeline to the start of our shot on Video 1A (the frame where we made our cut). You can get there quickly using the Previous Edit / Next Edit buttons on the monitor window:

8. Click Setup for the effect in the Effect Controls window to bring up the ZigZag Settings box, and set the sliders so the effect has no effect, setting the Amount slider to 0.

9. Also, set the other settings as we'll need them for the effect: Ridges to 8 and Style to Out from center. Now, the ripples will work properly when we animate them.

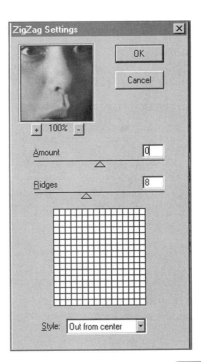

10. Click the OK button in the box, move to the end of the clip (click the Next Edit button twice), slide the Amount slider in the Effect Controls box right up to 100. Previewing the effect we can see that it's beginning to come together.

We now need to finish the shot by placing the same effect on the second video clip on Video 1B.

11. Drag ZigZag from the Distort folder and drop it on to Video 1B, and click the OK button. Turn on the Enable Keyframing animation button.

12. This time however, set the effect up in reverse. At the first frame of Video 1B, set the Amount slider to -100 (right to the left).

13. At the final frame, set it to 0 - so that the ripples have faded away, and the clip continues untouched.

Keyframes

Now that we can set up a simple animated effect, let's look at the way keyframes work to create more complex effects. The idea here is to take a landscape shot, animate a shooting star as it plummets to the ground, then create a ground shaking effect synchronised with a flash of light when it hits.

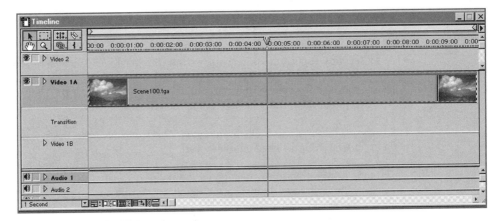

1. First we place our landscape onto Video 1A. To create the meteor, use a Lens Flare from the Render folder, which we drop onto our shot. When the control box appears, click on the image and move the center of the effect to the point at which the meteor will impact. Also set its Brightness to 30%.

2. Close the box and turn on animation. Then click the right facing triangle to the left of the timeline track, Video 1A. This should expand the clip on the timeline. As well as indicating the opacity of a clip, the line underneath the track can display the keyframes of our animation.

3. Move to about five seconds into the shot, and click in the square to the left of the track to add a keyframe:

    A keyframe is any position in the clip where an effect's value has been altered. Between keyframes, Premiere calculates intermediate values so the effect changes gradually from one keyframe to the next. There are automatically keyframes at the start and end of a clip. We've now created one in the middle, and can see it as a white diamond:

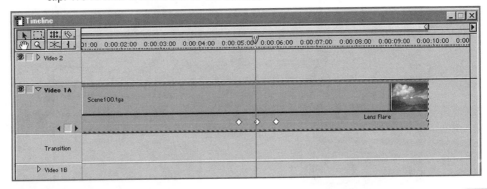

4. Move on a little – to about five and a half seconds, and increase the Lens Flare's Brightness to 200%. A new keyframe automatically appears.

5. At six seconds, reduce the Brightness to 10% (the minimum value we're allowed).

6. Finally, move to the start of the clip, and click the Setup box for the Lens Flare effect. Here we can position our lens flare at the top left of the screen.

Previewing the effect, it looks pretty good. The light falls from the sky, and impacts, flaring briefly. We now need another effect.

7. This time it's the Transform effect under the Perspective tab. As soon as we drop it onto our clip, the keyframes disappear and the effect's name appears at the bottom of the clip's video track.

> *If you click on the effect name on the track, you can choose to switch between viewing keyframes for all the effects you've applied (Transform and Lens Flare in this case). We've now switched to Transform, and so the Lens Flare keyframes are no longer visible. That doesn't mean they've been removed – they're just hidden, and they still have an effect on the clip.*

8. Scale the Height and Width sliders to 115% to expand our shot a little beyond the edges of the screen, then turn on animation. Moving to our point of impact (about five seconds into the effect), we set a keyframe.

9. Next, move one frame further on, and click the effect's Position button. A crosshair appears at the center of the Monitor window.

10. Click just next to it to move the entire scene just off center. Now move forward one more frame and do the same – moving the image slightly in a different direction.

11. Create a few more keyframes in the same way. The result is that the instant the meteor hits, the image on the screen shakes – just a little – for a few frames before settling down again - as though the impact was so strong that the camera was jolted.

The result is a powerful effect, but it's been created with nothing but a still photograph, and a couple of effects.

> *It's worth a mention that if you place a keyframe incorrectly, you can simply click and drag on it to move it. You can also delete it by moving the timeline over it, and un-checking the tick box at the left of the timeline. You can also move easily between keyframes by clicking the forward and backward arrows next to the same box.*

Playing with Time

In addition to the effects, Premiere also lets you alter footage by manipulating time. Here we'll look at various things you can do to speed up, slow down, and stop time.

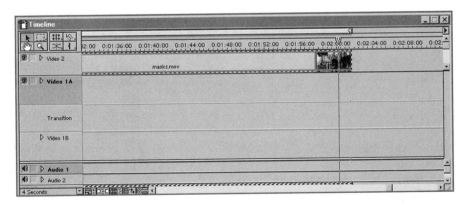

First, let's make a simple freeze-frame. We want this scene to be the final shot of our production. We want it to play, then freeze on its final frame, and fade out. Drop the shot onto the timeline on track Video 2.

1. Using the Razor Tool make a slice in the shot about five seconds in and, selecting the piece we've just cut, use Edit > Copy to paste a copy of the piece at the end of the clip.

2. Now right-click on the end shot, and select Video Options > Frame Hold. This brings up the freeze-frame dialogue. Here, next to the Hold On text, use the drop–down menu to choose to hold the shot either on the In Point, or the Out Point – choose the Out Point so that the second showing of our clip becomes a freeze frame of its final shot.

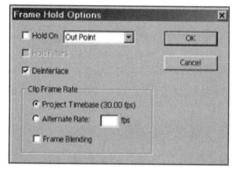

3. Also, check the Deinterlace box because frozen video can sometimes produce flicker unless we deinterlace it.

4. The Frame Hold box also lets you change your shot's frame-rate for stop motion type effects. The frame blending option can make lower frame rate shots appear smoother.

5. Close the box. We can create our fade-out over the still we've set up by opening the video track, and dragging the Opacity rubberband (the red line beneath the track) down at the right hand side so the clip fades to black.

Our second job is to create a slowed down version of this stunt. It's a jump, and will have a lot more impact if it's done slowly.

6. Drop the clip onto the timeline, right-click, and choose Speed. This allows us to change the speed either as a percentage, or as a duration:

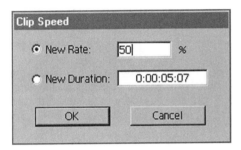

Right now, a percentage is fine – we can slow the clip to 50 percent of its rate, and it will play at half the speed. Of course, this also means that there will be half as many frames per second, so if you slow the clip down by more than about 50 percent it starts to become obvious, and motion becomes more and more jerky.

The Duration field is more useful if you have a gap of a certain length to fill in your production – say you're editing a music video, and want something to happen in an exact time frame. You just need to fill in the appropriate length, and the clip will be slowed down accordingly.

If you type a percentage above 100 percent into the dialog (or fill in a duration that's shorter than the original clip's length), the clip will play faster instead of slower.

Finally, if you want the clip to play backwards, just type in a negative percentage figure. -100% makes the clip play backwards at full speed.

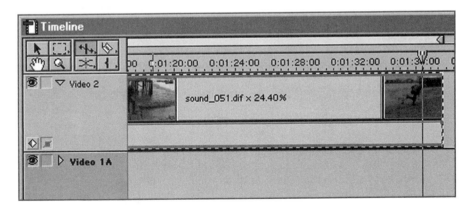

7. There's also a tool in the palette at the top left of the timeline which lets you change the speed of a clip by dragging its end. This can be more interactive than the Clip window method. The Rate Stretch tool is hidden underneath the Rolling Edit tool, so you'll have to click and drag that tool to bring it up.

> *Note: if you get flickering, or jerking of the image when you render a slow or fast shot, you may need to alter the* Field Options. *Right-click on the shot, and choose* Video Options > Field Options, *then experiment with the settings for the best result.*

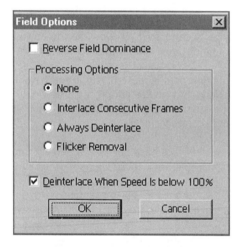

Summary

What we've seen in this chapter is an overview of what can be achieved with effects in Premiere:

- Applying a simple effect to a clip

- Animating an effect

- Using keyframes to make an effect change over time

- Changing the speed of a clip to produce different effects

You can find the full range of Premiere effects in the Effects appendix at the back of the book. Each effect is explained in detail with screenshots so you can see what it looks like.

Effects are a powerful tool with which you can really bring life to your movies. Very powerful indeed. So powerful that they can become overwhelming. Don't just apply every effect you can lay your hands on – use them subtly. Where effects are concerned, it can be a case of 'less is more'. Think about how each effect will affect your movie. Remember, movie making is an art, not a science.

11 Animating a Clip

When most people think of animation, they think of hand-drawn animation, of cartoons, and of 3D-modeled animations. Whilst these are all types of animation, they are by no means the only kind of work that goes under that heading.

- Whenever a title scrolls across the screen, it needs to be animated.

- If you have an effect that changes its nature over time, then it's an animation.

- Even stop-motion video footage is a kind of animation.

In Premiere, an animated shot is one in which we need to produce an effect applied differently at different points on the timeline. Any kind of change – be it a change in placing on the screen, in an effect, or even in the volume of a sound – which we have to apply to a clip during editing is animation.

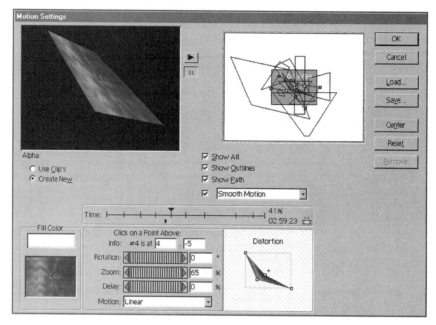

The basic concept behind animation is the idea of **keyframes**. We've touched on keyframes in previous chapters, and used them quite extensively in the previous chapter on effects. However, it's worth being clear on exactly what they are, and what they do.

Keyframes

Say you're trying to create an animation – you want an object to move from one side of the screen to the other. Now, it's not practical for you to go through your shot, one frame at a time, and position the object where it needs to be on every frame. Instead, we simply specify two frames - in this case the first and the last – and tell Premiere where we want the object to be on those frames. These are our two keyframes, and Premiere will work out what happens in between them using a process called **tweening**, or **interpolation**.

If you want the motion to be more complex, you just put in more keyframes. For example, if we want the object to move down to the bottom of the screen as it moves across, then go back up again – in a V shape – we need to set a third keyframe in the middle of the animation, and position our object. Premiere then tries to make a smooth motion path that moves the object between the three points.

This same process can be applied to any animated aspect of Premiere's behavior - whether it's the size of the object, the position of the Brightness slider in a brightness and contrast effect, or the stereo position of a sound. You just set your keyframes, and Premiere interpolates the values of every frame between them.

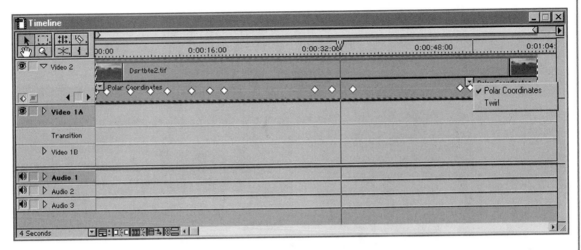

This can produce problems – for example, you might want your object to change direction suddenly (as in a V shape above) or smoothly (as in a U shape). Both shapes take in the same 3 keyframes. The difference is in the type of interpolation Premiere uses. Some basic tools are provided to let you pick the interpolation, but often, you just have to live with the results the package gives you, or create more keyframes to smooth out the curve.

There are two main tools for animation in Premiere:

- Effects - which we've looked at already.

- The Motion window – which allows us to animate the position, rotation, distortion and scale of any clip so that it can be flown through and round the screen.

Together, they offer a very powerful set of abilities. However, you really need to know what you can achieve and how you're going to do it before you start work, because animation can very easily go wrong if you haven't thought through your production in advance. In general, it's best when working on a complex shot, to start by adding just the most important keyframes, to sketch out the entire scene, then move in and add detail, tweaking the effect until it's perfect. There's nothing worse than painstakingly setting up a set of synchronized effects only to discover, when you make one small change to one part of the shot, that everything else needs to be re-done from scratch.

Performing a Simple Animation

The Motion window is a very powerful animation tool, but it can be a little daunting when you first meet it. This quick tour should get you used to the basic functions of this important window:

1. Place a clip onto the timeline. The image itself isn't that important, but make it around 10 seconds long to give us something to play with.

2. There are a couple of ways to get to the Motion window. We can either right-click (or COMMAND+CLICK on the clip itself and select Video Options > Motion, or simply click the Motion Setup in the Effects Controls window while our shot is selected (shortcut is CTRL+Y or COMMAND+Y).

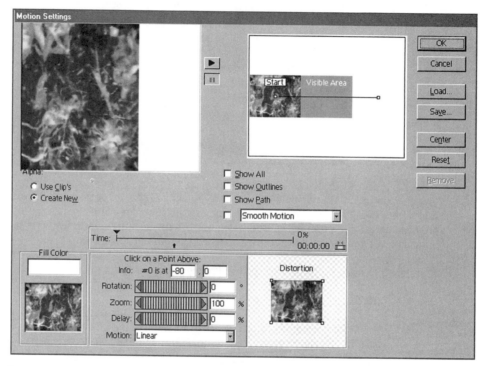

3. When the window opens, the default animation is shown – the monitor in the top left shows the image scrolling through the screen from left to right (if it's not moving, you'll need to press the Play button to the right of the monitor.

4. It's worth taking a little time to get to know the Motion window. To the right of the monitor window you can see how the motion displayed is created. The Visible Area of the screen is marked as a gray square in the middle. Our shot is positioned as it is at the beginning of the animation (just off the screen to the left).

The motion path of the image is displayed as a black line through the visible area - this indicates that our animation is currently a straight line directly through the screen. At either end of the line are dots. These represent keyframes. As explained before a keyframe is a point in time when we define a change in the direction of motion (or some other aspect of our clip).

Right now, our clip has just two keyframes – one at the start of the animation, and one at the end. The word Start, and the image of the shot indicates that the currently selected keyframe is the start of the animation, and shows us the size, rotation and distortion of our clip at that keyframe.

5. Click on the start point and drag it. By doing this you're setting the starting position of your clip's animation. By clicking and dragging the end point, you can change where your image ends up.

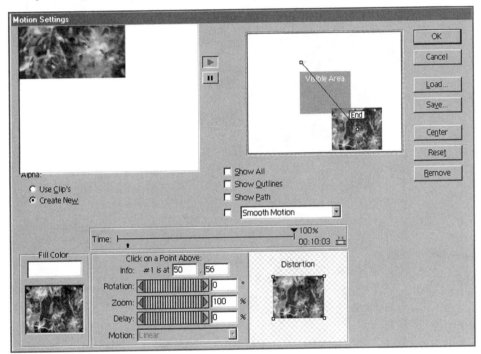

6. Now try clicking somewhere in the middle of the motion path. Another keyframe appears, and you can drag this wherever you like. You should now be able to create whatever motion path you'd like for flying your clip through the screen.

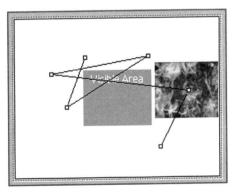

7. Below the motion path viewer are four check boxes. The first, Show All changes the view in the monitor area. Instead of simply animating a still of the first frame of our scene on a colored background, the window displays the entire shot as it would appear – playing back against a transparent backdrop through which you can see any other clips placed below it on the timeline.

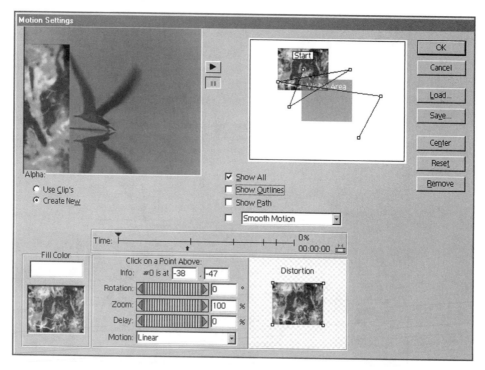

The disadvantage of this is that it tends to slow the computer down, creating jerky playback. On modern computers, however, processing power is usually great enough to have Show All turned on all the time.

8. The next box Show Outlines gives a more graphical view of the keyframes. A wireframe shape shows the position, rotation and scale of your image at each keyframe - useful when working on complex animations.

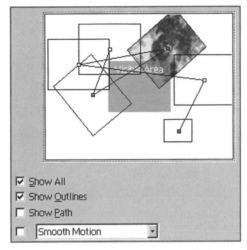

9. Show Path gives some indication of the speed your clip is traveling by displaying tiny diamonds along the motion path. These are equally spaced in time - so where the image is moving slowly, they'll be very close together, and where it's moving fast, they'll be further apart.

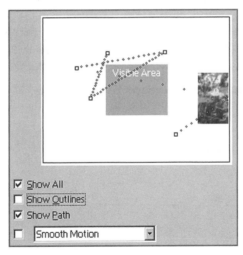

10. The final box lets you smooth the motion of your clip in various ways, and below this is a representation of the timeline. The upward arrow underneath the line is the playback head which can be dragged back and forth through the clip. The vertical marks on the timeline are the keyframes. Clicking above the line lets you add, or drag keyframes. A downward arrow above the timeline indicates the currently selected keyframe.

11. Below the timeline, is a set of controls for defining the motion very specifically. The two numbers in the Info box let you specify the *x* and *y* positions of the current keyframe. This is especially useful if you need to be very precise – or copy position information from one keyframe to another so that the image returns to its original position.

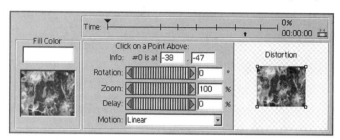

12. The Rotation control comes next – you can drag on the bar to spin your shot at the selected keyframe, or enter specific rotation values. The Zoom control lets you move the shot into or out of the screen.

13. The Delay control lets you set a time during which the clip remains stationary before it begins to move towards the next keyframe position. The time is defined as a percentage of the length of the clip. In other words, say you've got a clip with keyframes at the beginning, middle and end, and you select the first one, and start adjusting its delay. If you bring it up to 25 percent, the clip will spend the first quarter of the clip at the first keyframe position, move to the second keyframe, and then on to the third. If you set it at 50 percent, it will stay still for half the clip's length, then jump suddenly to the second keyframe position. You can't extend the delay beyond the next keyframe.

14. You can also change the Motion setting for the keyframe – to define whether you want the clip to accelerate towards the next keyframe, decelerate, or move smoothly over the course of the motion.

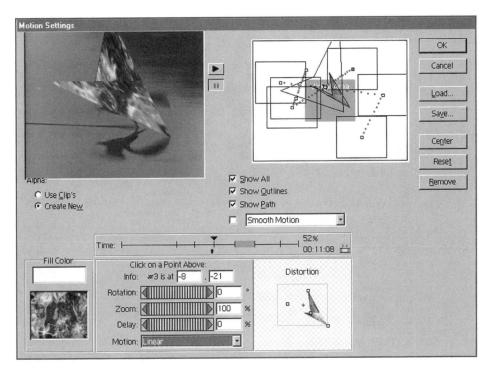

15. To the right, the distortion control lets you drag the corners of the image to define the way the shot is distorted at each keyframe. This is useful for creating perspective effects, and faking 3D motion.

16. To the left, the final area of the window lets you pick a fill color for the background if you choose to have the animation against a flat color (Unless you've placed the video shot in track 1A or 1B, the background will be automatically transparent).

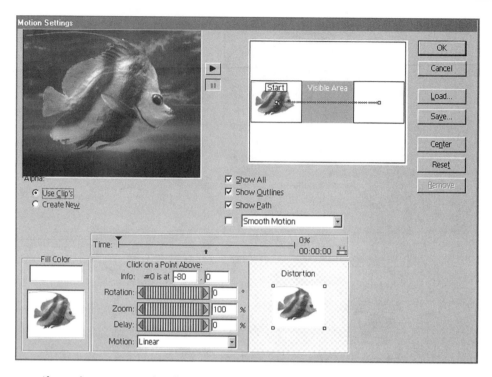

If you choose to use the clip's alpha (and if it has one!), the clip will be superimposed without its background – otherwise only the area around the clip will be transparent, and the clip will always be rectangular.

It's worth remembering that you can't use the Undo function in the Motion window. There is, however a Reset button which removes all distortion, zoom and rotation settings from your keyframe.

17. Now we've got a basic idea of how the Motion window works, let's see what it's capable of by trying out a few of the preset motion paths Adobe has included for us with the package. Click the Load button, and locate the Motion folder in your Premiere directory.

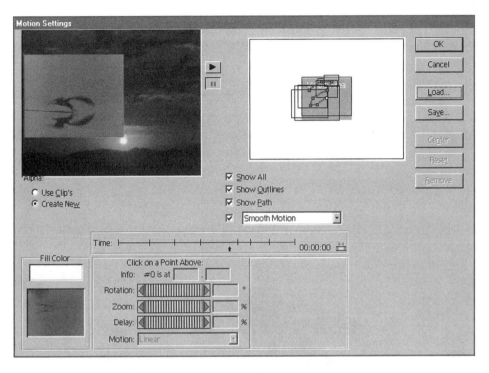

This should contain a selection of preset motion paths. Load in a few of them, and take a look at how they work. Here, we've loaded in the Whoosh path which brings our clip into view from the distance so that it ends up covering the entire screen.

When you create your own motion paths, and animations, you can save them in just the same way – so that you build up a library of your own effects. This allows you to use the same effects time and time again in a production – creating a "house style" for your shows.

Producing a 3D animation

Now we know our way around the Motion window, let's try creating an animation. The idea is to use a still image of a spaceship, and a still image of stars to give the craft a realistic motion path as it flies around the sky.

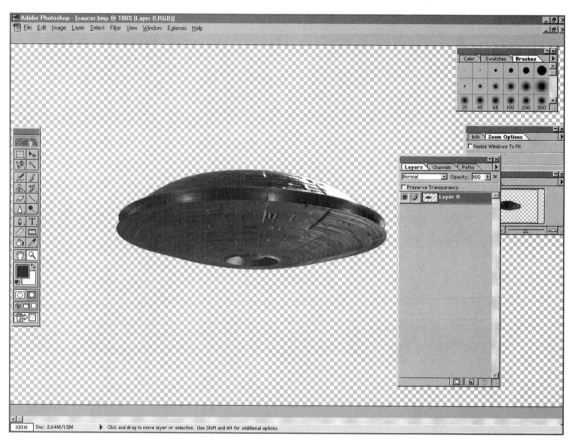

1. We import the foreground (spaceship) and background (sky) images, and place them onto the timeline with the saucer in the top track. The images should run parallel, and be stretched to about 20 seconds.

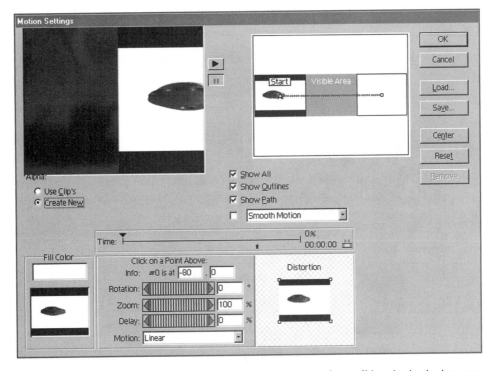

2. Next we open the Motion window (and make sure the Show All box is checked so you can see the background image behind the ship). The default animation has our spaceship flying from left to right, but because the alpha (underneath the monitor) is set to Create New, the transparency of the ship's background isn't in place. We just change the setting to Use Clip's.

3. Immediately, the ship begins to look good - it's superimposed correctly, and flying straight. However, we want the movement pattern to be a little more sophisticated.

4. Click on the first keyframe – either by selecting it in the motion path viewport at the top right of the window, or by clicking on it on the timeline in the middle of the shot.

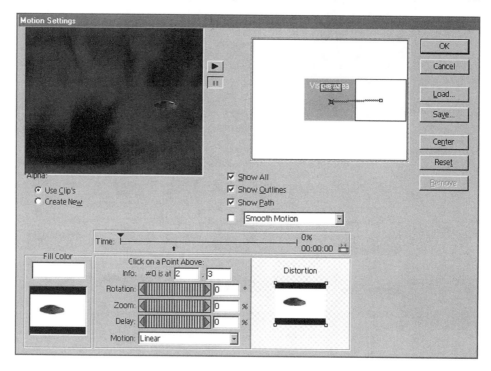

5. Now, reduce the size of the image with the Zoom control – take it right down to 0 percent, so the image vanishes, and drag it to the center of the screen. Playing the animation, the ship now shoots towards us as it rushes off the right hand side of the screen.

> *Note, the timing isn't right – The* Motion *window doesn't give you an accurate picture of how long your shot will take. You'll just have to guess at the appropriate speeds.*

6. Click on the timeline about a third of the way into your clip, and a new keyframe is created and selected. Drag the Zoom slider up to 60 percent and move the image over to the top right of the visible area.

7. Set up another keyframe about two thirds of the way through with the ship at the bottom of the screen in the middle, and finally, drag the end keyframe just above the top of the screen, and set the Zoom right up to 500 percent.

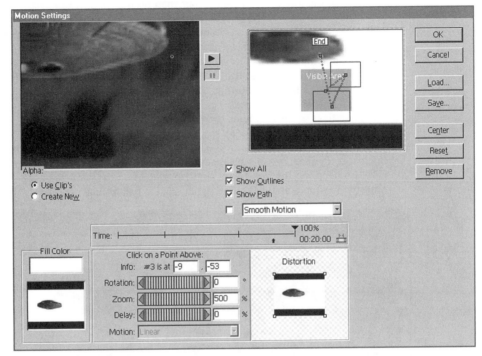

8. The ship now rushes around the screen before flying off over the top of the camera. However, the motion isn't too believable. The changes of direction are far too rapid. We can help this a little by checking the Smooth Motion box, and selecting Averaging-high from the drop-down list. This rounds the corners of our keyframes a little.

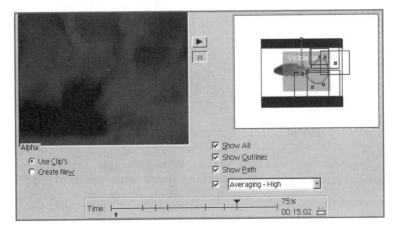

9. If we want to smooth the motion more, we'll have to add more keyframes. Here, you can see we've placed an additional keyframe at each side of the two angular changes of direction. This smoothes the whole animation out. It was easier to do this by clicking directly on the motion path view rather than on the window's timeline

10. Now let's work on our first keyframe – the spaceship shoots from the distance to the foreground completely evenly. This doesn't happen in real 3D space. Perspective means that objects which are further away appear to be moving slower – the craft needs to accelerate as it approaches us. Luckily, that's easy to do. Just select the first keyframe, and use the Motion drop-down list to select Accelerate.

    Three settings are available in this box: Linear, Accelerate, and Decelerate. They can help to make many animations more realistic. For example, using Decelerate on one keyframe, and Accelerate on the next makes an object slow to a stop, then move off increasing its speed – like a ball being thrown into the air, and falling back down. If you set Accelerate on the first frame, and Decelerate on the next, then the object crashes into the keyframe and is fired off again – like a ball hitting a wall.

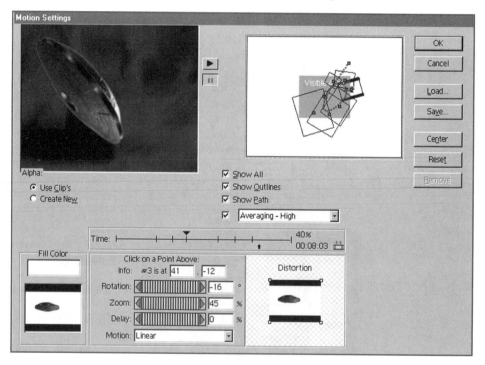

11. Now let's do a little rotation. As the ship turns at the bottom of the screen to make it's final zoom out towards us, we can emphasize the motion by making it appear to bank. We select the keyframe we've already placed, and drag the rotation slider to twist the ship.

12. You might need to experiment with the placing of rotation frames and the degree of rotation to get the best possible look to your shot, but basically, the ship should bank by twisting downwards into the direction of the turn as the turn begins, then flatten out more slowly on the way out of the turn.

13. Finally, we save our motion path (in case we want to use it on another clip later, like a chasing ship!) and hit OK to close the Motion window. We can now render our effect. In this shot we've also added a lens-flare effect to the background image for extra effect.

Animation with Effects

Several of Premiere's effects are designed with animation in mind. With them, you can create several types of 2D and 3D motion which can help to create impact and enliven otherwise uninteresting footage. The first thing I'll show you how to make a still image into something a little more interesting.

1. This landscape shot has to be on screen for 20 seconds, and would look pretty dull if it was just left there without any animation.

2. The image is a photograph, and luckily we were able to scan it in at high quality. This means that we can zoom in on the image. If it were a simple video capture, then zooming in close would reveal the poor quality of TV images.

3. Placing it onto the timeline, we add an Image Pan effect. This lets us select just a portion of the image to fill the screen. We'll also be able to animate the shot so the camera will effectively be roving over it during the course of the shot.

4. We click the box to the left of the effect's label in the Effect Controls window to turn on animation, and move the playback head to the start of the shot. We then click Setup for the effect to bring up the effect control window. Here we can drag the corners of the first image to define the portion of the screen we want to focus on at the start of the shot.

> *If you shift-drag the corners, then the shot's aspect ratio will be maintained. In other words, you won't distort the image by creating a different shape to the shape of the video screen.*

5. Closing the control window, we re-position the playback head to about half-way through our clip, and then open the control window again to set another view of the image.

6. Previewing the shot, we can see the scene we've created. We start off close, pan across to the other side of the image, then zoom out to view the whole picture.

Our only problem is that the shot is too short. We should have extended it before we started, but we didn't. If we just drag out the shot, the scene will extend, but the keyframes will stay where they are. Clicking the triangle by the track label opens up the shot so we can see the keyframes (if you see the red opacity rubberband instead, click the white diamond at the bottom left of the track to switch to keyframe mode).

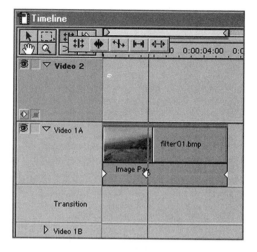

The Rate Stretch *tool (underneath the* Rolling Edit *tool) lets you stretch or compress the shot – speeding it up or slowing it down. This means that the keyframes will stretch, so the motion is scaled accordingly.*

7. Our next job requires us to take the shot we've just animated, and make it tumble backwards out of shot. We're going to use the Basic 3D effect to create the illusion.

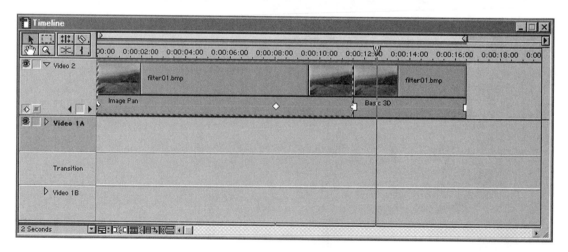

8. We place another copy of the image onto the timeline directly after the first, and place the Basic 3D effect onto it. The controls let us tilt, swivel and zoom our shot.

9. Turning on animation, and moving to the last frame of the shot, we set the value of the Zoom control to 1000. We can't do this with the slider, we have to click on the number above it, and type the figure in numerically.

10. This sets the zoom up – we just need to create our tumbling animation. We set the Tilt and Swivel values to 810 degrees, so the image is side on to the camera, and appears invisible.

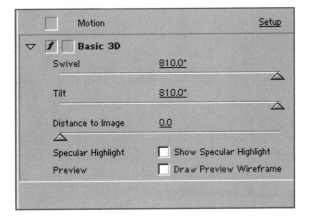

11. Scrolling through the animation, we can see the image tumbling backwards. If we want a more complex motion, we can always insert more keyframes, or combine the effect with the functions of the Motion window, or another effect.

12. With the Camera View effect, we can achieve a similar result. This time, the idea is to take the shot, and shrink it to a horizontalline before making it vanish to a dot – as though it was being shown on a TV which is suddenly turned off:

13. We place the image in exactly the same way as before, and add the Camera View effect. We set the fill color for the effect to black, and put the playback head at about half way through the scene. We then turn on animation for the effect.

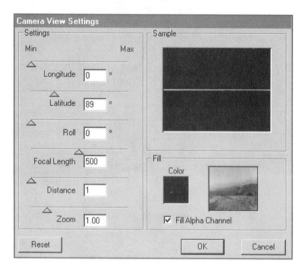

14. Clicking Setup, we set the Latitude to 89 degrees. This rotates the image horizontally so it looks like a line across the screen.

15. Moving to the last keyframe, we set the Zoom and the Distance sliders on the effect to their maximum values, and set the Latitude to 90 degrees.

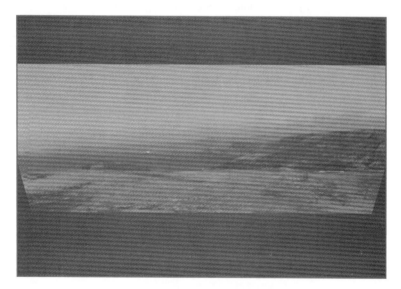

16. The scene now works, but may need to be shortened to produce a realistic effect. Here we've made it a little more realistic by placing an image of horizontal lines (as you'd get on a TV screen) on a track above the shot, and decreasing the opacity to about half way.

17. Finally we'll take a look at the Transform effect. This allows you to do some basic scaling and motion, but its unique function is its ability to set an anchor point – or center of rotation for its transformations. Here we're going to animate a strange surreal creature:

The hand, upper-arm, and body have been produced as separate layers in Photoshop. This means that they can be animated separately.

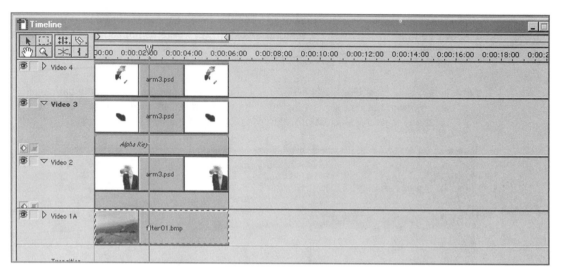

18. We load them all into Premiere, and, adding two extra video tracks, we place them into the timeline as shown – with the body at the back (in front of a still image we're using for a backdrop), the arm on the middle layer, and the hand at the front.

19. Transform effects are placed on the arm and hand tracks, and by clicking the Anchor Point button for each, we can pick on the monitor window where we want each element to be anchored. We choose the joint around which we want each to rotate, so for the hand object, the anchor point is set at the elbow, and for the arm, it's set at the shoulder.

We also need to set the position for each element once we've set the anchor point - just to put the arm and hand back in their correct places.

20.   Animating the hand to wave is now just a matter of altering the rotation slider - the hand rotates about the elbow. Animating the motion of the upper arm is more difficult, as you need to change the position of the hand layer to follow the rotation of the arm.

Picture in Picture in Premiere

Picture-in-picture shots are easy to achieve in Premiere. You can create them in a number of ways. Here are a couple of different methods – each of which has its own advantages.

1.   To start with, we'll create a picture within a picture using the Transform effect. We place the two shots one under the other on the timeline. The background image is placed on track 1A and the foreground on track 2.

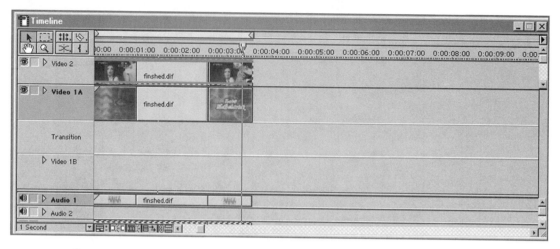

2. We drag the Transform effect onto the top track, and use the Scale height and Scale width sliders to shrink the image. We then click the Position button, and click in the Monitor window to place the center of our shot on the screen.

3. This places the shot, but it appears against a black background. To make that background transparent, we click Transparency Setup in the Effect Controls window. This brings up the Transparency window, and we select Black Alpha Matte as our transparency type.

That's one method. It's quick and easy. However it's not too flexible, and you can't use varying degrees of transparency. If you want a more organic feel, you can use an Image Matte:

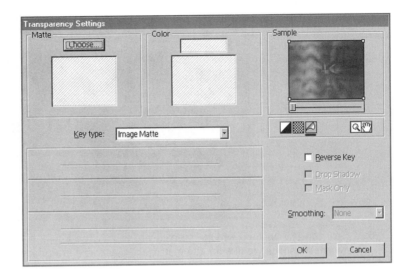

4. We place the shots as before, but don't use any kind of effect. Instead we go straight to the Transparency window, and select Image Matte.

5. Clicking choose, we locate our image matte on disk. This is a black and white image we've designed in Photoshop – notice that the edges of the box are blended in gray – the grayer the image gets, the more transparent it will be in Premiere.

6. We can use an Image Matte to control the way the image is faded in. We can draw whatever shape we like for the matte, and use partial transparency.

For our third method, we'll use the Motion window. If you need your image to move, this is often the best system to use.

7. Again, we place the shots onto the timeline, with the foreground on the higher track. This time we right click to select Video Options > Motion.

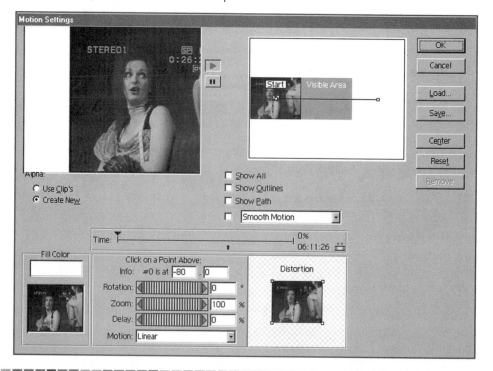

8. With the first keyframe selected, we use the Zoom control to reduce the size of the shot, then drag it into position at the top left of the screen. Right now, this looks OK, but playing through the animation, we see we've got some unwanted motion.

9. The ending keyframe hasn't been changed, so the image drifts off across the screen. We could click on it and type in the correct Zoom and Position figures so that the second keyframe was the same as the first.

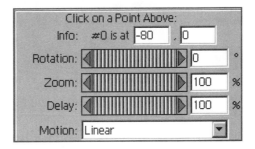

10. However, there is an easier way. We just drag the Delay control right up to 100 percent. This means that our shot will stay at its first keyframe position throughout the entire clip. Closing the Motion window, we can lengthen or shorten the clip as much as we like, and the picture-in-picture shot will remain still.

Split Screen

Here we're going to do a rather complex job. We've got several shots, and we want to combine them into a single scene. The result is going to be a split screen display in which shots are flown in, positioned on screen to form a pattern, and then replaced.

We need to do a bit of pre-planning for this effect. There's so much going on, that we can't just do it and hope that it works. Just a sketch of how you expect things to come out will be very useful, and it doesn't even matter that you stick to your original plan when you find a better way of doing things. It's still useful to have one so you know where you are, and what you're trying to achieve.

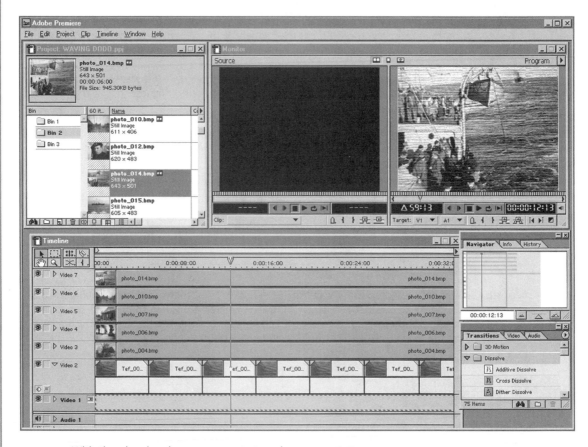

With the planning done, we can start work.

1.   We add four more video tracks and place all our images onto them – with the backdrop we're using in the lowest track. Remember, the order in which the images are placed on the tracks will determine which is on top in the final scene.

2.   To make our shots stand out a little, we're going to bevel them. We drop the Bevel Edges effect onto the top shot, setting the edge thickness to 0.07 and the light intensity to 0.8. This gives a nice 3D look to the shot.

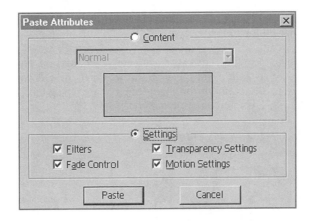

3. To save us some effort in reproducing the effect, we can just copy it from one shot to the next. With the top image selected, choose Edit > Copy. Now select the next clip, and go to Edit > Paste Attributes. The box which appears lets us choose whether to paste the clip itself, or just its settings. We choose Settings.

4. We carry on, and paste the bevel onto all our images. Right now, that gives us a shot of our top picture. What we need to do is to shrink and arrange the images so they appear in the correct positions. We bring up the Motion window for our top image, and start to work on it.

5. First, we use the Zoom tool to set the size of our shot to 40 percent of its original size. We need to do this at both the start and end points of the animation. We then click on the timeline about 10 percent of the way along it. This becomes the keyframe on which we want our shot to arrive in position, so we place it in the top left of the screen at this keyframe.

6. Because we want it to remain in place, we drag the Delay control to 75 percent. The blue bar on the timeline represents the amount of time the shot remains stationary.

7. We could now alter the start and end keyframes so as to create the arrival and departure animations for the shot, but we don't. Instead, we close the Motion window, and set up the positions for all our other shots. Doing this gives us a much better view of the way the animation will look in the end.

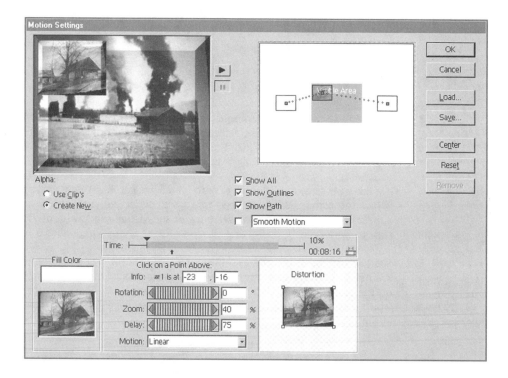

> *Note: because all the shots arrive and depart at the same time, we can save our motion path, then load it back in for every shot so we don't need to set it up over and over again for each clip. All we'll need to do is change the position of the second keyframe (the place on the screen where the shot settles).*

8. Our scene is looking pretty good already. However, right now, the images are simply flying in from the left, and disappearing to the right. We want them to be a little more interesting. We select the first track and go back to the Motion window.

9. The first shot will zoom in from above, so we select the start keyframe, place it just above the visible screen, and drag the Zoom control to 0. It's as simple as that. We then take the end keyframe, place it to the left of the screen, and again drag Zoom to 0. The image now zooms in, pauses, then zooms out to the left.

10. Next, we open the second image motion controls. We'll do something a little different with this. We drag the Start keyframe to exactly the same position as the middle one. We then use the Distortion section of the window to drag the two left hand corners of the shot over to the right, positioning them just between the two right hand corners.

11. The shot now starts completely flat against the right hand edge of the screen, and swings into view as though in perspective. Doing exactly the same with the End keyframe, we create the illusion that the image has folded itself away at the end of the shot.

12. For image three, we place the Start keyframe in the center, zoom it right out, and type 1000 into the Rotation field. This spins the shot out from the center of the screen. The End keyframe we place right out to the left of the screen, and zoom into it to 300 percent as we rotate it, so the image flies out towards the camera.

13. Finally, with the fourth image, we decide to add a few more keyframes. We click on the motion path between the first two positions, and drag the shot to another point on the screen. This creates another keyframe. We put in a few more to give the shot a really complex motion path into and out of the screen.

14. We also click and drag the keyframe in which the shot is in place, and shorten its Delay so that the shot arrives after all the others, and starts to move of before the rest.

The result is a very intricate set of moves which creates an interesting animated display for our images. Very useful in a slideshow, or a menu ident for a magazine-style program. Other interesting effects to add might be an Echo effect to emphasize the movement, providing trails, and a drop shadow so the scenes would cast a shadow on their background.

Still Image Animation

Finally, let's combine some of the techniques we've learned to do some more traditional animation. The idea is to have a pair of fingers walking down a hand-drawn high street. It's quite a difficult job, and will involve effects, compositing, and the Motion window used in tandem.

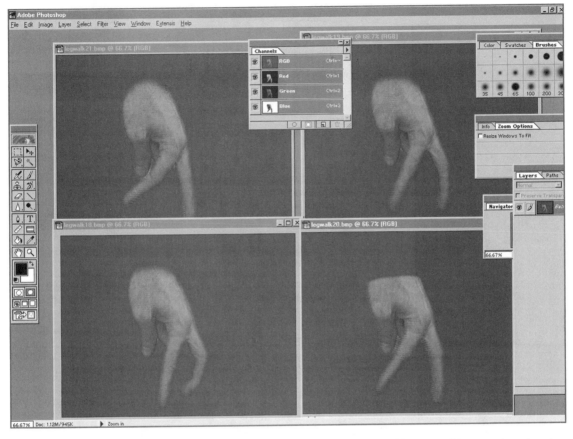

1. We've taken several shots of the walking fingers in different positions, and captured them as still images. These have been imported into Photoshop and cut around – with the background replaced by solid blue so the scene can be easily *chromakeyed*.

2. We've created one walk-loop (enough images to show the fingers taking one step), and named them sequentially as walk01, walk02, walk03, etc. They have been saved as bitmap (BMP) files.

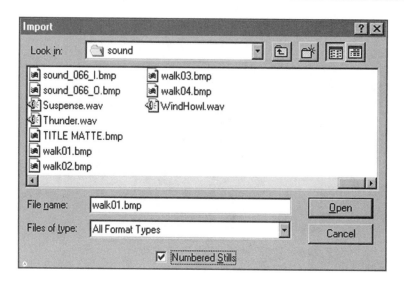

3. When we import them into Premiere, we can select just the first image, then check the Numbered Stills box, and the shots will be loaded in as an animation rather than a collection of stills.

4. What we have is a single step. What we need is several, so when we place the shot onto the timeline, we copy it about twenty times, placing the shots one after the other. We then use the Export Timeline tool to save our repeating walk cycle out as a video clip.

5. We can now start a new project, and load our clip into it along with the background onto which the fingers will be superimposed.

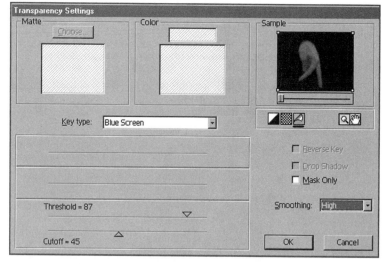

6. Our first job is to drop the fingers onto the timeline and open the Transparency window. We use Blue Screen transparency to remove the blue background so that our image can be composited with its background.

7. We then need to do a little animation. We open the Motion window, and use it to set up an animation where the fingers start about a third of the way across the screen, and end up about two thirds of the way across. It's easy enough. The default animation is a horizontal journey across the screen, so we just need to click on the start and end points, and move each in a little.

8. Click the Show All box if it's not already ticked. This will display the shot as it will be seen. Right now, there is no background, so the backdrop will be black. We also use the eyedropper tool to set the background color to chromakey blue by clicking on the background in the image at the window's bottom left.

9. We want the fingers to be a little smaller than they are right now, so we select each keyframe in turn, and use the Zoom control to reduce its size to 80 percent. With that done, we close the Motion window, and preview to see our fingers walking slowly across the screen.

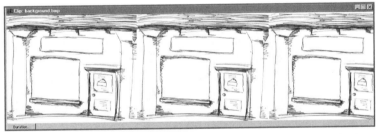

10. Next we place the background in track Video 1A. As you can see the background shot is actually far longer than the screen. This is because we're intending to scroll it behind the walking character as it moves, creating the effect of greater speed.

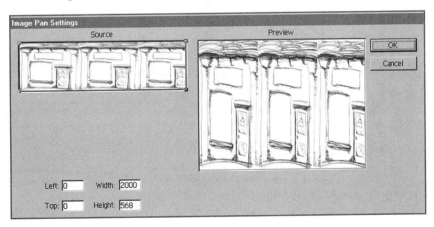

11. To do this, we drop the Image Pan effect onto our scene. We've used this effect before, but this time, the shot is a completely different shape to our TV screen. The image on the left is the correct shape for the backdrop. The image on the right shows the screen itself, and the way the backdrop is currently crushed into it.

12. If we alt-drag the corner of the left hand image, the box will automatically change to the shape of our TV screen. That way, the image will never be distorted. We set the effect to display just the left hand portion of the image, then close the box.

13. Now we turn on animation by clicking the stopwatch next to the effect's label, and move the playback head to the final frame before clicking Setup to bring back the Image Pan control box. Here we slide the left hand box over to the right of the image, creating a pan along the length of the drawing.

14. When we click OK, the animation is complete, and the hand walks across the screen while the background scrolls behind it. Combining several techniques and effects in the same effect is often the best way to get the result you're looking for. It just requires that you think through your animation before you start.

Summary

This chapter has shown you how easy it is to bring animation to your movies. You've learned how to:

- Perform a simple animation using the Motion window

- Give the impression of 3D animation using perspective

- Animate a sequence in conjunction with some effects

- Create a picture-in-picture effect

- Put together a montage of animated clips

- Animate a series of still images

By now you've learned all the major techniques of how to create a professional looking movie with Premiere. However, there is one major step left to consider – the process of exporting your work to the outside world. This is what we will cover in the next chapter.

12 Titling

Everything needs credits – even this book (go on, look them up!). Video productions are no exception and in this chapter we'll learn how to create credits and titles to enhance your projects and give credit (and maybe blame) where it's due.

But titles aren't just restricted to names and jobs; titling covers any text that needs to appear on-screen during a program. This can be anything from the simple white-on-black printing of the programme's title, to scrolling credits, info-bars, subtitles, name captions, or entire intro sequences involving 3D animation, video, and special effects.

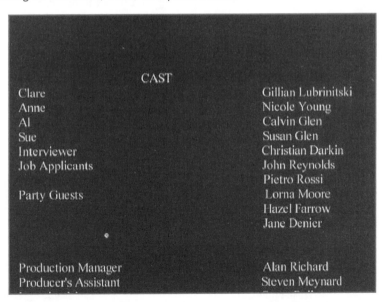

Creating a credit sequence is a job which needs to be done carefully and sensitively. You can't just throw together a list of the people involved in your production. You need to give a little thought to the order and grouping of your names; I'd be a little miffed if friends of ED left my name off the cover of this book, and so will your cameraman if he's credited just below the dog wrangler and caterer.

Credits Where Credit's Due

Most documentaries and factual programmes have credits only at the end. The on-screen presenters are usually credited first. Then, the various departments are credited in groups with the most senior workers at the top of the list, heading their various areas. The camera crew are usually followed by the sound operators, anyone involved in the construction of rigging and working with the equipment, and anyone else on the shoot. Researchers and advisors are usually in their own grouping, as are the editing and post-production staff (including those designing the credits themselves!)

As a rule of thumb, precedence is given to those people who have a greater creative impact on the screen. Thus, the music composers, directors, graphic designers, cinematographers, writers, etc. are generally separated in the credits – even if it's just by a blank line, they tend to stand out.

Writers, directors, and producers tend to be credited either at the very start of the end credits sequence, or at the very end. Where you place them tends to depend on how you expect people to be watching the production. On TV, the last credit is often the most memorable because it's the still on which the program is faded out. In the cinema, the final credits are rarely seen because viewers have generally left the theater and are hailing a cab by the time they come up.

Makers of factual programs tend to end up needing to thank a lot of people – either for giving them access, or setting up interviews, or just for going out of their way to allow them to film. It's perfectly right, and generally good practice to give a "With thanks to" credit to any person or organisation who's lent a hand, or been helpful. Do be careful, however – if you end up leaving anyone out, you'll be less popular than if you'd put no credits in at all!

In a film, things usually follow the same basic groups. There's often a sequence of credits at the beginning of a film, listing the principle actors, writer, director, producer, musician, and any heads of department who had a particularly significant input into the creative matter of the film.

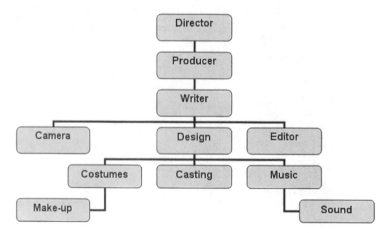

A Typical Set of Drama Credits

The end of a film lists everyone else. Sometimes names are duplicated at the beginning and at the end. Other times, people get just one credit. Sometimes the cast can be listed in order of importance, but whereas it's quite easy to place the lead characters in this way, things can get a little muddled when you get to the level of "third thug from the left" or "newspaper salesman". Many producers cut through the whole tangled mess and avoid upsetting actors by listing the cast in *order of appearance.*

If a person has more than one job on a film, it's quite acceptable for them to be credited more than once. In fact it's quite common for the director, producer, and writer to be the same person. That said, if you credit the same person with too many roles, the limited nature of your production team and budget may become apparent to the viewer, and this kind of thing often looks messy anyway.

Often, there will also be final mandatory credits. People or organizations you've got to credit because of agreements you've made. Music credits need to be very specific, as do logos for companies you've agreed to mention. This kind of credit can apply to even the smallest production if it's going to be shown in public. Contractual credits can often get forgotten by local TV companies, and others who really can't afford to ignore them.

Captions

MATT COSTAIN

John McLean

MEL YOUNG
PUBLISHER/DIRECTOR BIG ISSUE

Name captions are another common use for on-screen text. They too have their conventions. The first time an interviewee or speaker appears on screen, a caption is usually placed giving their name and their job (or the reason they're on the program). If they appear again, there usually isn't a caption – program-makers tend to assume viewers will remember who's speaking, although often, captions are repeated after a commercial break.

> *Captions tend to be placed right at the bottom of the screen while the person in question is shot as a medium close-up.*

Subtitles

If your production needs subtitling – either to make it clear what's being said in another language, or to make up for poor sound or a difficult accent, remember what it is you're trying to achieve with them. You have to find a balance which makes sure the subtitles are readable to anyone who wants to look at them, without letting them intrude on the action. Subtitles are usually printed in either black or white, and positioned at the bottom of the screen. An easily read sans serif typeface is most often used.

The problem comes when considering the subtitle's background. You can't rely on the background being of one color throughout the production. If it becomes a light color, then white writing will be invisible. Likewise, if the shot is a dark one, then black writing will be lost. You can't keep changing the color of the text throughout the production, so you have to pick one or the other.

A third way is to place the writing in white on a black block. Unfortunately, if someone is speaking rapidly, the block can be so large that it blocks out important pieces of action. Subtitling will always be a compromise. Sometimes the solution is to make the block semi-transparent, or replace it with a slight outline around the letters that lifts them slightly from their surroundings – a black border to white letters, or vice-versa.

> *Subtitling is actually a fine art in itself. Usually, it's impractical to write on-screen every word that is said, so part of the skill in good subtitling is getting the point of the dialog across in as few words as possible – communicating the message without expecting the viewer to spend all their time reading.*

Intro Sequences

On-screen text isn't always as simple as putting white writing on a black background and making it large enough to read. The style, colors and animations of text can have a major impact on your production. They work together to provide a **house style** which marks your program out from others, and they're also a way of setting the mood for your show, and tie all its elements together. For example, if you turn on any random news program, you'll know as soon as an interviewee name caption, or a stock market figure, or a Breaking News tickertape appears on the screen, which channel you're watching, and which program. It's all in the graphics – the way they're presented, the colors, and the typefaces.

Animated intro sequences may start life just as a way to carry the title of the program in an interesting way, but they can easily become the trademarks that let you know exactly what you're in for. Say the film you're watching opens with a white circle in the centre of the screen, a man walks into the circle, turns and fires a gun towards you, and the screen fills slowly with red. You probably don't need to know any more than that to be able to describe the plot of the film, to know who the hero is, how many girlfriends he's going to have during the film, how the movie ends, and how the lead character likes his drinks.

> *OK, now we've had the theory, let's have a look at Premiere's titling capabilities in more detail.*

Basic Titling

Premiere's built-in titling package is simple and unassuming. However, if you're looking for quick production of relatively ordinary single color titles and captions, it's perfectly adequate. In this example, we'll produce a page of credits, learn to fade it in and out, and make it scroll up the screen.

Let's start with something simple – a one word title, fading in, and then fading out:

1. We bring up Premiere's Titler from the File menu (or the Project window's context menu) with New > Title. The Titler window appears. Its central area represents the screen, and this is where you compose your text.

    Notice the two dotted lines around the window. These represent **safe areas** of the screen. TV sets are all different – they don't all show the whole image, and each clips the shot at the top, bottom, left, and right to a different degree to produce a slight curving in the corners of the visible area. Titles which are written right to the edge of the screen run the risk of being cut off on all but the flattest most modern sets.

    The only way to get around this is to make sure you keep your titles within the central portion of the screen. There are two safe areas marked – the title-safe zone and the action-safe zone, the recommended minimum areas for displaying titles and subjects respectively.

    > *Premiere's safe zones have been set up for NTSC TV pictures (the US broadcast format), and while other systems such as PAL and SECAM are pretty much the same, they're not exact. However, if you're creating your video for CD or Internet distribution, you can pretty much ignore the safe areas.*

2. We want our title to be on a black background – rather than the white one currently displayed. By right-clicking or control-clicking on the page, and selecting Title Window Options…, we can bring up a dialog which will let us choose the color and shape of our screen. We can use this to pick any background color or resolution we like. However, for a black or white screen, there's a shortcut – whilst in the main title area just press B or W on your keyboard for the appropriate color!

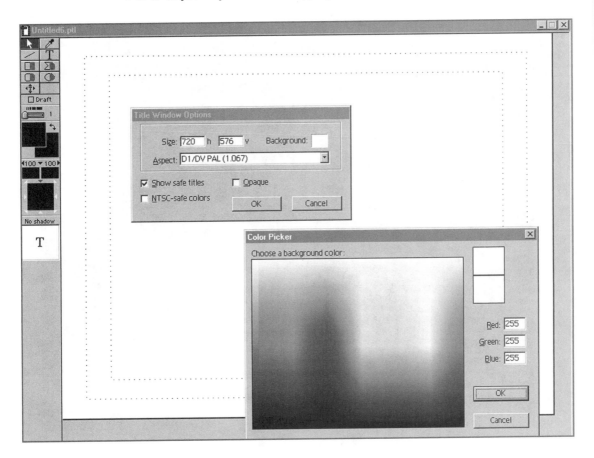

3. By default, the type color is black. We want it white. The top color selector on the left of the window lets us choose the object color (the text color) and the shadow color behind it.

4. We can now type our caption. Select the Text tool, and click anywhere in the safe area to start typing. Once the title is finished, we click elsewhere on the screen to deselect it. The tool changes to the Arrow tool, and we can start to manipulate our text.

5. Dragging the center of the text box moves it around the screen. Dragging the corners enlarges or reduces the box. This doesn't, however, alter the size of the text. To do that, we right-click or control-click to bring up a context menu:

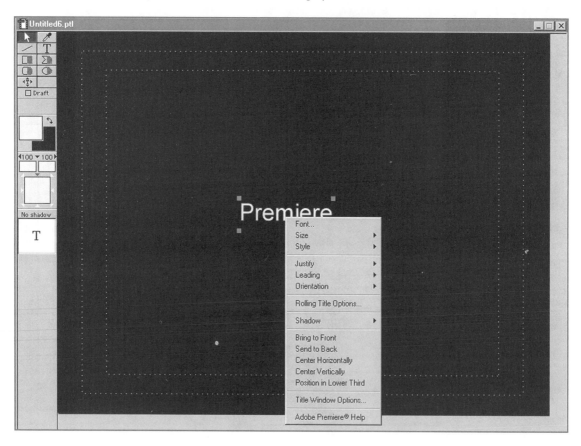

6. The first item on the menu is Font. As I'm sure you guessed, this lets you alter the size and typeface of your text. We pick a nice large, spangly font.

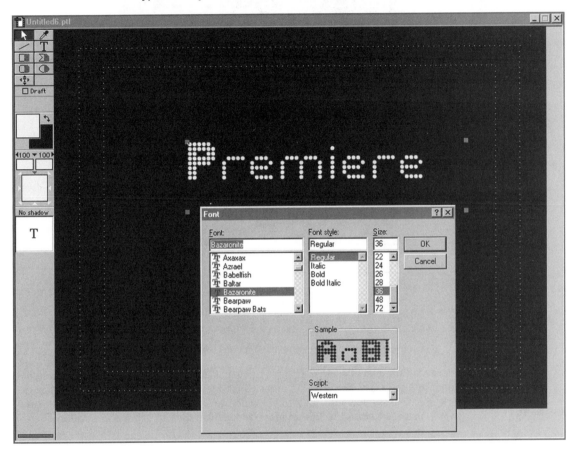

When we close the Font window, we need to alter the shape of the text box so our new larger words fit into it.

7. We can get the title centered exactly on the screen by selecting Center Vertically and Center Horizontally from the context menu.

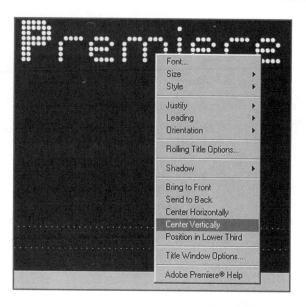

We can also use the Position In Lower Third *option to place the text in the ideal position for a name caption or subtitle.*

8.   In order to use our title, we must save it just like any other piece of footage. Saving is done from the main Premiere File menu. Once the screen is saved, you can just drag it from the Title window into the Project window, or down onto the timeline. With the shot in place, we close the Title window, and we can see our caption in position.

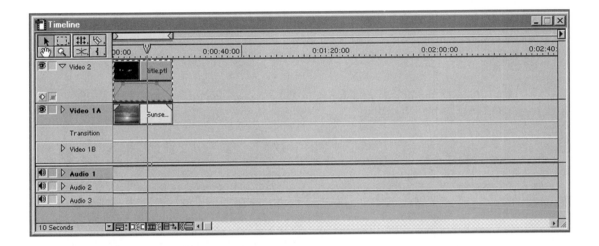

9. Placing the title in track Video 2 and another clip in a track below it, we can see that our text automatically has a transparent background. We can easily make it fade in and out by clicking the triangle next to the track label at the left of Video 2, and creating the fade using the opacity rubberband which appears beneath the shot.

This is great for our opening titles or our captions, but what about those closing credits?

Rolling Credits

Now we've got the basic idea of how to put words on-screen, let's do a typical end-of-production rolling credits sequence. We've already composed our credit list, making sure everyone we need to mention has been credited. Now all we need to do is put it on-screen and make it fit the length of the music:

1. Bring up the Title window as before. If the background isn't already black, hit the B key to get a black backdrop.

> *Because a title works just like any other video or still image media, it's perfectly possible to create a moving title by simply saving the shot, then using filters (like the* Image Pan *filter) or the* Motion *window to control its movement. If you want a complex motion for your title — for example, if you want it to loop the loop before centering itself on the screen — then these animation tools are probably the best method.*

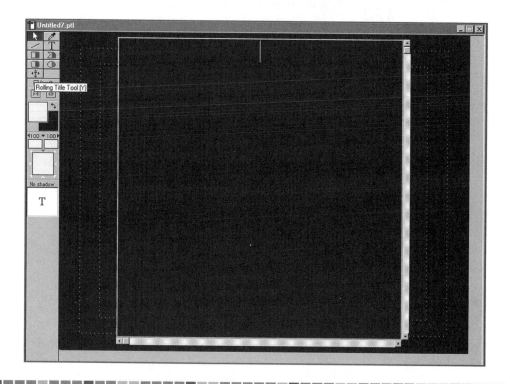

2. For the moment we just want our credits to roll from the bottom of the screen to the top – just like they do in the movies. No fuss, and no fancy movements. For this effect, there's a Rolling Title tool at the bottom left of the tool box.

3. We select this and drag to draw a box which covers the vertical length of the screen. Into this we want to type our text. We could go right ahead and do that now. However, as text editors go, the Title window is pretty poor; it's got no spell-checker function and laying out our screen can be a bit of a pain, so we simply type the text in our favorite word processor, and copy and paste it into the text window.

4. We can then go in and alter the typefaces, scale, and layout by selecting individual words, and right-clicking or control-clicking them. Once we've got the layout we want, we can set the credits in motion. Right- (or control-) click again and select Rolling Title Options. We want the text to move upwards, so we simply select Move Up, and close the box. It's as simple as that.

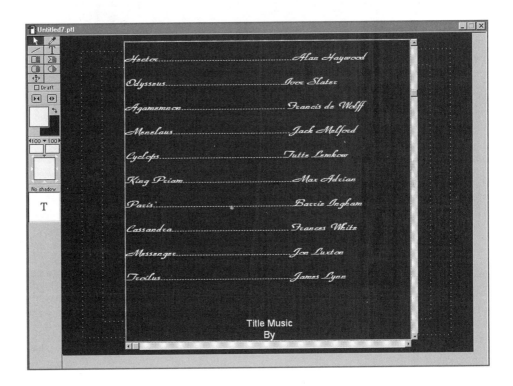

5. We can see how this has worked by dragging the slider at the bottom left of the window. This lets us scroll through the sequence, and allows us to see what the roll will look like – it doesn't tell us the speed because that will depend on the way we place the title on the timeline.

6. What we've got doesn't work quite right. We want it to start with a blank screen onto which the credits roll, so we click on the text box, and add enough blank lines to force the first credit off the bottom of the screen (by hitting RETURN a number of times).

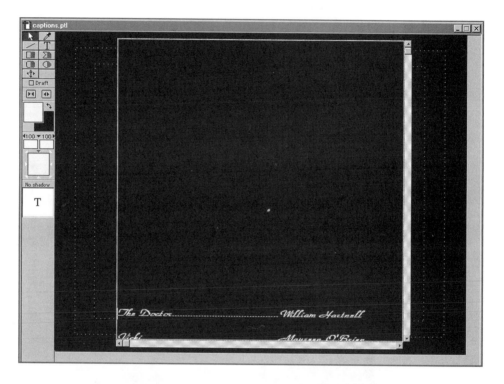

7. At the end of the sequence, we want the director's name to appear on a page of its own, so we hit RETURN a few times between it, and the credit preceding it, and a few times after it, so the title continues to scroll until the name appears at the center of the screen.

8. We also want the titles to stop rolling with the director's name in the center of the screen. We want it to hold this position for a few seconds while we fade the shot out. All this requires is a couple of adjustments in the Rolling Title Options window.

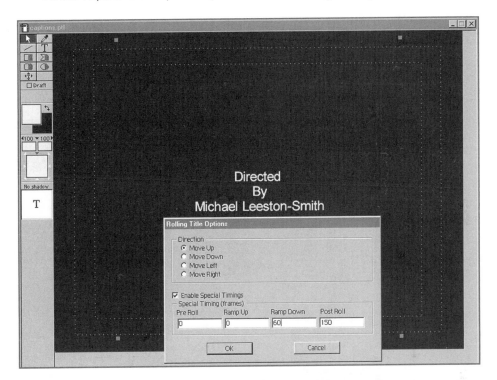

9. We bring this up, and check the Enable Special Timings box. In the Post Roll box, we enter the number of frames for which we want the director's name to be held. 30 frames is one second (on NTSC video), so let's say 150 frames. In order to make the scroll slow naturally to a stop rather than just freezing, we enter 60 into the Ramp Down box – this means that the credits will slow down over 2 seconds.

10. Finally, we save the credits and drop them onto the timeline. We can drag to change the length of the sequence, and thus, the speed of the scroll. This means our credits can last just exactly as long as our title music, or closing shot.

Graphics and Shapes

The Titler doesn't just produce text. You can also create graphics. The tools available seem pretty primitive at first, but with a little effort, you can create some neat effects. Here, we're producing a name caption for an interviewee.

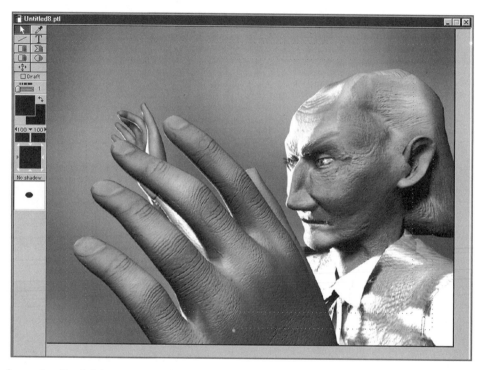

1. Our first job is to create a backdrop for the caption, so we bring up the Titler window. We want our interviewee in the background so we can check the positioning of the caption, so we drag his footage in from the Project window. (OK, so our interviewee isn't actually a real person...)

2. The graphics tools are pretty simple to operate. We use the box and circle tools to draw a frame around our interviewee, then create a filled box at the bottom of the screen into which the name will be written. The slider underneath the shape icons defines the thickness of the line used to draw your graphics.

> *Because each part of the graphic design is stored as a set of points – rather than an image – you can click on each element and edit it if you don't like it. It's not as flexible as something like Illustrator, Photoshop, or Flash, but it's perfectly tweakable.*

3. To add a bit of interest, we can make the caption bar at the bottom of the screen into a color gradient. We select the box, and move to the gradient settings at the left of the screen. Here, we can use the two color selectors to choose a start and end color for our gradient, and the arrows around the box beneath to define the direction of the color gradient.

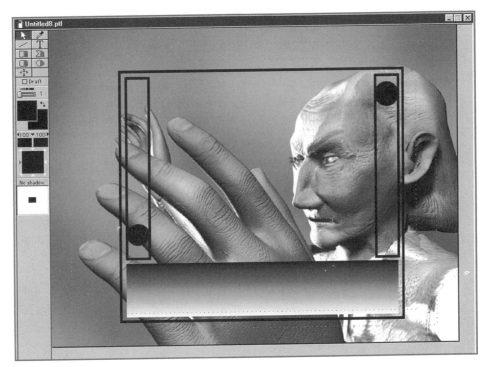

4. Additionally, if we click the number 100 above each gradient color picker, we can set the opacity of that color. We choose a left to right gradient, and set the right-hand color to 50 percent opacity. Now, the caption bar starts solid at the left of the screen, but fades out to the right.

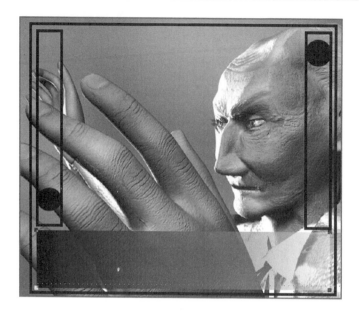

5. We now add the text. Clicking on the Rolling Title icon, we draw a text box within the caption area. We type in the interviewee's name, followed by a couple of returns. We then right-click or control-click and pick Rolling Title Options which we set up as below:

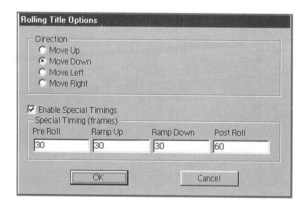

6. When we click OK, we notice that our caption is almost invisible. That's because we created it with the same gradient settings as the background. Click on the object color, and set it to pure white, then we alter the opacity setting for the right-hand gradient color back to 100.

7. Finally, we set the writing apart from its background with a drop shadow. Simply click on the T image at the left of the window, and drag to position your shadow.

You can alter its color with the Shadow Color picker (positioned behind the Object Color picker), and you can change the type of shadow by right-clicking on the text.

8. When we drop the caption onto the timeline, we can see how it behaves. The graphic appears, then the text scrolls in from the top. Once in the center, the name comes to a halt, allowing us to fade the caption out. Perfect.

Premiere's built-in caption maker is installed automatically when you install Premiere. However, it's not the only package supplied on the disk. You'll need to go back to your Premiere install disk to put *Inscriber Title Express* onto your system. Once you have, it will add a whole new dimension to your titling.

Using Inscriber Title Express

Let's start with a simple overlay.

1. Position the playback head over the place in your production where the title will eventually go. Now, if the package has installed correctly, you should be able to choose File > New > Inscriber TE Title, and the titling plug-in will launch, with your original footage loaded in as a backdrop.

2. You can start typing immediately if you want to, and your words will appear at the top left of the screen. However, we're going to start by using one of Title Express' presets. Click the drop-down list at the top of the screen, and you're presented with about 200 titling templates for various styles of caption. As you run the mouse over them, a thumbnail is displayed to indicate what each type will look like.

3. We've chosen a caption descriptively entitled Lower Third 145 which turns out to be a rather romantic typestyle embellished with a yellow lily ... well, it'll do for now!

4.   All we need to do is click on the default text, and type in our own, then save the title, and Title Express will close, giving us our title already loaded into Premiere's Project window ready for use.

Now, we've got an idea of the package, it's time to create our own title screen for a recording of a play. We're going to create our own type style for the production!

5. First we open Title Express on an empty timeline. We type the title and author credit on separate lines. By clicking the box surrounding each line, we can drag the text around the screen, positioning it however we like.

6. The caption doesn't look very special right now; certainly not good enough for the opening of our production. So let's select the title and drag the cursor over the word the way you would in a word processor. Now, take a look at the tabs at the bottom of the screen. These allow you to alter the text in a wide variety of ways.

7. Click the Styles tab. In the same way that Title Express contains a range of templates for captions, it also offers a range of preset typefaces. By right-clicking or control-clicking on any of them; you can load in over 100 more styles from disk!

8. Unfortunately, none of them are particularly suitable for our project. We're going to have to create our own. Switching to the Attributes tab, we can set a suitable font and size for the title and author credit.

9. We can also set up glows, embossed, outlined or bevelled text or add a shadow. In addition, clicking the Color tab lets us alter the parameters of the face, edge, or shadow on your text.

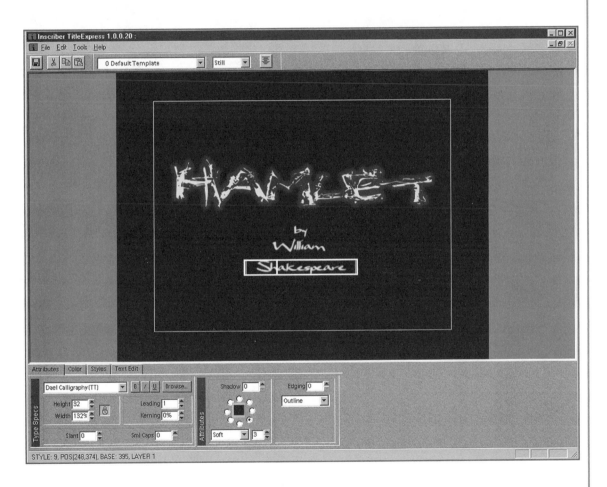

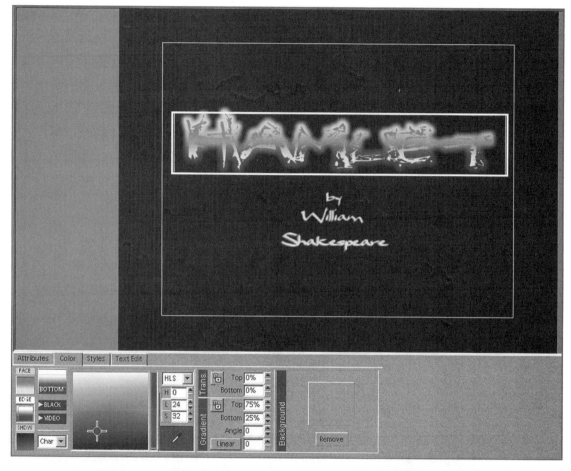

10. By setting the top, and bottom colors of the face, you create a color gradient on the image. Clicking the Edge or Shadow boxes at the very left of the screen lets you place gradients or change the solid color of the other aspects of your font.

11. The angle and other parameters of any gradient you place on your title can be altered at the right of the Color tab, as can the transparency of any attribute. All the type styles within Title Express are created simply by combining the fonts, gradients and effects.

> *If all this up to now doesn't fully meet your titling requirements, you'll be glad to know your Premiere CD has another hidden treasure, in the form of TitleDeko...*

Using TitleDeko

TitleDeko is another titling package which doesn't automatically get installed with the program. Like Title Express, TitleDeko also isn't mentioned in the Premiere manual. However, it's another pretty powerful captioning package with a few special skills, and who needs the manual anyway when you have friends of ED...

1. TitleDeko is launched in the same way as Title Express – just click File > New > TitleDeko. You should be getting used to the way titling packages look by now, and it should be pretty easy to recognise the main elements of the display.

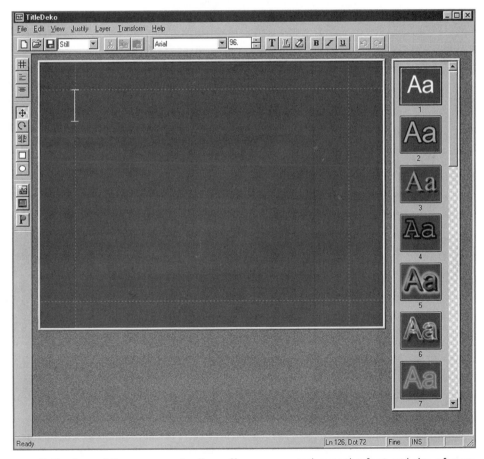

At the top of the screen, a toolbar offers you control over the font and size of your text. The buttons and drop-down lists will be familiar to anyone who's used a word processor. Down the left-hand side of the screen, the buttons control the placing of the text on screen – so you can have it justified in any number of ways.

At the right-hand side, another window offers you a range of preset Looks – each of which can be modified. You can bring up more Looks by clicking the red L icon on the menu bar. TitleDeko's Looks are just like Title Express' Styles. You can pick from the presets, or create your own as you need them. You can even go to the web site (www.titledeko.com) and download more!

2.   So let's create a title page. We'll start with the opening screen to a magazine programme. We type the program's title onto the screen, then we can start moving it around.

3.   You can select text in a number of ways in TitleDeko. Double-clicking on a word selects just that word. Click for a third time, and you'll select the entire line of text. Drag the cursor over any number of letters, and just those letters will be selected. Selected letters appear with a transparent blue highlight box.

This is a very flexible system, because selected letters can be altered in size, color, or font. They can even be dragged around or rotated, but still collectively group-selected if need be later. Here the word is easily selected as a single entity even though its letters have been spread around the screen.

4.   We continue by selecting all our text and choosing an appropriate Look. The red L button brings up a range of choices. We pick a neon look for the word Morning, and a more restrained glow for the other words.

5. We then alter the type face and size to get a reasonable title. The simplest way to alter the size is to select the text, and drag the corners of its box. This lets you stretch the text, expanding or contracting it horizontally and vertically. Here, we've increased the size of the capital letters out of proportion to the rest of the words.

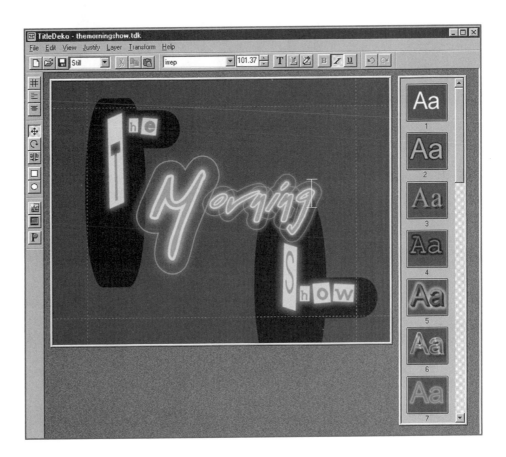

The other titling packages can only write in straight lines, but for our title, we want to arrange our letters around in a curve. By selecting each letter, and using the movement and rotation buttons at the left of the screen, we can create our shape easily. The Rotate button can also be used to skew (slant) letters. Just select the top right corner of the selection box, and drag!

If you do this kind of work a lot, it's worth remembering that TitleDeko is a cut down version of TitleDeko Pro – a much more powerful titler which, amongst other things, allows you to place text automatically along a curved line.

7. Our title screen is beginning to look OK, but it's now time to add another element to the scene. Clicking the Replace Background icon – the second to last button on the left-hand toolbar – we choose Background is a picture and select our image from disk.

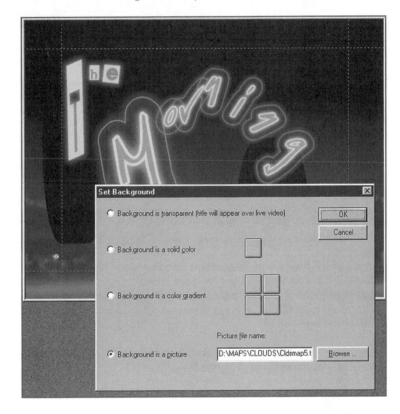

8. Just as we can add background images in TitleDeko, we can also add other pictures. Just click the Add Picture icon, and import an image. Unfortunately, you can't preserve the transparency of objects, so they'll always be rectangular.

9. When we load our image in, it's right at the front, and covers some of the text. This is not good. We want the picture to be placed at the back, so we highlight it, and select Layer > Send To Back. You can use the Layer menu to place any title objects in front of or behind any others – just think of each object as being printed onto acetate which you can shuffle around at will.

You can see how a little imagination, coupled with Premiere's various titling solutions, can create a pretty dazzling title or ident for your production, but what if you need more. Well, of course you're not limited to using any of Premiere's internal titling packages to create a title, because you can also import still images into the package, and you can create captions and screens in any still image package you like.

Let's keep our minds focussed on the practical side of things and launch straight into another tutorial – ok, maybe after a coffee break...

Titling With Images

Here we're using our old friend Photoshop to do a few things even Premiere's various titling add-ons would have trouble with.

1.   Loading up Photoshop, we create a new image at the same resolution as our TV image (720x576 for PAL, or 720x480 for NTSC). What matters here is not the resolution – anything larger than the screen will be re-sized to fit – but the aspect ratio of the image. If you create an image of the wrong shape, it will be squashed to fit into the TV screen shape. Make sure you set the Contents setting of the image to Transparent in the New Image dialog.

2. We're going to create our title on several layers. That way, when we load it into Premiere, we'll be able to have control over each layer separately. First we put in a border – this will allow our title to be transparent in the middle so we can have video playing behind it.

3. Clicking the Text tool and starting to type gives you a new layer in which you can create text in any font or size. You can then right- or control-click on the Layer icon to add effects like glows, shadows, and bevelling.

4. Now we add an image – opening it up on another layer, we drag it into our shot, and place it. The image has its own transparency, so our composition can be a lot more interesting than it would be if we were just using rectangular images (as in TitleDeko). In addition, because the layers will be preserved when we enter Premiere, we can continue to work on, and animate, the title.

Note that because we've applied some effects to our text, and Premiere won't recognise these effects, we need to convert the text object into a simple image before we start. The easiest way to do this is to select the text layer, choose Layer > Effects > Create Layer, then with only the text layers and their effects visible, select Layer > Merge Visible to flatten them all into one layer.

5. We now load the layers individually into Premiere along with the background video we'll be placing behind them. We add another two video layers to the timeline and place all our elements in parallel on separate layers. Be careful to get the order right so the text is at the front (track Video 4), then comes the car, then the border, and finally the video (on Video 1A).

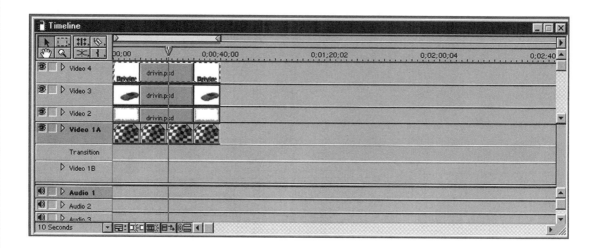

Basically the layers in the Premiere timeline should be in the same order as in the Photoshop layers palette to preserve your composite!

6. Because everything is on separate tracks, we can control each element on its own. We continue by opening the opacity rubberband on the top (text) layer by clicking the triangle next to the track label. This lets us drag the red line underneath the image to define the transparency of the text at any point.

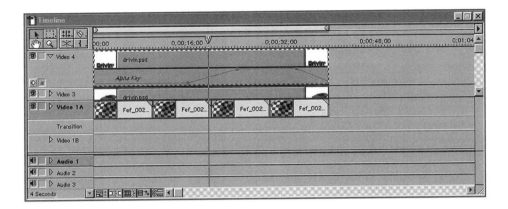

As you can see here, we've set it up so the text is invisible at the start of the sequence, then fades in over time before vanishing again at the end of the shot.

7. The car requires a different effect. We've already learned to use the Motion window in the previous chapter, so why not use that now to do a quick animation to bring the car into shot. We use the Razor tool to cut the shot about half way through – we don't want the car to take the whole length of the title sequence to arrive. We're only applying the motion effect to the first half.

8. Select the first part of the car layer, and click Motion Setup in the Effect Controls palette to bring up the window. Selecting the End keyframe, we type in the ending position for the shot (position 0,0). We then click on the Start keyframe, and set the car's position somewhere off the right-hand side of the screen.

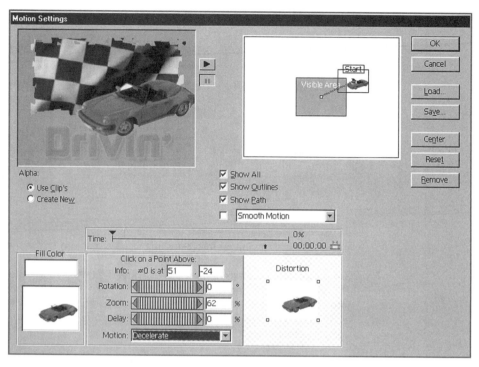

9. In addition, we set the Zoom control to about 60 percent – to give the animation a 3D effect, and set the Motion type to Decelerate so the car slows to a stop rather than just freezing suddenly. Previewing the shot, we can see it looks pretty good.

The only thing left to do is to apply a couple of filters to the frame of the shot, and render out our animated title sequence. It takes a little practice to work out just what parts of your effects are best done in a still image package, which are best done in Premiere itself, and which are best done in a dedicated titler. However, a good rule of thumb is to keep all the elements of your production as separate as possible for as long as possible – that way, you've always got the option of changing things without having to redo your whole effect.

Titling Tips – Please Dos and Just Don'ts

There are some things you should just not do if you want to create a successful caption or title. Some are obvious, some are less so, but all are worth considering...

Some colors just don't look good together. Complementary colors – like red against a green background can sometimes work, but if the colors are too bright, you'll get a very unpleasant **bleeding** effect. Also shades which are different colors, but at the same brightness, can be poorly defined. One of the best ways make text stand out is to give it a higher degree of saturation than its surroundings.

Whatever TV system you're using, it will have its own way of producing color. This will be a slightly different method to the computer's (which mixes colours using 256 shades of red, green and blue). The result of this is that it's quite possible to produce colors on your computer which can't be displayed on your TV. This is rarely a problem with captured images (unless you add color filters to it), but can happen very easily with titles and computer-generated footage.

Problems manifest themselves most often when you produce very bright pure saturated colors. You won't damage your equipment by using these colors, but they will be poorly reproduced. You'll probably not notice the difference in most cases, but you may see color bleeding, or certain shades may be slightly wrong.

> *If you find you're having difficulties with unsafe colors, you can use the* Broadcast Colors *filter to ensure all your colors are correct.*

Be careful not to use typefaces which are too clumsy. TV screens don't produce very high quality images and fine, fiddly typefaces can be difficult to read. In addition, they may even produce interlace flicker. This phenomenon is caused by the way TV screens scan horizontally to build up an image. If a very high contrast line is drawn on the screen, it may appear to flicker constantly. You can solve this by playing with the Field Options dialog (Clip > Video Options > Field Options).

There's a great temptation when you're presented with such a range of typefaces and styles to use them all. It's usually a mistake to fill your screen with dozens of different typestyles. It tends to confuse and distract the eye. One or two is usually enough. Try using different sizes of the same style rather than several different styles.

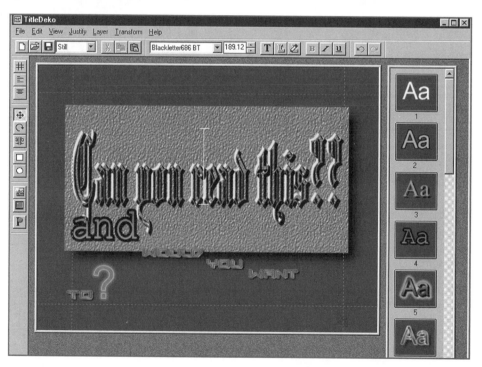

Try not to use too many colors either. You need to know exactly what information you're presenting and in what order you expect it to be read. Make it very clear from your design and layout what the viewer's eye is supposed to go to first, and what the most important information is.

Boldness and simplicity are the most important things to bear in mind when designing a title. That's why so many films are given a simple, title screen placed in white in the center of a black screen. Even those sequences which involve masses of images and elements are designed to make sure that what's important is brought to the forefront. By reducing the color saturation of the background, or darkening or blurring it, or even by simply choosing background and foreground colors to complement each other, what's important can be brought into sharp relief.

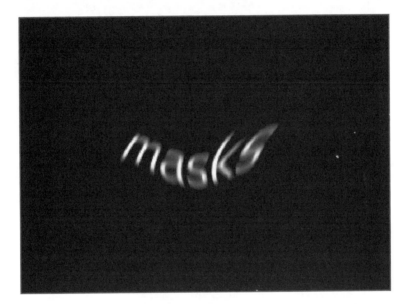

> *When animating your titles, do it to focus the viewer on what is important, not to distract them from it. Make sure the viewer has time to read the text. Don't just create motion for its own sake. Think of your animation as a scene in itself. Use it to create expectation, tension, and atmosphere!*

There is definitely a fashion in title screens – in the colors and animations which are used, and most obviously in typefaces. You can create the atmosphere of a given period in time very easily using an appropriate typeface. However, this can work against you too. Your work will become dated very quickly, if you use certain styles, and it's easy to create something which looks like it was designed for another era.

Keep an eye out for the way people are using text in modern work, and see if you can tell when a film was made just by looking at the style of its title sequence. The intro to the original *Star Wars* film is a classic sequence of its time, but when they repeated the style twenty years later, it looked strangely quaint. Likewise, the title sequences for *Hammer House of Horror* movies now look laughably melodramatic. Even Hitchcock films - which are recognized as classics - are placed quite definitely in time by their graphics.

One final note. When composing a caption, bear in mind what goes before and after it. Try not to create something which grates with everything else around it. The title of a film, etched in shining metal, which crashes onto the screen amidst showers of sparks, and the sound of a slicing blade might work very well as the intro to an action spy-thriller. However, place it at the opening of a romantic comedy, and you'll almost certainly ruin the entire film by setting up expectations which are never fulfilled.

Summary

You probably didn't realize there was quite so much to consider when producing titles, captions or credits for your video project. Hopefully, though, in-keeping with the style of the book in general, you've not only learned the hard facts of **how** to title in Premiere, but you've also seen the **why**s and picked up some tips, tricks, dos and don'ts along the way.

We've looked at:

- Basic functions of the Title window

- Rolling credits and adding graphics

- Creating more visual titles with TitleDeko and Inscriber

- Adding more flair by bringing in external packages

They say a picture tells a thousand words? Well, you've seen in the last thirty-or-so pages how a well-placed and carefully thought out word on-screen can do the job of a thousand pictures, even if they are at 24-per-second.

13 Exporting Finished Movies

Having finished your Premiere production, logically you'll want to distribute it. There are a couple of ways to do this – recording it to VHS, recording it to DV, producing a multimedia CD ROM or DVD, or even placing a version of the programme onto a web site for anyone in the world to watch.

Premiere offers a wide range of output types to suit everything from Internet distribution right up to broadcast television. The method you choose, and the set-up of your output parameters, will depend on your own hardware and software, as well as the audience you're aiming your work at.

Most productions will need at least two types of output.

- The first is the master copy. For your own benefit, and just in case you need to produce further copies, you should archive a copy of your programme at the highest possible quality.

> *Any video you produce is likely to generate a whole load of extra files - images, mattes, titles, animations, batch files, Premiere files, and so on. These don't usually take up too much room, so if you can, it's worth archiving them on a CD, just in case you need to come back and work on the project further at a later date.*

- The second is the distribution format. Most productions will need to be seen by somebody, and because not everyone has access to a DV playback deck, or a broadband Internet connection, you'll need to create a lower quality copy (on VHS, CD ROM, or an Internet file) which can be viewed by your audience.

If you can import and export your production in a DV format through a FireWire port, then the image quality should be just as high when you've finished work on your project, as it was when you first shot it. If you're using analogue capture cards, or compressing your video for CD, DVD or the Internet, then you start having to make compromises.

During this whole process, the more you have to compress your video at any stage, the more you'll compromise its eventual quality.

There are certain aspects of your image which will affect the quality of your finished video. If you're rendering for output to DV, image quality is rarely a problem. Other formats such as CD-ROM or internet video are more demanding on the compression of the scene.

Because a video image is made up of 30 or 25 frames per second (depending on your TV system), and each frame is a still image, the quantity of data it would take to store it perfectly would be huge. As a result, compression has to be used. There are various ways of compressing an image, but basically they all reduce the size of a video file by storing only part of the action. Put simply, they store the first image completely, then only store what changes between that and the next frame.

This means that if you've got for example a shot of a newsreader sitting still, talking to camera, you can get away with a lot of compression. Only a very small portion of the screen (the newsreader's mouth) is changing from one frame to the next. Even at a very high compression, you'll get quite a sharp image.

On the other hand, if you've got an action scene – where the camera is moving, or an actor is running through the shot – then virtually every pixel of the image on each frame will be different to the last. If you're trying to reduce the size of the video file significantly, there's only so much data Premiere can use to represent this change. The result is that the image begins to break down. Detail is lost, colors blur into each other, movement becomes jerky, frame rates are reduced and blocks start to appear.

In addition, compression will start to show itself, first in the areas of your shot where detail is high, then where the shades of color are very subtle. Shadow definition is often the first thing to go when you compress video, and you can sometimes see the effect of this even in DVD or cable TV transmissions.

Connecting Up

If you're recording your movie digitally, from your PC to a blank tape in your camcorder, setting it up is pretty easy. The FireWire cable you've used to capture your video works as both an input and an output. All you need to do is connect it up as you would for capture. You can then put your camcorder in VCR mode, and hit the record button on its player control panel. If your camcorder doesn't have a RECORD button, then it's possible you'll be able to record using controls on the software supplied with your capture card.

It's also quite possible that your camcorder isn't enabled for recording from a **digital input**. Many camcorders just don't have this function, and although manufacturers could very easily make all their products video-in enabled, some – especially on their cheaper models – simply don't do it. The situation is improving, and more video-in enabled camcorders are coming out all the time.

If you want to record to an analog device, connection can be a little more complex. There are three basic options.

- If you have an analog capture card (i.e. not a simple FireWire card, but one which has Phono plugs for video input and output on it), you should be able to plug these straight into your VCR (usually using a Scart socket).

- If you have a video graphics card (the card that attaches to your monitor) which has TV outputs, then you can plug this into your video. It will provide you with a copy of your monitor screen on your TV. All you need to do then is get Premiere to play back your show as a **full-screen display**, and hit record.

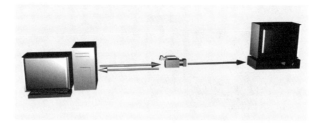

- If you're using a standard FireWire connection, and have a digital camcorder, you can connect this up as you normally would, and set it to VCR mode. All domestic camcorders have analog outputs, so when you connect these to your video, it should display an image of whatever's coming into the camera. Thus, by connecting to your VCR through the camcorder, you get the camera to convert the computer's digital signal to an analog one, something your VCR can record.

Recording Your Video to Tape

As mentioned before keeping a digital copy of your production at the highest possible quality is a good idea, even if it's just for archive purposes. Unfortunately, the sheer volume of information in a video production could make it impractical to keep all your old projects on your PC. If this is the case, you'll need to export your work to videotape. Here is a list of possible storage formats:

- **DV tape** is the highest quality storage medium you're likely to get access to right now. If you've recorded your original footage on DV, and you've edited in that format, it makes a lot of sense to put your finished piece back onto DV tape for posterity. From there, you can make VHS copies, or even re-capture the show to your computer without losing quality. Even if your original material isn't shot on DV, it's still best to archive the show on DV because you don't lose quality when transferring it.

- **DVD** is a little expensive as an archive medium, but it is digital, so despite the quality being slightly lower than that of DV tape, it will make a pretty good alternative when it eventually becomes more cost effective (see later on in the chapter for a discussion on DVD export)

- **SVHS** and **HI8** are the formats many video cameras record on; some VCRs can even record SVHS material. They're analog formats, so you will lose some quality in both your sound and video each time you transfer material from tape to the computer, or vice-versa. As well as this, you can't re-capture your footage unless you have an analog capture card, or a digital camera with an analog input.

- **VHS** – Try if possible to avoid archiving your masterpiece solely on VHS. It's fine for producing copies to distribute, but if you're using a VHS master tape, remember you'll need to copy from that to another VHS to make your distribution copies. The result is a third generation recording with the image being noticeably worse.

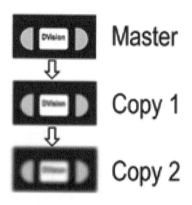

Master

Copy 1

Copy 2

> *In order to play back your video through your capture card, it needs to be compressed correctly for that card. Otherwise, it will simply play back on the computer screen.*

Rendering Your Movie

There are two ways you can export your work to video. The first option is to render out your finished movie, and play it back from disk so you can record it.

This creates a massive file containing your entire video production which you can then play back any time you like for recording, either from within Premiere, or using your capture card's own software – or the standard media player utilities on your computer. This can be useful if you've got a lot of short productions you want to put together on tape, or if you need to be able to access them on disk quickly.

However, remember that video – especially if it's high quality DV format material – is going to produce some huge files. 1Gb of disk space is going to equate to about 4.5 minutes of video. If you've edited your program down from a lot of raw footage, then that's going to have to be on your system while you're rendering too. As you can imagine, you can end up running out of space pretty quickly.

In addition, there's a size limit to files on Windows platforms. Windows 98 and NT limit your files to 2GB in size (that's about 9 minutes of video) and Windows 2000 limits them to 4GB. If your video is longer than this, then you'll have to render it in pieces, and play them back in order. Most capture software should be able to do this seamlessly, but do check before you commit yourself to rendering.

1. To render out your movie, select the portion of the timeline you want to render. Use the Work Area Markers (the yellow bar above the timeline) to mark the start and end points.

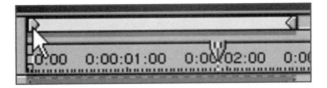

2. Go to File > Export Timeline > Movie. This will bring up a file selector where you can choose where you're going to place the finished movie.

3. Type the name, and click the Settings button to bring up the format options for your movie.

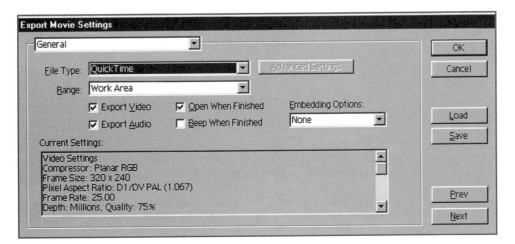

4. In the Range selector drop-down menu, choose whether you want to render the entire movie or just the preview area (area you have covered with the yellow Work Area bar).

Many capture cards, when you install them, will place presets into Premiere, which will allow you to easily set up your system for outputting their own form of video.

5. Click the Load button, if there's an appropriate preset there, then you won't need to worry about any of the rest of the settings, just select it.

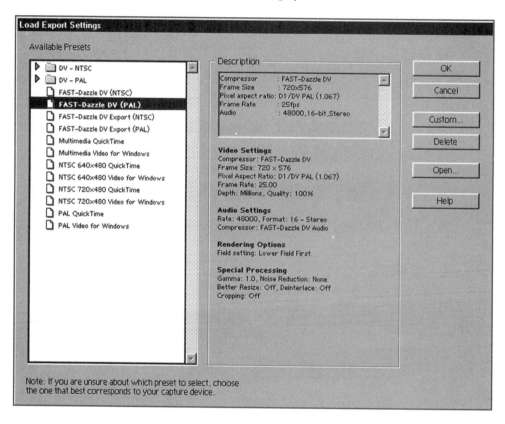

If there's no preset, you'll have to create the output settings manually. The way you do this will vary from one hardware setup to another. You'll need to consult the manual of your particular capture card for details. However, there are a few rules.

6. Click on the File Type drop-down menu first. There may be a format designed specifically for your capture card. For generic FireWire cards, you might find a setting like Microsoft DV AVI.

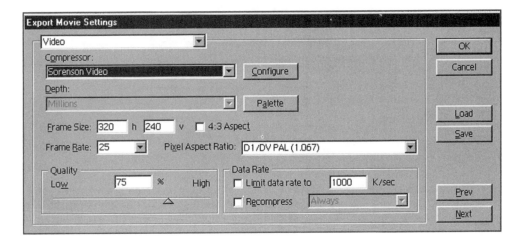

7. Select Video from the drop-down menu at the top, changing the window to the video settings.

8. Now look at the Compressor drop-down menu in the Video settings – if your capture card wasn't listed in the File Type list, it might be here as a Compressor for a file type of either AVI, or QuickTime. If your card was listed, you might be offered a choice of compressing for NTSC (American) or PAL (European) video.

    It's quite possible that your card won't allow you to choose other options in the Video box. In any case, DV cards are usually limited to the TV resolutions of NTSC (720x480 pixels) or PAL (720x576). Likewise, the Audio panel will probably be limited to only the audio formats supported by your card.

    > *If in doubt about any setting, you may get clues by examining the properties of video you've already captured. Right-click on a clip in the timeline or the project window, then click on Properties in the drop-down menu, and examine any settings you're concerned about. Make sure your output settings are exactly the same as the settings you're capturing with – otherwise you could be re-processing your clip unnecessarily and losing quality.*

9. When you're happy with your settings, click OK on the Export Movie Settings panel, and hit Save. The movie will begin rendering. This can take seconds or hours, depending on the length and complexity of your movie. Detailed info on how the rendering is going can be seen by clicking the right facing triangle in the Exporting window, next to the Frame progress information.

If you stop rendering while the movie is being processed, it won't do it any harm - you'll still be able to play back what you've rendered so far. However, you won't be able to get it to carry on from where it left off later. As well as this, if the computer crashes mid-way through rendering, you won't be able to play back the resulting file.

It is worth noting that if you've got effects, filters, transitions, transparency, or captions applied to a shot, the rendering will slow down. If you've got none of these, and the video is going out correctly in the same format that you've imported it, then it should fly through the rendering because it's not having to re-compress anything.

If your rendering is going slowly despite having only done straight cuts to your video, it's usually a sign that each frame is being re-compressed. This usually means you've set up the render incorrectly, and your video's quality may be being reduced as each frame is being un-compressed and re-compressed.

Once you've got the settings right, use the Save button on the settings panel to save the setup so you can call it up again instantly next time you want to render a video.

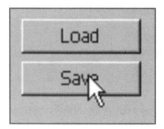

For our second recording option, Premiere offers you the ability to play your movie back from beginning to end directly from the timeline. It can do this to your computer monitor, or through your capture card to an external recorder. You can set it to include a few seconds of black tape before recording begins, and you can tell Premiere to automatically set your DV camcorder to record before it starts playing back.

If your project includes effects, transitions, titles, multiple sound channels, or footage in a format other than your capture card's (in other words, if you've included multimedia files from other sources, or still images, or animations) then it will need to render some portions of the programme before it plays them back. Basically, anything that needs to be previewed will need to be pre-rendered.

If the project has a lot of effects, or filters, the preview files created will take up almost as much space as if you'd rendered the entire sequence out.

1. To play back from the timeline, you first need to ensure that your and audio output settings are correct, as we previously discussed. Select Project > Project Settings > Capture to bring up the Project Settings window, then choose the appropriate settings for your capture or output hardware. If you're playing back through a TV attached to your monitor's video card, then this won't matter, but otherwise, you need Premiere to compress your work in the correct way.

> *If you've been editing with a TV attached, and have been rendering previews which play back successfully on the TV, then your settings should be just fine. If your previews only play back on Premiere's on screen monitors, then your settings aren't right! Check your capture hardware's documentation for details.*

2, Once you've set up your hardware and software to work together, select File > Export Timeline > Print to Video. The dialogue box that appears lets you set some options:

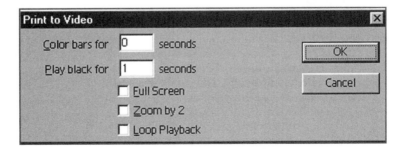

- Color bars for _ seconds: lets you produce a few seconds of color bars on tape before your production begins. This allows anyone playing back the tape to calibrate their equipment. It's not really necessary for domestic use.

- Play black for _ seconds: plays out a number of seconds of black video before the production begins. It's well worth putting at least 10 seconds of empty tape at the beginning of any production, just to avoid any noise at the start of your video tape, and allow for the time it takes to start up recording equipment.

- Full Screen and Zoom by 2: controls the size of the playback on the TV and your monitor. Not all capture cards support changing the size of playback for your video, and in any case, there's very little point in playing it back at anything other than full size.

- Loop Playback: keeps repeating the video sequence until you stop it. This is useful for creating multiple copies, or producing tapes which repeat the same video over and over (like promo videos in shops).

3. To start the process, click OK in the Print to Video window. If your video contains no un-previewed effects or transitions, the screen will clear, and it will start playing immediately both on your computer monitor, and through the capture card. If Premiere needs to render some effects before it can begin, then it will do this automatically, and will give you an estimate of how long it's going to take.

4. When you see the production start to play, just hit record on your VCR or camcorder. If you want to stop playback of your video mid-way through, just click Escape.

> If your computer can't handle playing back through the monitor as well as through the capture card, you'll have to disable the playback on the monitor by unchecking the Desktop Playback option. This can be done in the Project > Project Settings > General panel using the Advanced Settings or Playback Settings button, depending on your hardware.

5. If playback is still interrupted, or jerky once you've disabled simultaneous playback through the computer monitor, and you're using an analog capture card, you may be able to reduce the quality settings of your movie so it doesn't put such a strain on your computer's resources. If you're using a digital capture card, you won't be able to change the quality of playback.

*If your capture card is recognised by Premiere as a standard FireWire card, and your camcorder is **video-in enabled**, then you should also be able to pick Export To Tape instead of Print To Video. The effect is exactly the same, except that with Export To Tape, Premiere will take control of your camcorder, starting and stopping it's recording automatically at the beginning and end of the video production.*

CD and Hard Disk Playback

There are plenty of situations in which you might want your finished movie to be played back on a computer screen rather than a TV. Recordable CDs are cheap, light, and, as long as you get the compression right, they can be of reasonable quality. You can also play them back on most computers anywhere in the world.

There are several video formats around the world that are not compatible with each other. If you send a tape from the USA to the UK for example, it won't play back even though it's a standard VHS or digital tape. Unlike tape, computer disks have no such limitations.

If your video is for work, and it's part of some kind of presentation or demonstration, you can dovetail it more closely with the rest of your presentation if it's on CD. It can be included in a **PowerPoint** demo, or even a word-processing document, and it can be stopped, started, and repeated at a second's notice. In addition, if you need to be flexible about where and when you show the video, you'll find far more workplaces have far more computers than they do video players.

If your movie is intended for distribution on CD, or will be played back from hard disk, there's a whole range of new considerations you have to think about. CD ROMs can only store a certain amount of data – **700mb** is about the most. That would be only just over *3 minutes* of video at standard DV compression. Clearly, that's not enough for most purposes. They also only produce a limited throughput of data. The exact bandwidth (the amount of information you can read from them per second) varies from model to model, but the bottom line is that even a good one (50x or 60x speed) can't play back fast enough to play full quality video.

If your video is too high quality for your CD drive, it will keep freezing during playback.

To get decent playback on most machines, you should be aiming for your video to be running at about **300k per second**. That's less than one tenth of the data rate you need for DV. If you're creating a video for CD ROM, then is all about compression. The idea is to get your data rate as low as possible without loosing too much of your video quality, - this can be a very fine balance indeed.

Unfortunately, Premiere doesn't have the best CD export tools available. No matter how you tweak the settings, sometimes your results will be disappointing. This is why dedicated compression packages like **Media Cleaner Pro** have been developed. A limited version of Media Cleaner has been included with Premiere, and will have installed itself with the package. This is designed for producing video for streaming from Internet sites but does have some settings that can produce decent CD files.

For a quick and easy output of CD files, choose File > Export Timeline > Save for Web, and pick one of the CD ROM settings on the Settings Wizard. You'll be guided through the process of creating a file, involving choosing a name for your file and waiting for it to render. The result will probably give you decent playback, however, you won't be able to alter some of the finer settings to optimized your work. More on this is covered later on in the chapter.

If you really want to get to grips with the way your file is produced, you'll need to use Premiere's built-in output tools.

When you click File > Export Timeline > Movie, and choose a filename for your finished project, click Settings in this window to move to the Export Movie Settings dialogue. If you've not tried to export video for CD before, the first thing you should do, is click the Load button at the right of the window.

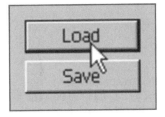

You should be presented with a Load Export Settings window. Depending on where you got your copy of Premiere, and what other hardware and software you've installed, you may find a list of presets for common rendering jobs. If you're really lucky, there might even be presets for multimedia productions of the kind you're trying to create. Try them out, and see if they produce the kind of effect you're looking for.

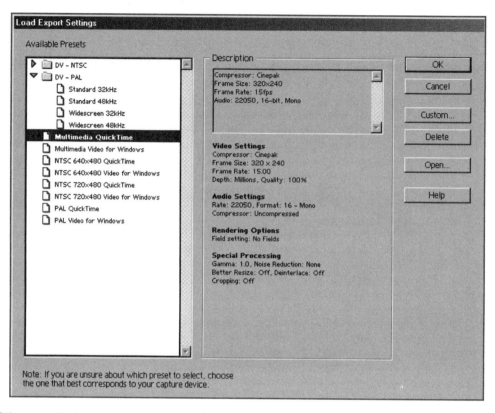

If there aren't, then as you work out the best settings for your productions, you can save them as presets so you can call them up again whenever you need them.

Export Movie Settings: General

When exporting, the first thing to consider is the type of movie you're trying to create. Under the Export Movie Settings window and General, File Type has a drop-down list with a series of options (there may be extra items in the list if you've got certain capture hardware which requires its own output types):

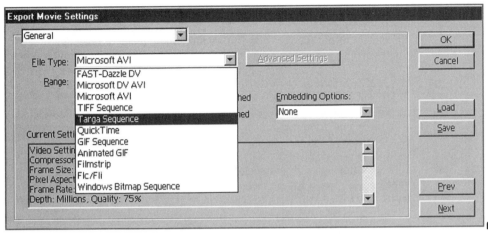

Microsoft AVI - the AVI format is a pretty standard video file type. It plays back through the Windows Media Player which is installed on virtually every PC. Use the AVI format if you want to be able to play back your video on any PC even if it's never been used for video in the past.

■ Tiff, Targa, Bmp or Pict sequence are not strictly video files, they're **still image** file formats. Pick one of these, and Premiere will render the video of your production as a numbered series of still images, with each frame as a separate still. However, this means *sound will be ignored*. Obviously for video playback, this is no good at all. However, if you're doing an effect, or want to edit a (short) sequence of frames in a still image editor, it's often a good way to export the clip as it lets you work with it one frame at a time.

■ QuickTime produces files with a .mov extension. QuickTime files are one of the most flexible formats you can export in, and the vast majority of CD video presentations are QuickTime files. They can be played back on PCs or on the Mac, and can be rendered at qualities ranging from very high (DV quality and higher) right down to the extreme levels of compression needed for internet playback. The disadvantage with MOV files is that you need to have a QuickTime player installed on your computer to use them. The player is freely available, but not all computers have it as standard.

> *If you intend to distribute your video on CD-ROM in QuickTime it is possible to ask permission to include QuickTime itself on the CD. You might have noticed that many multimedia CDs (including those with friends of ED books) come with QuickTime.*

- Animated GIFs are designed for very small, very short animation loops that form moving images on the Internet. They're not a lot of use for video, as they are completely silent. You can, however, reduce the number of colors in an animated GIF (right down to just 2 if you like) to make it smaller.

- Filmstrip is a format designed simply for transferring short video clips to and from Adobe PhotoShop. The scene is rendered as a single long thin image with each frame placed in sequence along it. Because you can load filmstrips into PhotoShop, you can edit them one frame at a time for very fine control over effects. This process is called **Rotoscoping**.

- FLC/FLI is a rarely used animation format. Images can be of high quality, but tend to be large because they can't be compressed. Sound is not included. Use this only if you're trying to transfer your work to a package that won't accept any other format.

> *You might notice that MPEG export is missing from the above list. MPEG is the video format used by DVD players, and many professionally rendered CD movies use a reduced quality version. You can create MPEG files with Premiere using the Save For Web option. The tools aren't very well developed, but they're pretty good for CD-ROM quality work.*

Other options in the Export Movie Settings window, let you choose whether to output Video, Audio, or both, and from the Range drop-down menu, whether you export the Entire Project, or just the Work Area (the portion of the movie enclosed by the preview bar).

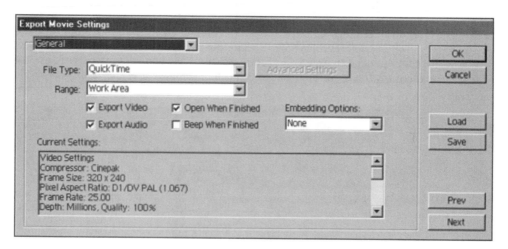

Export Movie Settings: Video

Once you've picked your File Type, move on to the Video Options section – either by clicking the Next button or choosing Video from the drop-down list at the top of the window.

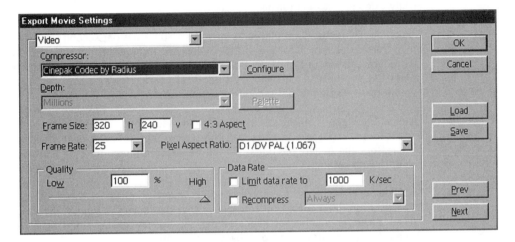

The page that appears is the most important dialog in controlling your image quality. The first choice we have to make is which compression method we're using. If you click the drop-down Compressor menu, you'll see a list of options. AVI and QuickTime are the most common options for CD-ROM video, but AVI can be unsuitable as it requires very high data rates for good playback. Each has a number of different compression **codecs**.

Codec stands for **Co**der-**dec**oder; the coder sits at the production end and the decoder at the viewer end. A codec is basically an algorithm the system uses to compress your video frames. Which codecs are available depends on your own system; some are common to every installation of Windows Media Player or QuickTime, others aren't and need to be downloaded before you can play compressed video with them. The result of this is that if you compress your video with some of the more exotic ones, it might look great on your system, but won't play on other computers.

> *If you attempt to play a file using Windows Media Player, but the correct codec isn't installed, Windows will attempt to download it for you.*

Cinepak is a good compressor for CD quality video, and it's available on everyone's system. **Sorenson** and **Indeo** are other commonly used and very successful compressors.

Once you've selected an appropriate codec, you need to specify the rest of the settings.

- Frame size: There's no point in giving your CD video the same dimensions as the TV version. Reducing its size can dramatically reduce the data rate you'll need to get a good image. Most multimedia video is rendered at either **320x240** pixels for medium quality video or **640x480** for high quality video.

- Frame Rate: TV pictures are played at the rate of 30 frames per second for NTSC video (or 25 frames per second for PAL video). Reduce the number of frames per second and you reduce the amount of video that has to be stored, processed and displayed. 15 frames per second gives a relatively smooth playback. However, you might want to bump it up to 25 frames per second for action sequences.

- Quality: The higher you set the quality of your video the more disk space it will use, and the longer it will take to compress. This setting doesn't have a huge effect on most compressors, the quality of your video will be affected much more by the **resolution** and **data rate** settings.

- Data Rate: One of the most important settings in any video where bandwidth is limited is the data rate limit. Here you can specify that the images in your video should not exceed a certain number of kilobytes per second. DV footage runs at 3,600k per second. Most hard drives can play back at that rate quite easily. CD drives are much slower, but all but the oldest can handle a rate of 300k per second. At that data rate, using Cinepak, Indeo, or Sorenson compression codecs, you can get a pretty decent picture. Most current multimedia CDs are using 300k per second as a standard.

> *Two things are worth remembering when setting the data rate. Firstly, the setting relates only to the video portion of the file. The rate of the audio also needs to be taken into account. Secondly, you can work out the file size from the overall data rate. At 300 k per second, you'll get about 36 minutes of video on a CD. At 100k per second, you'll get nearer 110 minutes. At Internet data rates (as low as 4.5k per second) you'd get 40 hours - although you wouldn't want to watch it!*

- Recompress: turn on the recompress control to ensure your video is kept to the data rate you specify. There are two settings: Always – which re-compresses every frame; or Maintain data rate – which only compresses frames that need compression to fit within the data rate.

Generally, you should set it on Maintain data rate for the best quality results, and to save time in rendering. If you're exporting video which is going out in the same format that it came to Premiere (captured video destined for video output, or multimedia video destined for CD), de-select the option. This will prevent Premiere from re-compressing (and thus lowering the quality of) video that you haven't actually altered during editing (by adding effects or transitions).

Export Movie Settings: Audio

With the important video options covered, we can move on to the Audio window. Again, you can select this from the drop-down menu at the top of the window, or just click the Next button.

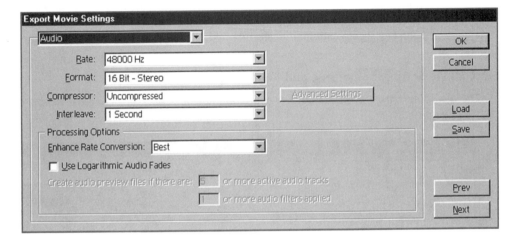

- Rate: This controls the sample-rate of the audio you're producing. It affects both the quality and the file size of the audio. Commonly used settings are: 8000Hz for Internet audio, 11000hz for low quality multimedia, 22050Hz for radio quality audio (usually perfectly OK for multimedia video clips), and 44100Hz or 48000Hz for audio CD quality sound.

- Format: You can choose here to have your video in Mono or Stereo. Stereo is better quality, and lets you include stereo effects. However, it takes up twice the data rate. You can also pick 8 Bit or 16 Bit audio. This affects the quality of the sound - 16 bit sound is of higher quality, but takes up greater bandwidth.

- Compressor : Just as you can pick a compressor for video, you can also use an audio compressor. This can reduce both the size and the quality of the audio portion of your files. If you're having trouble with the sound reproduction on your finished clips, it's often best to just stick to no audio compression.

■ Interleave: Specifies the way audio and video are stored together in the file. Change the setting here only if you're having trouble with audio breaking up, or going out of sync during playback.

■ Enhanced Rate Conversion: The audio on the timeline might be made up of any number of different audio formats – depending on where you've got it from. This control sets the way Premiere handles merging all this audio into the format you've chosen, using the settings above. The higher you have this setting, the longer rendering your movie will take. However, the difference usually isn't that great, so it's a good idea to just leave the setting on Best all the time.

■ Use Logarithmic Audio Fades: If you check this box, the changes in volume on your audio will be turned from the sudden sharp changes in the increase or decrease in volume which are produced by the volume rubberbands to a more natural sounding curve. This makes changes in volume sound less artificial, but can result in the audio sounding slightly different in your finished piece to how they sound on the timeline.

Export Movie Settings: Keyframe and Rendering

The next option from the drop-down menu is the Keyframe and Rendering panel. This offers a selection of options:

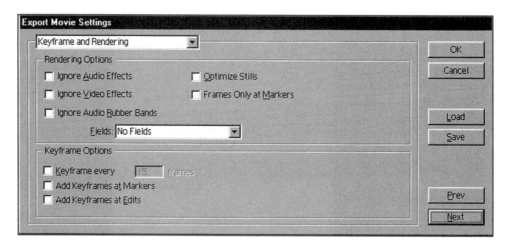

■ Ignore Audio Effects, Ignore Video Effects, and Ignore Audio Rubber Bands: These three boxes let you turn off the effects of filters and volume changes. It's only useful to do this if you're producing a rough-cut of your project because it saves time in rendering. Most users will never need to tick these boxes.

- Optimize Stills: Generally keep this option selected. It makes the best use of your data rate by exporting one high quality image of any stills in your video, rather than a load of poor quality video frames. Imagine you've got a static credits page with a lot of small writing on it and it's on screen for 10 seconds. With Optimize Stills un-checked, the writing might well be unreadable because it's exporting dozens of low quality images of the same shot. With it on, the data rate is "saved up" to give you one decent quality rendering of the shot, that's held for 10 seconds.

- Frames Only at Markers: This option is rarely used as it can be of little use most of the time. The idea is that you can place markers on the timeline and Premiere will only produce a new frame when it hits one of these markers. It is probably most useful if you're creating a slideshow.

- Keyframe every _ frames: This can be quite an important setting. A keyframe in rendering is a frame on which the compressor pays special attention to the whole of the image. When data rates are low and the compressor is made to work hard, images tend to become sharp at the keyframe, then slowly lose resolution, blurring out until the next keyframe brings everything back into focus again. Too few keyframes and the image will become very indistinct – too many and the data rate won't be sufficient to provide sharp keyframes. Use about 2 or 3 keyframes per second for a reasonable result.

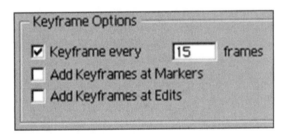

- Add Keyframes at Markers: If, after a few tests, you find there's a point in your video where the compression really isn't working, try checking this, and placing markers on the timeline around the poor compression area. This forces keyframes to be created at these points.

- Add Keyframes at Edits: Because of the way keyframes work, if a sharp cut occurs between two keyframes, there sometimes isn't enough spare bandwidth available to handle the amount of change in the image from one cut to the next. Turn this setting on, and keyframes will automatically be put in at your cuts.

Export Movie Settings: Special Processing

Moving on to the Special Processing panel, click the Modify option to gain access to various settings which change the shape, and re-sizing of the video image:

- The top of the screen gives you a shot of the video – you can scan through it with the slider. Underneath, four controls let you crop the video at the top, bottom, left and right. You can also do this interactively by dragging the corners of the image. If you're rendering a widescreen image, there's no point rendering it square, and placing black lines at the top and bottom, you might as well crop out the unused space.

  Crop is also a useful tool for keeping the edges of your video tidy. If you have captured your source material from tape (particularly VHS) and are planning to export it for viewing on a computer, then you'll probably notice that the edges of the video are not tidy. This is because a television does not display the entire picture it receives – the edges go off the end of the screen (this is called **overscan**); a computer monitor displays the true image complete with wobbly edges. This not only looks untidy but makes the entire picture worse if you are exporting to a web format.

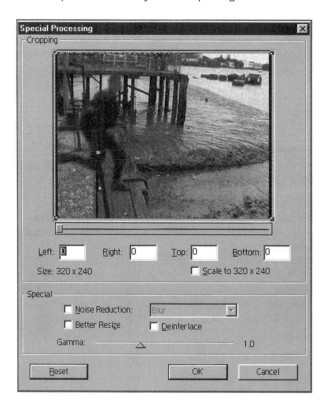

- If you select the Scale to (the frame size) option, the cropped video will be stretched to fit the measurements you specified in the Video options window. If you don't select it, when you crop the video, you're reducing the actual size of your finished video.

- The Noise Reduction selector lets you apply three different types of blurring on your image (but does nothing to the sound), before it's compressed. This smoothes out any grain, or video interference in the image so that the compressor doesn't have to waste data compressing tiny imperfections in the image. This can give a better image if you're trying to make very small files.

- The Better Resize box should be ticked if you're cropping the image, as it uses Premiere's own system for scaling the image rather than relying on the codec's which can sacrifice image quality.

- The Deinterlace button can be more effective at turning captured video footage into video suitable for playback on the computer screen. Use it if you find horizontal lines appearing in your rendered scene during fast movement of objects or the camera.

- Finally, the Gamma slider lets you brighten or darken the video shot. People will have their monitors and video cards set differently. Some videographers increase the gamma on their productions just in case their audience is watching on a darker screen, and can't see what's going on. It's a matter of choice whether you alter the setting. Many editors figure that if the viewer can't be bothered to set their own screen up so it can be seen, that's their own problem!

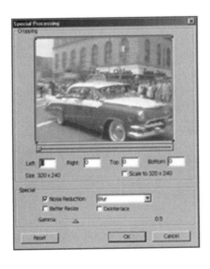 

Internet Video

It's now possible to put your video clips onto the Internet where anyone can download and view them. The problem with internet video is **bandwidth** - the amount of data a standard telephone modem can receive per second is minute compared to the amount needed to produce full quality video. A 56kbs modem gives you about *1000th* of the data rate of DV quality video, so as you can imagine, the compression needed to get any image at all needs to be quite extreme, and the resulting picture and sound quality tends to be very low.

There are two ways you can handle internet video: **Streaming Video** – where the viewer watches the video clip live as it's played from the website; and **File Download** – where the video is placed on the web site and the viewer downloads it to be played back later.

Each has its own advantages and disadvantages. Live streaming allows the viewer to see the video right away – it starts playing back as soon as the page is opened. It also allows the filmmaker to retain control over the material. If the viewer wants to see the clip again, they have to return to the maker's website. They can't keep it or make copies of it. However, the quality of the video is very low, and can get considerably worse if the Internet is having a bad day. Also, for best results, special streaming servers need to be set up at the web site hosting the file.

Downloadable files need to be completely loaded before they can be played. The larger they are, the longer this will take. In addition, the viewer ends up with a complete copy of the video which they can play whenever they like. Downloadable files don't have to be constrained by the data rate of the viewer's modem. You can set the data rate higher, and thus have higher quality videos. However, the video still has to be downloaded, so you still need to make it as small as possible.

> *The important thing to remember is short clips, low resolutions, and very high levels of compression. However, not everyone is limited to 56k telephone modems. Broadband, cable modems, ISDN, and intranets all offer much higher bandwidth, and are becoming increasingly common. Soon it will be possible to have much higher quality video online. Right now, however, you need to keep in mind the audience for your clip, and the level of technology they're likely to have access to.*

Premiere offers three different formats specifically designed for internet video:

Windows Media

The Windows Media format has been developed by Microsoft for video over the Internet. Media Player comes as standard with all Windows 9x machines and above. It therefore doesn't need to be downloaded, but it may require upgrading by downloading a newer version. When a Windows Media Server is in place on the web site hosting the file, it's able to choose from a range of copies of the video optimized for different connections. However, it's normally only able to do this for the video portion of the clip, and only at the beginning of transmission.

If the viewer's connection slows during playback, Windows Media can reduce the image quality, and the frame rate to keep playback going. It can also remove the video altogether, just playing the audio from the clip if the connection gets really poor.

Windows Media is supported on the Mac and the PC, but PC development is slightly ahead of the Mac, so there are slight issues of portability.

RealMedia

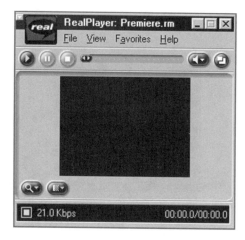

RealMedia files are one of the most commonly used video formats for the Internet. They are small, and can be set up relatively easily for a range of different connections.

Where RealMedia really comes into its own is when conditions on the Internet are poor. You are able to encode your file so that it plays back at different qualities, depending on the connection speed of the viewer. The really clever bit, however, is that the system can switch between these versions *interactively*. If there's congestion on the net, the viewer will get the lower quality version. When the congestion clears up, RealMedia will switch back to the higher quality version.

In addition, frames are dropped, or image quality is reduced if the Internet really slows down. This means that even under very difficult conditions, and on low bandwidth connections, RealMedia is able to keep a live image uninterrupted.

On the other hand, RealMedia files do need a special player to be downloaded by the user before they'll play back. In addition, once you've created a RealMedia file, you can't edit it and you can't import it into Premiere (or any other editing package).

It is possible to download a free compression tool from RealMedia at www.Real.com which lets you convert any movie to a .rm file. On the surface, this sounds like a good idea, and the **RealProducer** software is easy to set up and use. However, Premiere will produce far higher quality RealMedia files, so I would recommend this instead.

QuickTime

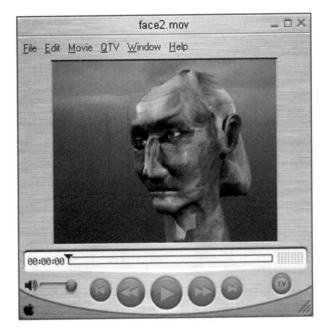

This can be a good choice for CD quality video and DV although QuickTime, as a web compression format, can have problems as it cannot negotiate rate changes during transmission. QuickTime files though can be made very small and tend to remain clear and sharp. You can play them back on most computers, PC and Mac, as long as the viewer has the appropriate version of QuickTime installed.

Viewing a QuickTime movie online can be frustrating if your system can't handle the bandwidth or if internet traffic causes your connection to slow down.

QuickTime movies work very well as files for complete download. They also work well for streaming on broadband connections. QuickTime movies can be created as 'alternates'. In other words, several versions of the same movie can be stored, each optimized for a different kind of internet connection. The correct quality version will automatically be played out for whoever wants to view the clip.

Exporting for the Internet

Whichever system you choose, Premiere will let you export your file through a plug-in which is automatically installed when you install Premiere. The plug-in is a cut down version of **Terran's Media Cleaner** – a tool for creating and optimizing video files – and we briefly mentioned it at the start of this section.

Select File > Export Timeline > Save for Web, and the Media Cleaner Wizard will open. The settings available here let you choose from a whole range of different formats, and the add-on will lead you through the process of creating your video file with a series of simple questions.

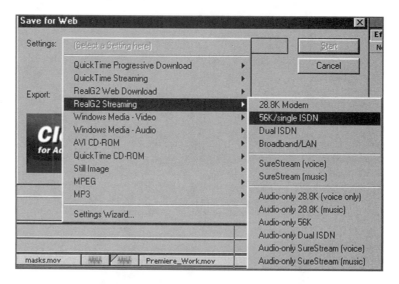

Some of the options presented are also suitable for CD-ROM and other presentations, and you may find Media Cleaner gives you a quick and easy way to produce these files too.

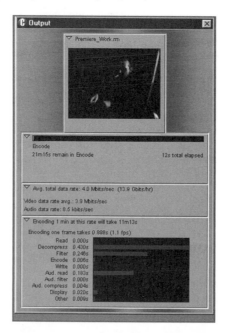

Once you reach the end of Media Cleaner's Questions, you'll be able to watch as your video is produced. You can see very detailed information about the way your file is being processed, and even see the frame that's being worked on at any time. The display, however, is of your original footage, and not the output quality, so you can't keep an eye on how your shot will eventually look.

If you're producing Windows Media files, and need more control over your files, try File > Export Timeline > Advanced Windows Media. This brings up a special dialog for creating Windows Media files, and offers you a lot of advanced control over the way your file will be constructed. If you are an experienced user of Windows Media Encoder, then this is an excellent utility and much more versatile than Cleaner EZ. However, there's little to choose between files created this way and those produced with the much simpler Media Cleaner Wizard – it's all a question of personal taste.

Creating Web Pages

Once you've finished your video, it's likely you'll want to embed them into a Web page. For downloadable files, this is easy enough. All you need to do is create a link to where the video files are stored, and the viewer can download them.

Streaming files are more difficult. Web design is a little beyond the scope of this book, but the Media Cleaner Plug-in does produce a basic HTML page whenever you render a movie for the web. This page can be examined to allow you to produce more complex pages of your own.

For more information, take a look at the documentation for whichever web authoring package you're using.

One neat trick worth mentioning when you're producing web video in Premiere is that when you're creating a video on the timeline, you can place markers containing web links. When the video's rendered out in an appropriate format (QuickTime for example) those marker links will be stored within the video file. Then whenever the file is played back, and reaches the frame with the marker in, the web address you've specified will automatically be called up. Thus, you can have an online presenter talking about a certain subject, and just as they mention it, a webpage about the subject can be called up. Or, you can have a video advertisement which brings up the product's webpage as soon as it ends.

DVD

The ability to burn DVD disks isn't something many people have right now. However, the technology is getting cheaper and cheaper, as are the blank disks themselves. Soon it's likely that home DVD recording will be very common.

A DVD disk looks exactly the same as a CD-ROM, and can be used to store exactly the same kinds of data. The only difference is that its storage capacity is much, much larger. You can store 4.7Gb on a DVD as opposed to 650mb on a CD.

If your DVDs are to be used on a computer, you can treat them in exactly the same way as CDs, so you can store any kind of information on them. If you want them to play on a DVD player, however, you need to create a certain kind of content.

A DVD production is made up of two types of content:

- **Video**: DVD video is compressed in the **MPEG2** format. This format offers very good picture quality with file sizes that let you place an entire film on a single disk. You can create MPEG2 video using Premiere but only the full upgraded version of Media Cleaner has this output setting. However, it's not a very flexible system. You can only produce files of a certain quality (about the quality you'd have on a CD ROM).

For true DVD production you'll need an add-on to Premiere which gives you access to the full range of tools for producing MPEG files.

- **Multimedia**: DVD movies are packaged using a kind of multimedia interface which can be created to allow you to select and view video files in whatever way you like. Some let you pick which scene or episode to jump to in a video file, others might let you choose to have commentary or alternative language sound tracks. Others still let you view extra footage, or additional programmes included on the disk.

If you were creating a DVD wedding video, you could let viewers choose to jump straight to the speeches, or view highlights of the ceremony. You could even present them with a sequence of snapshot images through which they could browse.

These interfaces need to be written with a DVD authoring package. Some are very complex and expensive. Others with reduced features are given away free with capture cards. **Minerva Impression**, and **DVDit** (both previously pictured) are two examples. They each allow you to import still images and video files. From these, you can create on-screen menus which allow the viewer to navigate the contents of the disk.

Both packages produce files which will run on a PC, or a DVD player, but will also let you produce small DVD projects which can be burned onto a CD (playable only on a computer), or run from the computer's hard drive.

This means that you can relatively easily create DVD type multimedia presentations for demonstrations, sales points, information kiosks and so on, without the need for either a DVD burner, or any particular training in multimedia design.

Summary

Exporting your footage is rightly one of the most important phases of your production. You need to make sure that your final material is of the appropriate quality and in the right format for whatever your destination medium is, whether that's the Web, CD-ROM or videotape.

You'll have by now discovered that there are a wide range of options available to you, including the ability to export for:

- Videotape, including DV and S-VHS

- CD-ROM

- Internet Video

- DVD

Whatever your destination format, Premiere has a setting for you, and the quality of your final exported video will no doubt do justice to all those long days you spent editing your video together!

14 A Step Further

You should, by now, know your way around Premiere pretty well. It's a huge and expanding package, and opens up creative possibilities for all kinds of video productions. However, Premiere alone is not a complete post production suite. There are many other software packages that can help, both with effects, and with other aspects of your production.

Once you've got your completed video, you're still not at the end of the process. For anything but the most private home video, getting an audience for your work is an issue that needs consideration. In addition, if the examples in this book have whetted your appetite for production, you'll want to know how to take your work to the next stage. You'll want to get in touch with like-minded videographers, and find cast and crew for your next production. You might also want to explore the plethora of resources available for the Premiere user, and for film and video makers in general.

This chapter aims to provide information, contacts, and resources to allow you to take your productions beyond Premiere. Here you'll find information on software which can both extend Premiere itself, and add to it to create a more complete post production studio. You'll find out what you can expect to achieve, and what tools you'll need to create different effects. As well as that, you'll find Internet resources to get you in touch with filmmakers and crew around the world, and find out more about the skills and technology available.

In addition, if you're looking to take your work to a wider audience, you could do a lot worse than submitting it to some of the film and video festivals listed in Appendix C. These provide a platform for your work to be shown, and some also offer the opportunity for you to meet with other videographers, and distributors.

Web Resources

The Internet is becoming the natural home of filmmakers. It's not only a great research tool for all kinds of filmmaking information, but also place where filmmakers can meet, recruit crews, and swap ideas. As well as that, it's quickly becoming a transmission medium too. You can already view short films and video productions online - in various qualities. You can also download clips and promotional material for many more shows.

There are even several online film festivals, and sites dedicated to showing new videos made by independent groups. Occasionally, these sites will pay for the films they show, but mostly funding models haven't proved themselves yet, and filmmakers need to decide whether they're prepared to provide their work for nothing to a global audience. There are good arguments for and against this type of distribution, and it's a decision filmmakers have to make for themselves.

It's well known that the Blair Witch Project made heavy use of the Net in its publicity - to the extent that there was already a series of fan sites set up and rumours were flying around cyberspace about the film long before it reached cinemas. Since then, more and more productions have used the Net as a free publicity machine, providing free images, screensavers, games and trailers to generate interest in a project.

The Internet, then, is a powerful tool for anyone involved in video. Here are a few sites which might be of interest. They should at least provide a start, and help to direct you to the thousands of sites and email groups representing hundreds of thousands of people online with an interest in video production:

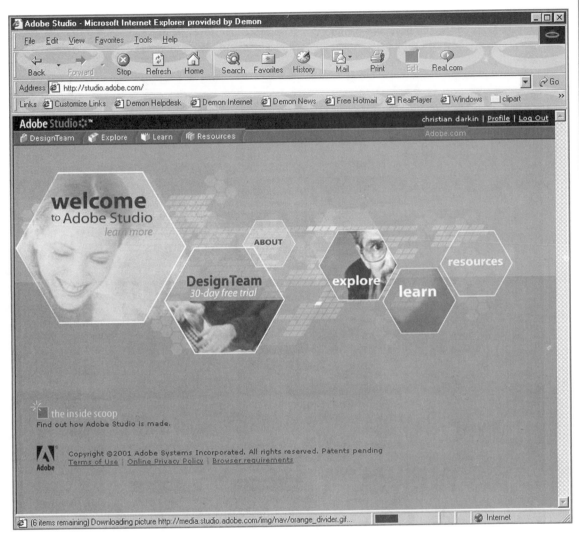

studio.adobe.com/expertcenter/main.html - Adobe's web page for Premiere users. The Expert Center contains information on all aspects of Premiere. There are also tutorials on how to achieve various effects. In addition, the site carries updates and bug fixes for the package, so you can make certain that your copy contains all the latest tools to keep it running smoothly, and allow it to integrate with the latest hardware.

www.nextwavefilms.com - An ultra-low budget film and video production site. Next Wave Films lets you submit your own projects, and the site contains advice and information for low budget filmmakers. They also provide small grants for finishing productions.

www.cyberfilmschool.com - A massive resource for filmmakers with articles, links, and advice. The makers of the site have also produced a CD ROM which is heavily plugged. On the site you'll find a whole host of useful links, which are well grouped and reviewed.

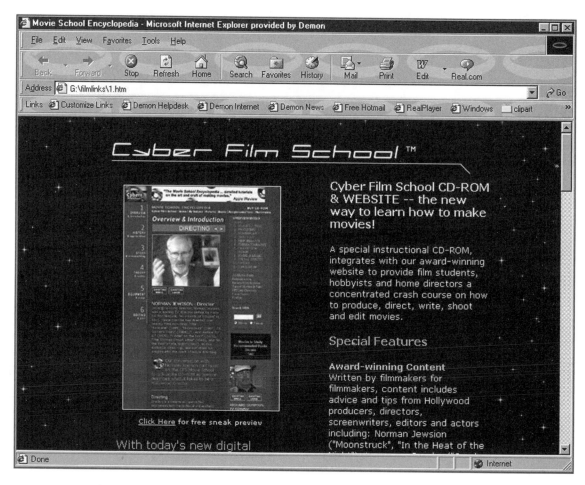

www.catharton.com- Search here for online resources on directors, Authors, musicians and artists.

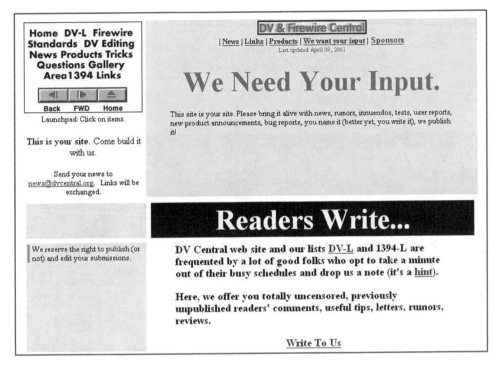

www.dvcentral.org - Mainly a hardware based site covering all aspects of digital video and firewire. It's quite technical, and covers a lot of new products like camcorders, and gives hints and tips on getting the best from DV.

www.shootingpeople.com - A UK site which allows you to register for 3 British email lists. These lists are very useful for establishing contacts between filmmakers (UK filmmakers network list), writers (UK screenwriters network) and actors (UK casting network). With over 17,000 members, it's one of the fastest ways to crew up for a low budget production, or get advice.

www.webcinema.org - This site lets you sign up to one of the biggest filmmakers groups in the world. Once subscribed, you can get quite a lot of mail (dozens of posts per day), but there are sub-lists for many countries so you only need to get email from filmmakers in your country.

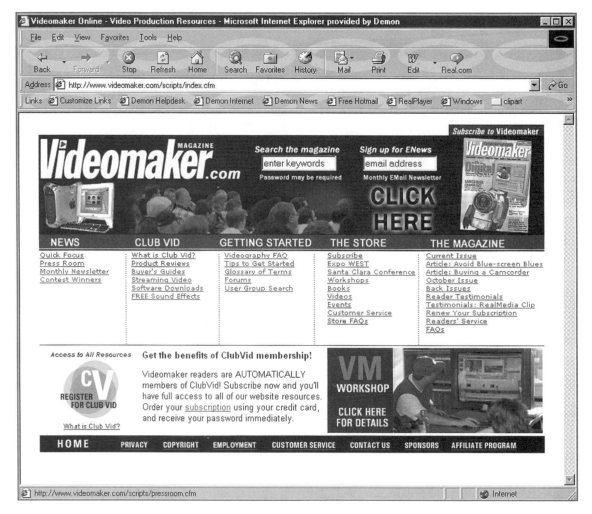

www.videomaker.com - The website of Videomaker magazine. The site is a large resource, drawing upon the experience of the magazine to provide a good archive of product reviews and FAQs.

www.filmmaking.net - A large resource containing news, articles, reviews of new camcorders, and a forum for buying and selling used equipment.

www.cinemedia.org - Basically just a huge resource of links. Cinemedia contains a well researched and ordered set of links for every aspect of filmmaking. You can search the database (of over 25,000 links) for any subject that interests you.

www.ifilm.com - A site which streams films and video clips live. It's like an ongoing film festival. You can submit your own productions for the site, and view and rate other people's work.

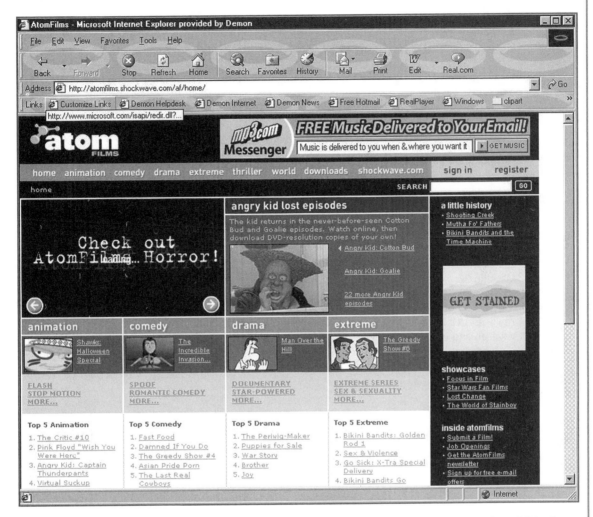

www.atomfilms.com - Another video site which shows short videos. Atomfilms is well established and is always looking for submissions from videomakers.

wwug.com/forums/adobe_premiere - A forum for Premiere users. Lively discussion on everything about the package from users all around the world.

Effects packages

Premiere has a good range of effects filters and animation tools, and you can add more. However, if you want to create more sophisticated effects, you'll have to move beyond it. There are dozens of effects packages on the market designed for different tasks. Some are complete programs in themselves. Others are add-ons to Premiere, After Effects, or other programs and you'll need to know exactly what you're trying to achieve in order to decide what to go for.

Basically, effects tools fall into two main categories: tools to create images and animations – 3D modellers, painting packages, titling packages etc. – and tools to composite clips and images together into more complex shots.

Effects work is a tough job. It's time consuming, often frustrating, and difficult. It's not unusual to spend days or weeks working on a single shot that will last for perhaps a second of screen time. You shouldn't go into it thinking it will take you a couple of days to learn the tricks either. It'll take months or even years before you really know your way around a good 3D animation or compositing package, but once you do, you'll be able to produce incredible results.

The programs listed here are certainly not a complete guide to special effects. However, they should give you a quick guide to what's on the market, and what you can expect to do with it...

Lightwave
Mac and PC
www.newtek-europe.com

You'll find Lightwave used in a huge range of TV and films. It built the spaceships in Star Trek Voyager, and is used in one way or another in most Hollywood effects movies. It's a very versatile 3D modelling and animation package, and it's updated regularly enough to keep it ahead of the competition. It's particularly good at producing smoke and fire effects.

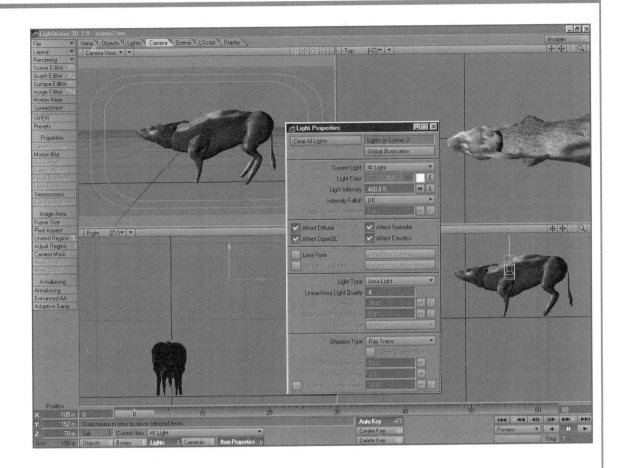

Revolutionary Premiere 6

Movie3D
PC
www.aist.com

Movie 3D is a very cheap, but very flexible 3D package. You can model using most of the modern techniques, and create simulations involving physics (so that if you position a ball over a solid surface, it will fall and bounce realistically without you having to animate every motion).

3DS Max 4
PC
www.discreet.com

3DS Max is another of the top animation packages. It's a little out of the price range of many users, but allows you to model and create animations very quickly, so it's often used in TV and film work where deadlines are tight. Its wide user base means there are dozens of plug-ins available to extend the program, and with it, you should be able to produce virtually any 3D effect you can imagine.

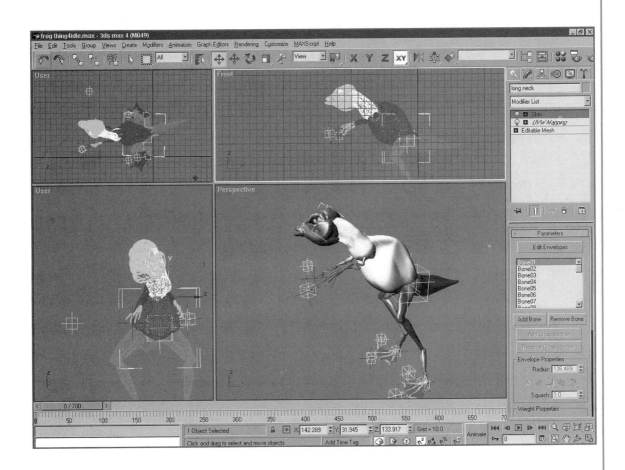

Vue d'Esprit 4
PC
www.e-onsoftware.com

Creating realistic 3D landscapes is a snap with Vue d'Esprit. The package is very easy to use, and very intuitive. You can create mountains, lakes, skies, and even plants and trees, then export your 3D worlds into another package for compositing, or further 3D modelling.

Poser Pro Pack
PC, Mac
www.curiouslabs.com

Poser is probably the simplest way to quickly create and animate 3D people and animals. It contains a range of models with interchangeable clothes, hair, etc. Each can be animated and posed into different positions, and given different hand and facial expressions. You can then morph between them to create animations.

After Effects
PC,Mac
www.adobe.com

Probably the single most popular effects package in the world. After Effects is made by Adobe, so it has a lot in common with the way Premiere and PhotoShop work. After Effects lets you apply filters and effects and keyframe them just as you would using Premiere. However, it also allows you to mask off areas so that effects only alter certain objects, or composite many elements together in much more advanced and complex ways than Premiere.

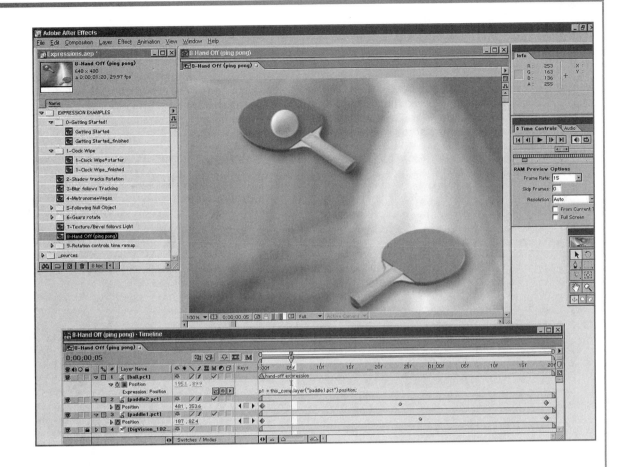

Commotion
PC, Mac
www.commotionpro.com

Commotion, like After Effects, is a specialised compositing package. It combines semi-automatic colour balancing between shots, the ability to create particle effects (like smoke and fire), and very good colour keying tools. Commotion started life as a video painting package and has a strong set of 'natural media' paint tools for altering video frames.

Cinelook
PC, Mac
www.digieffects.com

Many videomakers would like to be able to make their productions look as though they were shot on film. Cinelook is very good at doing this. It lets you set the grain, damage, and colour response of your film along with a huge number of other settings to create the ultimate film look. Cinepack is an After Effects style plug-in - it does work within Premiere, but is far better used within After Effects.

Boris FX
PC, Mac
www.borisfx.com

Boris FX is one of the most powerful add-ons you can get for Premiere. It basically gives the package some of the power and flexibility of After Effects. In addition, it adds several filters you don't even get in After Effects such as 2D and 3D particle effects (snow, and rain, for example), and 27 different compositing modes.

Aura 2
PC
www.newtek-europe.com

Aura is a compositor with a strong line in video painting. With it, you can manipulate individual frames of video in the same way you might work with still images in a paint package. In addition, you can do colour correction, text effects, and advanced masking within the program, and import PhotoShop style filters to apply to your video images. Aura's real strength is that it renders work as you go along, so you can see the effect of every change you make to a scene without waiting for it to be rendered.

Elastic Reality
PC. Mac
www.avid.com

Morphing is the art of transforming one image into another. It's often done with faces to produce a seamless merge between one person and another. The technique is also used as a transition to get from one shot to another similar one without anyone ever noticing that there's been a cut. Elastic Reality lets you have complete control over the way objects change, and use distortion to create the impression of a 3D morphing effect.

Macromedia Flash

PC, Mac
www.macromedia.com

Flash is traditionally thought of as a Web design package. However, it can output video files, so it can be used very effectively to create animated graphics, logos and title sequences. Because it's so good at creating animations, and producing interesting designs, and because those designs can be transferred as easily to the Internet as they can to video, the format is ideal for cross-media productions.

Photoshop

PC, Mac
www.adobe.com

A good still image manipulation package is one of the most important programs to have at your disposal when creating video. It can help you out in building masks, in isolating still images, in cutting out transparent pictures, and in creating text effects. PhotoShop is very well integrated with Premiere, and you can send files back and forth between packages very easily.

Pre-Production tools

Of course, post production isn't the only place the computer can help your video work. A good word-processor is essential for scripting your productions. You can buy dedicated script layout software, but in general, it's not worthwhile. On the Internet you'll find various templates for the most commonly used standard word processors (like Word). These let you lay out your script in forms which are standard for video production, just using a series of simple command keys.

Most of these layout templates have been designed by writers, and are available for free download. Scriptmaker is one of the best Word For Windows templates, and you can find it at many writers' sites - just type the name into any search engine, and you should be able to download it.

Budgeting software is also available, but again, for a small production, a copy of any standard spreadsheet should do just fine. There are templates available for filmmakers, and these can be a lot of help in setting up your budgets. However, each film is different, and has different requirements and restrictions, so you'll probably need to alter any standard layout you find considerably to make it suit your own production.

Complex scheduling and storyboarding packages are also on the market - letting you organize shooting days, and plan shots. These can be a lot of help on a complex production where dozens or even hundreds of people have to be scheduled on a complex shoot, but most tend to be out of the price range of individuals and small companies.

Film festivals

If your productions are anything other than pure home videos, it's likely that there'll be a film festival somewhere in the world to which you can submit them. There are literally hundreds of festivals taking place all over the world every year. Some specialize in feature films, others in documentaries, short films, animations, art films, or pop videos. Some are general, accepting submissions of all types and genres, whilst others specify very limited types of production. Limitations may range from a requirement that entries have a running time of less than 3 minutes, to an insistence that all productions must be promotional videos on the subject of dentistry.

All in all, you'll need to do some research to find out which festivals your particular work would fit into best. Some festivals are free to enter, others charge a fee, which the festival will keep whether your work is accepted into the event, or not. Many festivals are competitive affairs often attracting cash prizes, or (in the case of smaller events) free filmmaking equipment donated by sponsors. Others are simply a showcase for your production - providing you with an audience of filmgoers and other filmmakers and the opportunity of seeing your work on the big screen. Still others include film markets - where distributors and TV companies are out looking for work to purchase.

Some festivals will accept video productions. Others are a little snooty about it. Many filmmakers (generally those with the money to shoot on film) think of video as a second-rate medium. This is changing as more and more high quality productions (and even some top films) are shot digitally. However, the stigma still remains.

Although filmmakers tend to love film, it's not really a very manageable medium. Before you shoot it, it needs to be kept in a fridge. After you've shot it, you need to spend extra money having it developed. Editing on film involves physically cutting the negative up with a razor, and sticking it back together with sticky-tape (although nowadays, most film users have their footage transferred to video for editing because you can simply do a lot more with it using a package like Premiere!). Finally, when you come to make your production available on film, you can spend huge amounts of money producing even a single copy which then needs to be protected, and often insured.

Film festivals, and cinemas sometimes require film copies of your production. Often this is a purely practical demand - film projectors are a lot easier to come by than video screens. However, if you've edited with Premiere this means, you'll need to transfer your video onto film. This is an incredibly expensive process, so unless you really need to do it, don't.

If your production is accepted by a festival you'll often be asked to send a range of publicity materials - images from the show, biographies of the significant creative people involved, and sometimes a script of the work. Festivals are usually very pleased to welcome contributors to the event itself. The richer festivals will offer to pay for the travel and accommodation of visiting contributors, and may invite you to take part in a panel or some other event in connection with your work. The less well funded festivals should at least offer to help you find transport and accommodation for yourself - you are, after all providing that which the festival couldn't function without!

Finally

So that's it. We've taken Premiere apart and put it back together again. We've learnt how to build up a production from individual shots. We've tried out some flashy wipes and fades, and used special effects and animation to create titles, and picture-in-picture effects, and we've taken our video production from a set of rushes to a finished piece either on tape, or CD, or on the Internet.

We've learnt all the technical skills we need to begin creating our own video productions. However, editing isn't primarily a technical skill - it's a creative one. Knowing how to edit technically merely allows you to realise the production you've got in mind. It's the quality of your ideas that will actually determine whether anyone wants to watch the production.

The more you edit, and the more video you work with, the more comfortable you'll become with Premiere, and the more you'll be able to visualise your production as you're putting it together, and as you're planning it.

The key is to just get out there and try things out. Shoot, and edit anything you can. Video costs nothing to shoot, and takes only time to edit. If you've got an idea, try it out - if it doesn't work, try it a different way. The whole beauty of the medium is that you can work on it as much as you like, refining it, re-cutting it, and playing around with it until you get something that works for you. Once you master the basic editing tools you'll begin to be able to picture how the edit will work as you're watching your footage - or even as you're planning your shoot.

As your experience with video grows you'll start to visualise as you're filming where the cuts will go, what extra shots you're going to need, and how you can record material so as to give yourself the best range of choices when you get back to the computer.

The edit suite is where a production really comes together. Until you reach the rough cut, you're just working with elements, and shooting takes one at a time. When you sit down in front of the edit screen, all the ideas you had when you were originally thinking through your production - which were somehow overpowered by the frantic problem-solving of the shoot - will be right there in front of you waiting to be re-captured.

With Premiere, you have one of the most flexible storytelling tools ever created. You have the ability to capture the imagination of an audience, and to take them on a journey. Where you take them is up to you, but your ability to work in this powerful medium is dependent on the way you develop your own skills. So now's the time to start developing them. Pick up the camcorder. Pick it up now, and press the red button...

A Appendix A

Premiere has 74 video effects as standard, you can add to them as much as you like by including third-party plug-ins. Effects are organized into folders to make it a little easier to find your way around, but you can set up your own folders containing whichever effects you use most often.

These are the video effects Premiere ships with.

Adjust Folder

The **Brightness and Contrast** effect adjusts the brightness and contrast of the clip – you can also animate both functions. It's easy to use, but for more control, try using the Levels effect, which allows you to be much more specific in the way your changes affect the clip.

Channel Mixer allows you to make adjustments to the color values in the image, increasing or decreasing the amount of red, blue, or green based on contributions from the other colors.

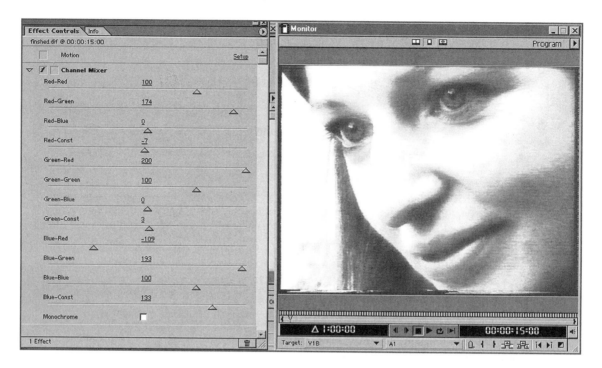

By playing around with the settings in the Channel Mixer, you can bring out and emphasize colors in certain parts of an image as well as changing the color balance of the whole picture. This allows you to create very different looks from the same basic clip. Distorting the color slightly can give the impression that the footage was shot on a hot, dry day, or focus the viewer's attention on a small detail of an image.

You can also create black and white images where you have control over the way each color is turned into gray.

Color Balance lets you increase or decrease the amount of red, green, or blue in the picture. Changes are made evenly over the whole image, meaning you can very easily create a sepia shot, or a wash of color.

It's also useful for correcting images which have been shot using the wrong white balance setting. Basically light is not the same color wherever you go - daylight tends to be much more blue, interior lighting is very orange and our eyes make the adjustment automatically. Camcorders do the same, but much more slowly. Often, a camcorder can be tricked, and end up with the wrong setting - so you get yellow, or blue tinted footage. You can often work wonders using the color balance effect to correct these images.

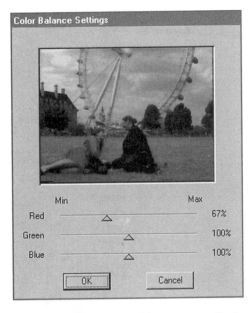

Convolution Kernel is a rarely used, but useful effect. With it, you can build your own effects based on the brightness of individual pixels in a shot. The grid of numbers shown represent the brightness adjustment made to each pixel in the image.

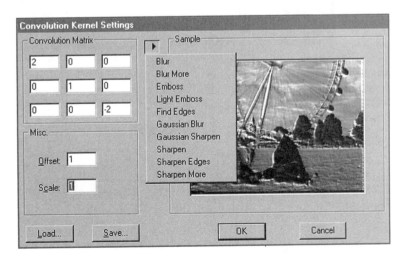

The middle box in the matrix represents the current pixel, and the boxes around it represent the surrounding pixels. As you fill in numbers, you increase or decrease the brightness of the pixel in question. The effect goes through your image, applying the rules in this grid to each pixel in the image in turn.

The practical result of all this is that if you put a 1 in the center of the grid, with a 10 to the left and -10 to the right, you create an embossed effect - because brightness is increased at the left of objects and decreased at the right creating the impression of light reflecting off a raised edge. On the other hand, if you raise the values at opposite sides of the box, the image will brighten, but become blurred.

Click the right facing arrow to the top left of the Sample Box, and the drop down list should get you started, by giving the set-ups for various common effects.

Extract turns color images to grayscale images. However, this is not like turning your image to black and white. The effect tends to be harsher and less realistic. It's useful for creating weird effects, and might help making mattes for compositing, but has only limited uses beyond that.

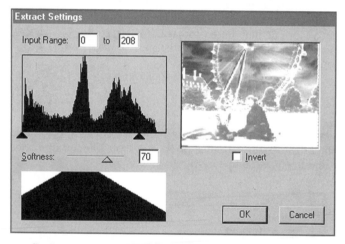

Levels is a far more flexible way to control brightness and contrast. You can adjust the brightness of the lightest or the darkest parts of your image, or adjust the brightness level overall. You can even alter the brightness of the red, green, and blue parts of your image independently.

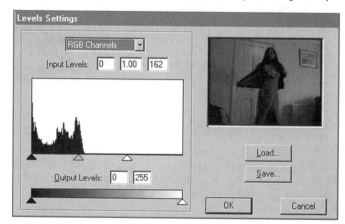

The graph represents the distribution of pixels with different brightnesses throughout your image. Here, we've chosen a particularly dark image - so we can see that there aren't many light pixels at all. To improve the contrast in the shot, we slide the white triangle under the graph to the left. This brightens the lightest parts, without altering the shadows, thus improving the spread of shades in the image.

The drop-down list at the top lets us choose to only affect red, blue, or green portions of the picture, so we could, for example, increase the brightness of just the actress' red dress.

Posterize lowers the number of shades in each color in the image. This makes an image appear as though it's been painted with felt-tipped pens, or like a poorly compressed Internet image. If you reduce the number to six (as we have here) you get six different levels of red, green and blue - so in this image, we can see the definite shades in the blue sky.

Blur Folder

Antialias introduces a very slight blurring to the image by softening the border between high-contrast areas.

Camera Blur simulates the effect of a camera going out of focus. This is a slightly different effect to the other kinds of blur effects - with objects retaining their straight lines even as they blur out. It's slightly more realistic than the Gaussian Blur.

Directional Blur creates the appearance of motion. Blur is applied at whatever angle you choose, and effectively smears the image in that direction. Here it's applied vertically at about 180°.

Fast Blur This effect looks pretty much like Gaussian Blur, but processes faster (a bit of a relief if you're rendering a long blurred scene. Fast blur can be horizontal, vertical or both.

Gaussian Blur is a slightly higher quality blur than **Fast Blur**, but with the same controls. You'll rarely notice the difference between the two apart from their processing times.

Ghosting creates echoes of the preceding few frames to show the movement in a shot. This effect is hard to control, and can't be keyframed, so if you need to be more specific, using the **Echo effect** may be advisable.

Radial Blur produces a zooming or swirling blur effect, useful for **tunnel vision** type effects. You can alter the center point of the effect, define how strong it is, and decide whether you want a spin (a whirlpool effect) or a zoom (as shown - where the viewer appears to be rushing towards the center point).

Because this effect requires a comparatively long time to render, there's also a quality setting. If you set the Quality to Best, you could be waiting several minutes for your previews to render - even on a relatively fast machine.

Channel Folder

Invert very simply reverses the colors in the scene. There are a number of different things you can do this with the Invert effect.

The default effect simply inverts everything. However, you can choose to invert just the Red, Blue, or Green aspects of the image, or the Hue, Saturation, or Luminance values for a different effect. You can also choose to use YIQ inversion - which lets you invert based on the method **NTSC** television calculates color.

One interesting and useful aspect of the **Invert** effect is the option of just inverting an image's Alpha channel. This has no effect on the colors of a shot, but if the image has transparency, the transparency will be reversed - so parts of the image which were transparent will become visible, and those that were visible will vanish.

Distort Folder

Bend applies waves to the image which can be controlled both horizontally and vertically. The Bend effect animates by default so that the waves travel across the screen, but you can still set keyframes for it.

You can set the intensity to control the height of the wave, the width to control its wavelength, and the rate to control its speed of movement in either direction. You can also change the shape of the wave - circle, or sine waves produce a natural looking ripple, whereas triangle and square waves look more artificial. In addition, you can alter the direction that the ripples travel - either sending them across the screen, or towards or away from the center.

Lens Distortion simulates the shot being taken through a distorted lens. You can set up fish-eye type effects, although the result won't be completely convincing as the package is working with a 2D image, not distorting the real world.

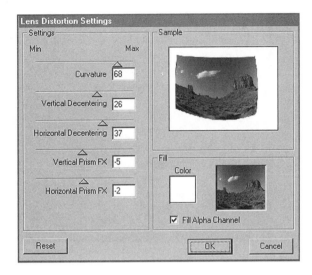

You can use the effect to create a range of distorted perspectives as though the shot is being played on a piece of bending rubber.

Mirror places a mirror effect down the shot, allowing you to create a lot of strange effects. By clicking on the crosshairs, then choosing a point in your monitor window, you can define where the mirror will be placed, and with the Reflection Angle slider, you can choose its angle (0 degrees creates a vertical mirror).

Pinch distorts an image around its center. The effect is either to bow it out to create a ball-like effect as though the center of the image has been inflated or as though it sucks it inwards as though the picture is being drawn down to a single point.

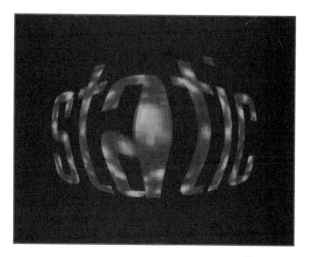

Polar Co-ordinates transfers the co-ordinates of each pixel of the image from polar to XY co-ordinates or vice versa. This effect does create a rather strange, hall of mirrors type effect, which can be varied in strength over time.

Ripple creates an animated ripple in the image. The controls here are the same as the **Bend effect**, and the effect is very similar. You can adjust the depth of the ripple, its wavelength and its speed as well as altering its direction. You can also change the wave type to Sine, Circle, Triangle or Square.

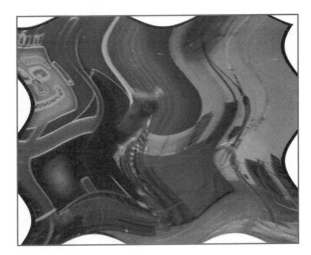

The one thing Ripple has which Bend doesn't, is the ability to pick a background color. This is because the Ripple effect distorts the edges of the picture so gaps are sometimes left behind which you can see, depending on the color you've picked.

Shear leans the image over to the left or right. By dragging the point at the top or bottom of the vertical line, you can change the position and slant of the shearing. You can also choose to have the effect in Repeat Edge Pixels mode - where gaps left in the sides of the image are filled with repeated pixels from the edge of the screen, or in Wrap Around mode where the shearing pulls parts of the image round from the other side of the screen to always leave a complete image.

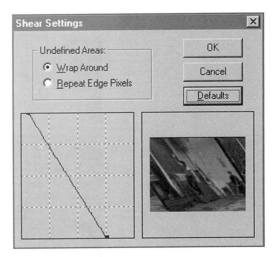

Spherize is very much like the **Pinch** effect. Spherize creates bulges and dents in the center of the image. The scale of the effect can be adjusted with a single slider. You can select to have the effect apply horizontally, or vertically to create a tube-like effect going up or across the screen.

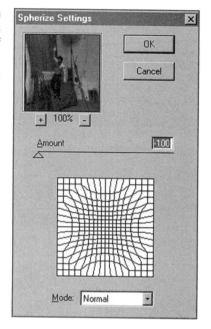

Twirl simply creates a whirlwind effect, as though the image has been stirred about its center point. The single control lets you control the angle and direction of the spin. Unfortunately, you can't move its center point, so you can't decide whereabouts on the screen you'd like the effect to happen.

Wave is another ripple creating effect. This one requires you not to be too heavy-handed with the sliders. It's very easy to increase the number of generators to several hundred. In reality, you only want up to about 20. The more generators you have, the tighter packed the waves will be.

The key trick with the wave effect is its ability to create waves with random wavelengths and amplitudes. Use the sliders to set the maximum and minimum values, and then click the Randomize button to create random waves. You can also switch between Triangle, Square and Sine waves.

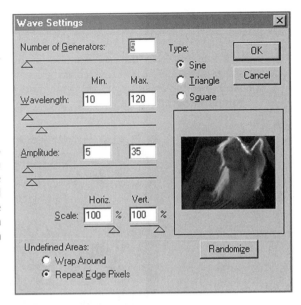

Zigzag creates concentric ripples as though a stone had been thrown into a pool. You can alter and animate the number and strength of the ripples, and you can choose whether the ripples go around the center, inwards or outwards.

Image Control folder

Black and White as the name implies, turns your footage into black and white. There are a number of ways you can create a black and white clip. This effect is the quickest, if you need more control over the way different color tones are transformed into black and white, try the using the **Channel Mixer** effect.

Color Balance HLS allows you to alter the Hue, Lightness and Saturation of the image. Sometimes you may want to increase the saturation of a clip in order to make it stronger and more vibrant. Other times you may want to reduce the saturation for a more subdued look.

A more unusual effect can be created with the Hue slider. This cycles the colors in the image through the spectrum.

The **Color Offset** effect allows you to take the red, blue or green portion of the image, and shift it a given amount to the left, right, up or down. The result looks like a badly tuned television. However, its real purpose is to create shots for viewing through 3D glasses.

3D glasses have one red and one blue lens. When you watch through them, the red image becomes invisible to one eye, and the blue becomes invisible to the other. The eye then assumes it's looking at a single image, and because they're slightly offset, the image appears to be in 3D.

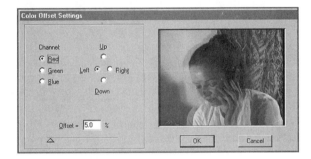

Color Pass is an effect for a very specific job. With it, you pick a color within your shot, then the effect makes everything but that color into black and white. The effect is the preservation of just one color or range of colors in an otherwise colorless image. The most obvious example of this kind of effect is the girl in the red coat in the film *Schindler's List*.

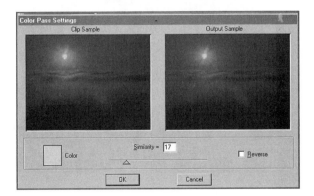

Color Replace allows you to select any color or range of colors in your image, and replace them with another color. The result however, is usually a little pixelated. By checking the Solid Colors box, shades are not preserved, and you simply get a smooth color.

Gamma Correction increases or decreases the brightness of a clip, but does it by affecting the mid-tones in the image rather than the whole image. By using Gamma Correction, you can preserve the tonal variation in an image whilst altering its lightness.

Median smoothes out an image by bringing the colors of neighboring pixels closer together. The result is a softer image. Here we've used it to remove the grain created by shooting on film. However, If you turn the radius right up, the image begins to look like a watercolor painting.

Tint quite simply 'tints' the image. You can use this to create sepia, or underwater type images. The effect maps light and dark areas of the image to colors you choose. This means that you can create some quite specific tints.

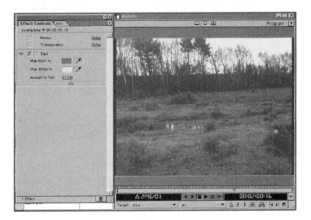

Perspective Folder

Basic 3D lets you move and rotate the image in 3D space. The Swivel control lets you spin the image about a vertical axis; the Tilt control rotates it around a horizontal axis. The Distance to Image slider allows you move the image in the Z axis (away from or towards the viewer).

You can also add a Specular highlight to give the impression of light reflecting from the image. This will only be visible as you tip the image backwards. If you find the screen updating only slowly when you use this effect, check the Preview box. This displays only a wireframe in the Monitor window while you find the right settings.

Bevel Alpha creates a bevel around any transparent areas of the image. It's often used on titles or graphical images to create a 3D look. You can control the depth of the bevel, as well as the angle and intensity of the light. You can also pick the color of the light.

Bevel Edges creates the effect of the entire clip being placed on a slightly raised platform. The Bevel Edges effect differs from the Bevel Alpha effect in that it always creates the raised edge around the sides of the image - whether parts of it are transparent or not.

You can adjust the bevel's depth, intensity, angle, and color of the light reflected from it.

Drop Shadow allows an object with an alpha channel to cast a shadow on the layer beneath it. You can control the distance between the shadow and the object casting it (in other words the distance the object appears to be from the background). You can also alter the Color of the shadow as well as its Direction, Opacity and Softness.

Drop shadow works best when placed after any other effects you add to a clip.

Transform lets you perform some scaling and skewing functions on the clip. You can adjust the horizontal (Scale Width) and vertical (Scale Height) scaling of the image, and Skew it. By clicking the Anchor Point button, you can position the point around which the image will be skewed or scaled. By clicking the Position button, you locate the center of the image.

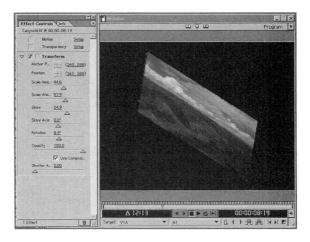

The opacity and shutter controls don't actually do anything - the effect was originally designed for After Effects, and although the controls work there, they don't have much effect in Premiere apart from causing a slight pixelation.

Pixelate folder

Crystallize creates a stained-glass window or painting type effect. The image is divided into randomly shaped crystals - each of a solid plain color. You can adjust the size of these crystals. Low values create a diffused or painted look - higher values are more abstract.

Facet is a slightly less sophisticated version of the crystallize effect. Facet creates the look of a painted image by making neighboring pixels share the same color - almost as though the image had been reduced in resolution and become pixelated. The result is a reasonable imitation of a painted scene, but there are no controls to the effect, so you're probably better off using Crystallize or Pointillize.

Pointillize is a effect for fans of Pointillist painters. The image is broken up into dots as though painted with the tip of a brush. You can control the size of the dots, and therefore the detail of the image.

QuickTime folder

QuickTime Effects are a range of effects that appear under this single effect as long as you've got QuickTime 4 or above installed. They're not strictly part of Premiere, but are free add-ons from QuickTime. Most of the effects are covered pretty well by Premiere's own effects, but one or two are worthy of note:

Cloud creates an animated cloud effect - where you can adjust the cloud's color and background as well as its rotation (which determines it's shape and density).

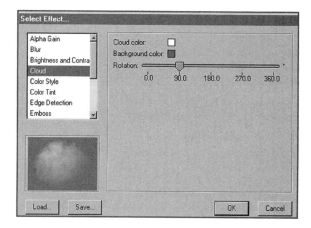

Film Noise is quite a neat little effect for producing the effect of an old film. You can adjust the number of hairs and scratches that appear on the film. For a really good film effect, you'll need to add some kind of texture effect too.

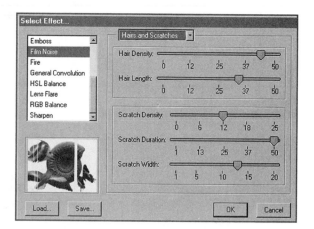

Fire simulates a fire set along the bottom of the screen. You can adjust the fire in several ways, but the most important slider is the Sputter rate slider that defines how high the fire rises. When using the fire effect in Premiere, you need to bear in mind that the preview and still image export functions don't work brilliantly, and you'll only usually get a couple of lines of fire at the bottom of the screen.

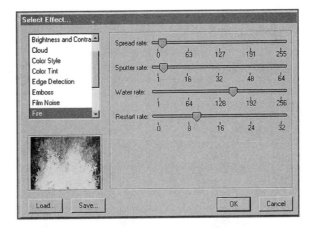

Lens Flare, as the name implies, creates a lens flare. The results of the QuickTime Lens Flare are different from the Premiere Lens Flare. It tends to be a little more de-focused and less realistic, but can create some interesting effects

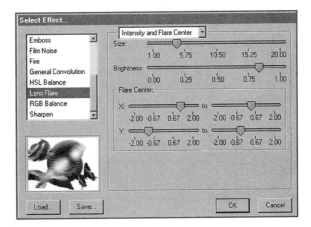

Render folder

This **Lens Flare** effect is more realistic and more controllable than that provided in the QuickTime effect. You can produce accurate looking flares for three different lens types - the principle difference between them being the kind of reflections they produce.

By clicking on the image displayed in the effect, you can set the position of the flare, and by changing the Brightness slider you can vary its strength.

Lens flares are useful in a number of situations. They can:

- Brighten an otherwise dull image

- Cover slight problems in a composite or special effect

- Produce eye catching animated light effects when used on their own

Sharpen folder

Gaussian Sharpen applies a large degree of sharpening to an image. The result is usually too extreme, and creates an unpleasant look. There are no controls - Gaussian Sharpen is either on or off.

Sharpen is a far more controllable sharpen effect than the Gaussian Sharpen effect. Sharpen lets you set or animate the level of sharpening. Used carefully, it can restore apparent detail to a blurred image.

Sharpen Edges applies a high level of sharpening to just those areas of an image where color contrast between pixels is high. The result is usually quite a stylised image with a lot of detail, but when viewed overall, looks blurred.

Stylize folder

Alpha Glow creates a colored fringe around a clip's alpha channel. The glow only appears around the transparent areas of the image - so if it has no transparency, then there will be no effect. You can alter the size of the glow, its intensity, and its color. You can specify two colors so that the glow fades from the first to the second the further it gets from the object. In addition, you can have the effect fade out at a distance from the object (as though there's a light behind the object) or end suddenly (so the effect is like a solid border around the object).

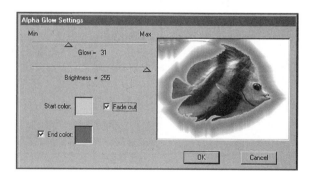

Color Emboss brings the image into relief. High contrast objects appear to come forward out of the picture a little. Unlike the straight **Emboss Effect**, Color Emboss preserves the original image.

You can alter the depth (Relief) of the emboss, the angle (Direction) of the light hitting it, and the Contrast. You can also Blend the effect to increase or decrease its strength.

Emboss embosses the image in much the same way as the color emboss effect, only it does not preserve the original colors. The result is an embossed image on a gray background. You can define the strength of the emboss, and its angle, as well as being able to blend it with the original footage to produce a color image.

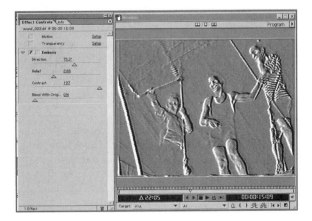

Find Edges looks for the boundaries between areas of high contrast in your image and replaces them with solid lines. This creates the look of an image that's been drawn in pen. You can blend the image with the original, to bring back some of the clip's detail, and you can invert the lines (to make them light instead of dark).

Mosaic effectively decreases the resolution of an image; it divides the image into blocks of color. By choosing the number of horizontal and vertical blocks, you decide how detailed the image will end up. Checking the Sharp Colors box increases the contrast between the blocks by not operating any blending before creating the effect. The result is a less distinguishable image.

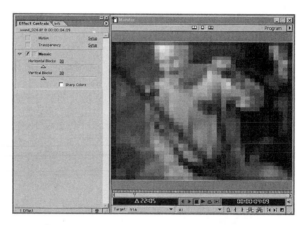

Noise creates random noise on your image. This is useful for giving video a film-grain look (especially when used in conjunction with the QuickTime Film effect), or creating static interference. The Amount of Noise slider increases or decreases the amount of noise on the image. If you're creating an effect of slight interference, maybe for film effects, keep the Clipping box checked - if you're want complete interference, uncheck this box, so your footage becomes totally masked.

Replicate simply duplicates and places multiple copies of the image on screen at the same time. Images are arranged in a block, and you can control how many rows and columns of images are created.

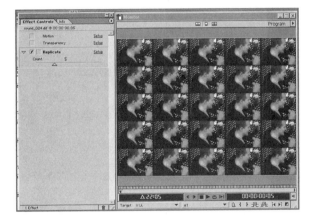

Solarize blends a negative and positive version of the image to produce an effect that alters brightness and color. It does this by progressively turning brighter colors negative. The Threshold slider alters the image from completely positive (or Min) at 0 percent to completely negative (or Max) at 100 percent.

Strobe creates a strobe effect on the clip. This effect turns the video to pure white for a fraction of a second every few frames. Basic settings are the Strobe Period (the gap between one strobe and the next) and the Strobe Duration (the length of the strobe effect), however it can do a lot more besides.

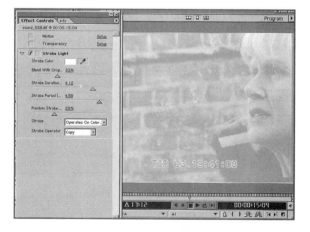

You can create random strobing with the Random Strobe Probability slider, and strobes of different colors using the Strobe Color selector. You can also change the Strobe Operator - so that the strobe effect inverts the image, or performs any of a number of functions on it.

In addition, you can have the strobe affect the transparency of a layer (as long as you've applied a transparency method to it before hand - like an alpha channel, or a Chroma key). However, care must be taken when using this effect, as overuse could prove annoying to the viewer!

Texturize creates a texture for a clip based on an image in another track. Using this effect, you can make your shots look as though they were painted on canvas, or emboss the shape of one object onto the image of another.

Using the Light Direction slider, you can control the direction of light, and through Texture Contrast, the strength of the effect. Through Texture Layer, you can also pick which track the texture information is to come from (the image or video clip has to be laid into that track at the correct point in the timeline).

Tile divides the screen up into a definable number of tiles, offsetting each by a definable amount. If you animate the offset, you can have a clip appear to break into squares and drift outwards. Between the tiles, you can have white, black, transparency or an inverse version of the clip itself.

Wind makes the image appear as though pixels are being dragged to the left or right, smearing the image. The result is effective for simulating poor TV reception, for example. You can choose from three different types of wind; Wind for normal, Blast for a more powerful effect, or Stagger for a slightly more subtle effect.

Time folder

Echo creates echoes in time. When you add this effect to a shot, each frame is given an overlay of several previous frames - to emphasize the effect of movement. You can set the Number of Echoes and their separation in time. You can even have echoes of motion before it happens.

The Starting Intensity and Decay sliders govern the strength of each echo and the way they fade out. In addition to this, you can also set the way in which the echoes are applied over the original clip. Careful setting of these values will ensure that the constant application of one image over another doesn't brighten or darken your shot too much.

Posterize Time lets you set the frame rate for a clip. You can use this to create stop motion effects (by setting the frame rate very low). However, you can also use it to give video footage a more filmic look by posterizing it to 24 frames per second.

Transform folder

For **Camera View,** imagine the video clip is a flat image, and we view it from a camera that is free to move and orbit around it. Camera view lets us change and animate the position of the camera in three dimensions. The Latitude and Longitude sliders orbit the camera around the clip vertically and horizontally, appearing to make it spin in space. The Zoom, Distance, and Focal Length controls let you move towards or away from the clip, and alter its perspective.

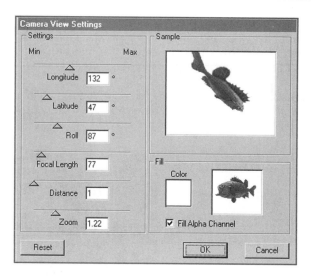

You can fill the background with a color, using the Fill Color box, or make it transparent so the clip can be superimposed onto another shot.

Clip lets you clip a shot, creating a solid border around it. The four sliders let you reduce the shot by different amounts at the bottom, top, left, and right. This is most useful when creating a widescreen effect for your productions (by slicing off the bottom and top of the image).

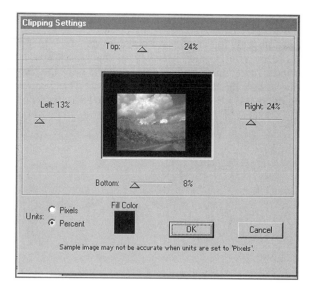

Crop lets you choose which portion of the screen is seen. The same four sliders - Left, Right, Top and Bottom - as are found in the Clip effect, appear here. This time they **stretch** the image so that just the portion you want of it is on the screen. With the Crop effect, you can zoom in on a single object in the shot, or re-frame it to cut out an unwanted object (like a boom microphone) or to get rid of any peripheral interference caused by bad tracking.

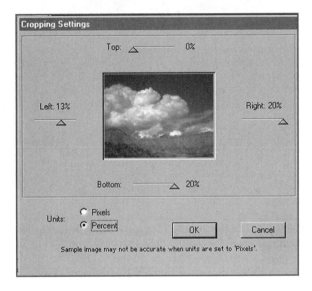

Horizontal Flip - flips the picture horizontally. This can be very useful when you've accidentally crossed the eye line during shooting, or need to reverse a shot to provide a better composite.

Bear in mind that when you do a horizontal flip, everything in the shot will be reversed, so writing will be backwards, and vehicles will appear to be traveling on the wrong side of the road!

Horizontal Hold creates the effect of a damaged TV - slanting the image. A slider controls the degree of slant.

Image Pan selects just a portion of the shot for viewing, and expands that to fill the shot. You can choose the cropping numerically, or by dragging the corner points of the Source window.

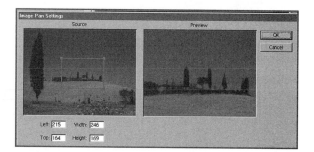

Image pan can be animated, so it's possible to produce roving, zooming, and distorting shots from a single still image.

> However, since you're expanding a small area to fill the screen, beware of the reduction in quality of your image.

Resize can be useful if you've got a clip or image that wasn't captured as video, it may be of a different resolution than a normal TV image. When you export the clip, it will be converted to the correct size for the screen, but using a resize effect does a better job of this scaling than exporting alone.

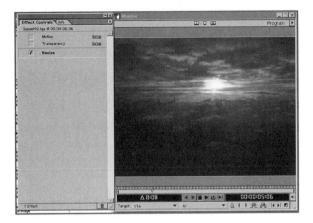

Roll automatically scrolls the image slowly across, up, or down the screen, using the Left, Right, Up, or Down Radio buttons. This simple control lets you pick which direction the image will scroll. This effect can be good for scrolling credits.

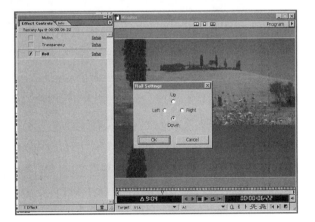

Vertical Flip quite simply turns the image upside down!

Vertical Hold rolls the clip vertically - as though it's being shown on a damaged monitor.

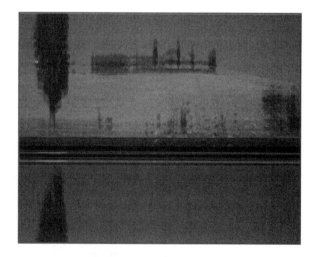

Video Folder

Broadcast Colors - Computers display and store colors differently to TV monitors. This means that some colors won't look exactly the same on your TV as they do on your PC or Mac. This applies mostly to highly saturated colors. The Broadcast Colors effect makes all the colors in your clip safe for video. It's not usually necessary to apply the effect, but you might want to if you find your shots look too different, or if the exact colors are critical to your scene.

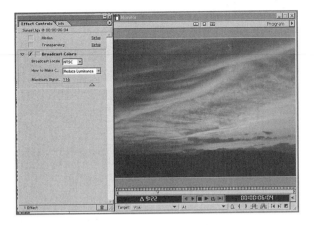

Field Interpolate tries to make up for fields of the video image missed during capture. It may be rare to find a situation where you'll need to use this effect. However, it can sometimes increase the quality of still image outputs.

Reduce Interlace Flicker deals with the long, thin horizontal lines - particularly those found in graphics, titles, or web images that tend to flicker on TV monitors. This effect softens the image so horizontal lines remain steady.

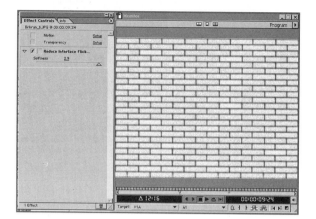

Appendix B

This appendix will give you a quick tour of the drop-down menus that appear across the top of the Premiere interface.

File menu

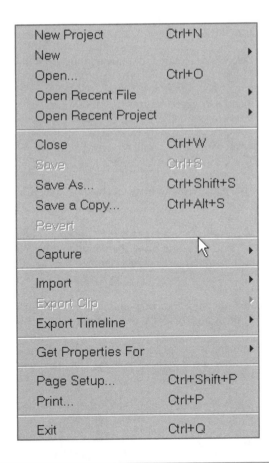

New Project	Ctrl+N
New	▶
Open...	Ctrl+O
Open Recent File	▶
Open Recent Project	▶
Close	Ctrl+W
Save	Ctrl+S
Save As...	Ctrl+Shift+S
Save a Copy...	Ctrl+Alt+S
Revert	
Capture	▶
Import	▶
Export Clip	▶
Export Timeline	▶
Get Properties For	▶
Page Setup...	Ctrl+Shift+P
Print...	Ctrl+P
Exit	Ctrl+Q

The New Project command is used for starting a new movie. It closes the current Timeline and Project windows and opens new, empty ones.

The New command allows you to create certain kinds of assets for a movie. It's similar to the Create Item button in the Project window.

The Open command allows you to open a previously saved Premiere project file. It can also be used to open a video clip or other asset. (Opening an asset with this command allows you to view it, but does not make it part of the current project. For that, use the Import command instead.)

The Open Recent File command lists the most recent assets you've opened in Premiere and allows you to choose one to re-open.

The Open Recent Project command is similar to Open Recent File, except that it lists recently saved Premiere project files.

The Close command closes whatever window is currently selected in Premiere. If the selected window is the Project window, the Close command closes the project.

The Save command saves the currently open project under its current filename. (If the project has not yet been named, Save defaults to Save As.)

The Save As command allows you to name (or rename) the current project, and then saves it under that name.

The Save a Copy command allows you to save the current project under a new name, but leaves the project open under its current name.

The Revert command eliminates any recent changes you've made to the current project, and returns it to the state it was in when you last saved it.

The Capture command is what you use to bring video and audio onto your hard drive from sources outside your computer.

The Import command allows you to select assets that are already on your hard drive – video clips, audio files, graphics, and so forth – and bring them into your Premiere project. You can also use Import to bring one entire Premiere project into another, thus combining the two projects.

The Export Clip command allows you to select an individual video clip in Premiere and save it in various formats, including standard streaming and non-streaming video formats. It also allows you to save an individual frame as a graphic file, or to output a clip to videotape.

The Export Timeline command is similar to Export Clip, except that it exports the entire Timeline (or the work area) rather than a single clip. This is the command you'll use to output the finished version of your Premiere project.

The Get Properties For command tells you everything you could want to know about a particular video clip, including its duration, frame rate, image size, and many other characteristics.

The Page Setup and Print commands allow you to print the contents of most windows within Premiere – you can even print an image of the Timeline. This can be especially useful if you've rough-edited a project in Premiere and need a visual reference to help you reconstruct the project on another system.

The Quit command shuts down Premiere.

Edit menu

Can't Undo	Ctrl+Z
Can't Redo	Ctrl+Shift+Z
Cut	Ctrl+X
Copy	Ctrl+C
Paste	Ctrl+V
Paste to Fit	Ctrl+Shift+V
Paste Attributes...	Ctrl+Alt+V
Paste Attributes Again	Ctrl+Alt+Shift+V
Clear	
Duplicate Clip...	Ctrl+Shift+/
Deselect All	Ctrl+Shift+A
Select All	Ctrl+A
Find...	Ctrl+F
Locate Clip	Ctrl+L
Edit Original	Ctrl+E
Preferences	▶

The Undo command allows you to undo the most recent actions you've taken in Premiere. The number of undo levels can be set in Preferences.

The Redo command allows you to undo the Undo command.

The Cut, Copy, and Paste commands are the standard commands found in other programs, allowing items to be copied to and from your operating system's clipboard. They can be used with any asset in Premiere – even video clips.

The Paste to Fit and Paste Attributes commands allow you to do specialized kinds of pasting within the Timeline. For example, you can use Paste to Fit to make a long clip fit into a short space, or you can use Paste Attributes to copy effects settings from one clip to another.

The Clear command is similar to the Cut command, except that it doesn't save a copy of the deleted item to the clipboard.

The Duplicate Clip command allows you to make a copy of a selected clip, and to choose the name and location of the copy, all in one step.

The Deselect All and Select All commands allow you to select or deselect all the items in a particular window — for example, all the clips in the Timeline or all the bins in the Project window.

The Find command is identical to the Find button in the Project window. It allows you to find an asset within your project based on any combination of criteria.

The Locate Clip command helps you maintain a correspondence between the Project window and the Timeline. If you select a clip in the Timeline, Locate Clip will find its source clip in the Project window. If you select a clip in the Project window, Locate Clip will find where it's used in the Timeline.

The Edit Original command allows you to edit a clip's original source file on your hard drive. (Ordinarily, when you make changes to a clip in Premiere, you're only editing a reference to the clip; the original file remains unchanged). This is a powerful command that should be used only with care.

The Preferences command allows you to customize certain aspects of Premiere.

Project menu

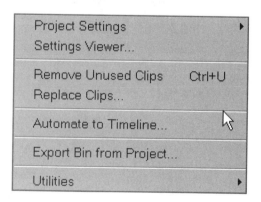

The Project Settings menu item gives you access to various submenus that allow you to make technical adjustments to your project.

The Settings Viewer command opens the Settings Viewer window, which allows you to see all your settings at a glance – not just the Project Settings, but also the Capture Settings, the Export Settings, and the settings for any individual clip.

The Remove Unused Clips command is a housekeeping tool – it removes any clips from the Project window that aren't being used in the Timeline.

The Replace Clips command allows you to replace older or lower-quality versions of clips with newer or higher-quality versions.

The Automate to Timeline command allows you to take a series of clips from the Project window or the Storyboard window and send them directly to the Timeline. This is a quick, easy way to create a rough version of your movie.

The Export Bin from Project command allows you to export the contents of any bin so that the assets in that bin are available to use in other projects.

The Utilities menu item gives you access to two useful tools: Batch Processing, which allows you to output one or more movies to various file formats in a single, automatic, unattended session; and the Project Trimmer, which allows you to make a streamlined, compact copy of your Premiere project.

Clip menu

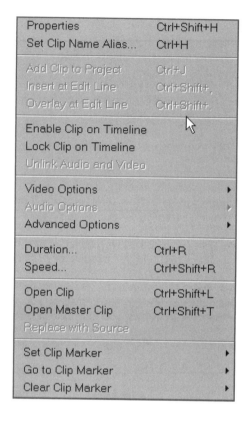

The Properties command gives you information about a clip. It's similar to using the Get Properties For command on the File menu.

The Set Clip Name Alias command allows you to rename a clip, or to give different names to different copies of a single clip.

The Add Clip to Project command applies only to a clip that has been opened via the Open command and that is currently visible in the Source monitor or in a clip window. It adds the clip to the Project window.

The Insert at Edit Line and Overlay at Edit Line commands are editing tools that determine how a clip is inserted into the Timeline.

The Enable Clip in Timeline command is a toggle. When there's a check mark next to it, the currently selected clip in the Timeline is active; when there's no check mark next to it, the currently selected clip in the Timeline is inactive, and can be neither seen nor heard.

The Lock Clip in Timeline command is also a toggle. When there's a check mark next to it, the currently selected clip in the Timeline can't be edited or moved; when there's no check mark next to it, the currently selected clip in the Timeline is free to have changes made to it.

The Unlink Audio and Video command allows you to edit the audio and video tracks of a clip separately.

The Video Options menu item gives you access to two powerful and important features of Premiere: the Transparency window and the Motion window. The other submenu items are less consequential: Maintain Aspect Ratio lets you 'letterbox' a clip that doesn't have the 4:3 proportions of a standard TV screen, and Aspect Fill Color lets you choose the color of the letterbox panels. Frame Hold allows you to set up a freeze-frame effect. Field Options allows you to handle interlacing in a way that best suits the technical requirements of your hardware.

The Audio Options menu item gives you access to submenu items that affect a clip's audio track. Audio Gain allows you to set the overall volume of a track; the other options affect the clip's panning (that is, whether the sound uses the left stereo channel, the right stereo channel, or both).

The Advanced Options menu item gives you access to various technical settings for a clip. Timecode determines how a clip's frames are numbered and displayed, Pixel Aspect Ratio determines whether a clip's pixels will be treated as square or rectangular; and Interpret Footage allows you to change a clip's frame rate.

The Duration command allows you to adjust a clip to a specific length by adding frames to or deleting frames from the end of the clip.

The Speed command allows you to adjust a clip to a specific length by speeding it up or slowing it down.

The Open Clip command is identical to double-clicking on a clip – it opens the clip in the Source monitor (or, if there is no Source monitor, in a clip window).

The Open Master Clip command is similar to Open Clip, except that if the clip has been trimmed (that is, had its in or out points changed), Premiere opens an untrimmed version of the clip.

The Replace with Source command is intended only for virtual clips. This command exports the virtual clip as an independent movie and then replaces the clip with that movie.

The Set Clip Marker, Go to Clip Marker, and Clear Clip Marker commands are identical to those that can be found on the Marker menu below the Source monitor. They allow you to identify and return to specific frames in a clip.

Timeline menu

Preview	[Enter]
Render Work Area	
Render Audio	
Razor at Edit Line	
Ripple Delete	
Apply Default Transition	Ctrl+D
Transition Settings...	
Zoom In	+
Zoom Out	-
Edge View	
✔ Snap to Edges	
✔ Sync Selection	
Add Video Track	
Add Audio Track	
Track Options...	
Hide Shy Tracks	
Set Timeline Marker	
Go to Timeline Marker	
Clear Timeline Marker	
Edit Timeline Marker...	

The Preview command plays whatever is currently in the work area of the Timeline. It's identical to pressing the Enter (Windows) or Return (Macintosh) key while in the Timeline.

The Render Work Area command causes Premiere to build the preview files that are needed to allow you to view effects and transitions in the work area. (As noted in Chapter 1, Premiere can't show you these effects in real time without creating preview files first.) Premiere automatically builds preview files whenever you issue a Preview command from the keyboard or menu, but Render Work Area allows Premiere to build these files without showing you a preview.

The Render Audio command causes Premiere to build preview files for the audio tracks in the Timeline. (Again, issuing a Preview command causes these files to be built automatically.)

The Razor at Edit Line and Ripple Delete commands are among the editing tools that were explained in Chapter 6.

The Apply Default Transition command causes Premiere to insert a transition between two clips. The default transition is normally a dissolve, but any transition can be made the default in the Transitions palette.

The Transition Settings command is identical to double-clicking on a transition in the Timeline — it opens the Transition Settings dialog box.

The Zoom In and Zoom Out commands have a function similar to that of the scale menu at the lower left-hand corner of the Timeline: they allow you to broaden or narrow the amount of your movie that can be seen in the Timeline at any one time.

The Edge View, Snap to Edges, and Sync Selection commands are toggles that affect the way clips behave in the Timeline.

The Add Video Track and Add Audio Track commands give you a quick way to add a single video or audio track to the Timeline. By default, Premiere offers two video and three audio tracks, but you can use a total of 99 video and 99 audio tracks in a project.

The Track Options command opens a window that allows you to add or delete multiple tracks in one step. This command is identical to clicking the Track Options button at the bottom of the Timeline.

The Hide Shy Tracks command allows you to use the Timeline more efficiently. Any video or audio track can be marked as shy by control-clicking (Windows) or command-clicking (Macintosh) the 'eye' icon at the very left edge of the track. When you select Hide Shy Tracks, those tracks disappear from the Timeline, but all clips in those tracks remain visible in the movie. This procedure allows you to move previously edited tracks out of sight, and to display only the tracks you're currently working on.

The Set Timeline Marker, Go to Timeline Marker, and Clear Timeline Marker commands are identical to those that can be found on the Marker menu below the Program monitor. They allow you to identify and return to specific frames in the Timeline.

Window menu

The Window Options menu item allows you to customize the Project, Monitor, Timeline, and Audio Mixer windows. These options can also be accessed by choosing Window Options from the drop-down menu at the upper right-hand corner of each individual window.

The Workspace menu item allows you to save and choose window layouts.

The Timeline, Monitor, and Audio Mixer commands allow you to open any of those windows if they've previously been closed. (The Project window is not included here, since closing the Project window closes the project.)

The remaining items on the Window menu allow you to show or hide the various palettes that are available in Premiere.

Help menu

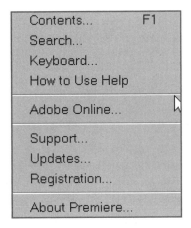

Premiere comes with an extensive help system which is displayed in your web browser. If your browser isn't open, Premiere will open it whenever you choose an item from the Help menu.

To find help on a particular subject, choose Help Topics. To search for help on a particular keyword, choose Search to see a list of keyboard shortcuts for many of Premiere's commands, choose Keyboard Shortcuts.

You can get help on using the Help system by choosing How to Use Help.

If your computer is connected to the Internet, you can also get help online. The Adobe Online menu item connects you with the Adobe website, where you can find tips, tutorials, and tech support.

The remaining items on the Help menu – Support, Updates, and Registration – connect you with specific areas of Adobe Online to get help with problems, update your version of Premiere, or register your software.

About Balloon Help and Show Balloons appear on the Help menu only in the Macintosh version of Premiere. They're required by the operating system, but they're not implemented in Premiere.

Appendix C

Here are a range of festivals taking place throughout the year which all accept entries on video. It's by no means an exhaustive list, but should give you a good start. Not all the festivals will be staffed all year round, but you should be able to get application forms from the addresses provided from about 2 months before the entry deadlines.

Transmedia International Media Arts Festival Berlin

February

All types of multimedia, video, innovative television, and installations. Entries must be in English or German, or be subtitled in one of those languages. Entries must have been produced in the 2 years preceding the festival.

Address:

Mediopolis Berlin c.V
Klosterstr.68-70
D10179 Berlin
Germany
International Amateur Short Film and Video Festival

Email: info@transmediale.de
www.transmediale.de

Entry Deadline: November

Yugoslav Documentary and Short Film Festival

March

Short films, documentaries, animations, and experimental productions. Work must have been produced during the 2 years preceding the festival.

Address:

Yougoslavia Film
11000 Beograd
Makedonska 22
Yugoslavia

Entry Deadline: February

New York Underground Film Festival

March

Features, shorts, documentaries, experimental films, animations. Subversive, innovative, or controversial productions.

Address:

New York Underground Film Festival
225 Lafayette St., Suite 401
New York NY 10012
USA

Email: festival@nyuff.com
www.nyuff.com

Entry Deadline: January

Festival of Video Creation

April

Video productions on Pal, SECAM or NTSC accepted. Competitive festival with cash prizes.

Address:

Videoformes
BP71
63003 Clermont-Ferrand Cedex 1
France

Entry Deadline: Varies.

Images - Festival of Independent Film and Video

April

Installations, animations, fiction, and documentaries on film or video. Work must have been made during the two years preceding the festival.

Address:

Images Festival Office
401 Richmond St, W. Suite 448
Toronto, M5V 3A8
Canada

Email: Images@interlog.com

Entry deadline: November

Onedotzero

May

Animation, digital video, pop promos.

Address:

14M Abbey Orchard St Estate
London SW1P 2DL
UK

Email: info@onedotzero.com

Entry Deadline February

Copenhagen Film and Video Workshop Festival

June

Each time it's held, the festival has a different theme and requirements. Contact them for details

Address:

Danish Film Institute Workshop
Vesterbrogade 24
DK-1620 Copenhagen V
Denmark

Entry Deadline: April

Festival Der Nationen

June

Non-commercial films and videos. Many film and video formats accepted with a maximum running time of 30 minutes. Entries must have been produced within 2 years of the festival. Every filmmaker who turns up at the event has the right to show their work. Amateurs encouraged.

Address:

Film Festival der Nationen
Gaumbergstrasse 82

A-4060 Linz
Austria

Entry Deadline: May

Montreal International Festival of New Cinema and New Media

October

Film, video and new media. Looking for productions which are visionary, challenging, provocative and pioneering. Work should have been produced in the 18 months preceding the festival and must not have been shown publicly in Quebec.

Address:

Montreal Festival Of New Cinema and new Media
2668 Boulevard St-Laurent
Montreal
Quebec H2X 2V4
Canada

Email: montrealfest@fcmm.com
www.fcmm.com

Entry Deadline: June

US International Film and Video Festival

June

Thirty-six different categories. Accepts most film and video formats. Entries must have been produced within 18 months of entry into the festival.

Address:

US International Film and Video Festival
841 North Addison Avenue
Elmhurst
IL 60126-1291
USA

Entry Deadline: March

Sydney Film Festival

June

Features, documentaries, short films. Send a VHS for selection. Non-English language films must be subtitled in English. Entries must not have been screened publicly in Australia before the festival.

Address:

Sydney Film Festival
PO Box 950
Clebe
NSW 2037
Australia
Email: info@sydfilm-fest.com.au

Entry Deadline: March

New York Video Festival

July

Video in all formats accepted.

Address:

70 Lincoln Center Plaza
New York
NY 10023
USA

Entry Deadline: May

International Student Television and Video Festival

July

Films and television programs, fiction, documentaries, animations, and video. Maximum of 40 minutes

Address:

FAMU
Smetanovo nabrezi 2
116 65 Praha 1
Czech Republic

Entry Deadline: April

Rio Cine Festival

July

Feature films, short films, videos, television programs. Works must not have been previously shown in Brazil, and must have been produced within 1 year of the festival.

Address:

Praca Mahatma Gandhi, 2/402
20018-900 Rio de Janeiro - RJ
Brazil

Entry Deadline: May

Canadian International Amateur Film Festival

September

Amateur and Independent filmmakers, and students. Productions should have a maximum running time of 30 minutes and be available on NTSC video or film.

Address:

Canadian International Amateur Film Festival
25 Eugenia St
Barrie
Ontario L4M 1P6
Canada

Email: ciaff@canada.com

Entry Deadline: July

Brisbane International Film Festival

August

World cinema with an Asian-Pacific focus. Short films and videos of all formats. English subtitles required for non-English language films.

Address:

Level 3 Regent Building
167 Queen St Mall
Brisbane 4001
Queensland
Australia

Email: brisfilm@thehub.com.au

Entry Deadline: May

International Amateur Film and Video Festival For Young People

August

Films and videos with directors under the age of 26. Maximum running time 30 minutes. Productions must be amateur, and not have been made for commercial purposes.

Address:

Organisationskomitee der Juvenale
Stockgasse 7
A 9020 Klagenfurt
Austria

Entry Deadline: July

Hollywood Film Festival

August

Shorts, features, documentaries, animations. Send a VHS (NTSC only) for selection. Usually screens 35mm or 16mm films, but occasionally accepts VHS or UMATIC productions.

Address:

433 N.Camden Drive, Suite 600
Beverly Hills
CA90210
USA

Email: awards@hollywoodawards.com

www.hollywoodfestival.com

Entry Deadline: April

International Festival for Student Films

August

All kinds of student productions, short films, features, documentaries, art films. Film or video formats accepted.

Address:

31 Lijuben Karavelov St
Sofia 1000
Bulgaria

Entry Deadline: May

Video Brasil: Electronic Arts International Festival

September

Video art, installations, fiction, documentaries, computer art, CD-Rom work, and animations. Many formats acceptable. Entries must have been produced within 2 years of the festival. Only Southern Hemisphere entries may be included in the competitive competition

Address:

Associacao Cultural Videobrasil
Rua Fernandes de Abreu
31, 1. Andar
Sao Paulo-SP
CEP 04543-070
Brazil

Email: info@videobrasil.org.br

www.videobrasil.org.br

Entry Deadline: July

Toronto International Film Festival

September

Features and Canadian short films. Work must have been produced within 20 months of the festival, and not have been screened commercially in Canada.

Address:

Toronto International Film Festival
2 Carlton St
Suite 1600
Toronto
Ontario M5B 1J3

Email: tiff@torfilmfest.ca
www.bell.ca/toronto/filmfest

Entry Deadline: May

BBC British Short Film Festival

September

Short films with a running time of under 40 minutes. Entries must be produced during the 12 months preceding the festival.

Address:

BBC British Short Film Festival
BBC Centre House Room B202
56 Wood Lane
London W12 7SB
UK

Entry Deadline: June

Festival of Short Films

September

Experimental, fiction, animation, documentaries. Film and NTSC video accepted. Maximum running time 35 minutes. Productions must have been made in the 18 months preceding the festival. And have to be subtitled in Spanish.

Address:

Festival Chileno-Internacional de Cortometraje Instituto de Arts y Comunicacion ARCOS
Campos de Deporte 121
Nunoa
Santiago
Chile

Entry Deadline: August

Chicago International Film Festival

October

Features, short films, Animations, TV productions, student films, educational films, TV commercials. Each category attracts a 1st, 2nd, and 3rd prize.

Address:

Chicago International Film Festival
32 West Randolph St, Suite 600
Chigago
IL60610
USA

Email: filmfest@suba.com

www.chigago.ddbn.com/filmfest

Entry Deadline July

Raindance Film Showcase

October

Features, shorts, works-in-progress, director's reels, documentaries.

Address:

Raindance Film Showcase
81 Berwick St
London W1V 3PF

Email: info@raindance.co.uk

www.raindance.co.uk

Entry Deadline: September

Kinofilm: Manchester International Short Film and Video Festival

October

All types of short films, animations, documentary, fiction, and experimental work. Special categories for Eastern European short films, and black cinema. Entries must be under 30 minutes running time.

Address:

Kinofilm
48 Princess Street
Manchester M1 6HR
UK

Email: john.kino@good.co.uk

www.kinofilm.org.uk

Entry Deadline: August

New Orleans Film Festival

October

Features and short films of all types. Music videos. Films must have been produced within 20 months of the festival.

Address:

Cinema 16
New Orleans Film Festival
225 Baronne St, Suite 1712
New Orleans
LA 70112
USA

www.nofilm.org

Entry Deadline: June

Co-op Young People's Film and Video Festival

October

Work from groups or individuals under 21 years old. Entries must be less than 6 minutes in length. No entries from professional filmmakers, or students at film school.

Address:

Co-op Young People's Film and Video Festival
The Co-operative
Freepost OL 5573
Sandbrook Park
Sandbrook Way
Rochdale
Lancashire OL11 1YD
UK

Entry Deadline: May

International Amateur Short Film and Video Festival

November

Experimental productions, fiction, non-fiction, animations. Running time must not exceed 30 minutes.

Address:

International Amateur Short Film and Video Festival
140 Rue Faidherbe
59150 Wattrelos
France

Entry Deadline: October

Video Film-Tage

November

Productions made by children, students, and other non-professionals. Entries must not have been released commercially.

Address:

Video Film-Tage
Landesfilmdienst Rheinland-Pfalz e.V
Postfach 3004
D-55020 Mainz
Germany

Entry Deadline: September

Brief Encounters - Bristol Short Film Festival

November

Films and videos under 30 minutes in length.

Address:

Brief Encounters
PO Box 576

Bristol BS99 2BD
UK

Email: brief.encounters@dial.pipex.com

www.brief-encounters.org.uk

Entry Deadline: July

London International Film Festival

November

Features, short films, documentaries, and animations. Film and video accepted.

Address:

London Film Festival
South Bank
London SE1 8XT
UK

Email: sarahlutton@bfi.org.uk

Entry Deadline: August

Hawaii International Film Festival

November

Documentaries, features, and videos. Competition for films either from or about Asia, North America, or the Pacific Rim.

Address:

1001 Bishop St
Pacific Tower, Suite 745
Honolulu
HI 96813
USA

Email hiffinfo@hiff.org

www.hiff.org

Entry Deadline: June

Caracas Short Film Festival

November

Fiction, animation, documentaries. Works must have been produced during the 2 years preceding the festival, and have a maximum running time of 30 minutes.

Address:

Cuarta Avenida Entre 5ta y 6ta Transversal
Qta. Yayagua
Los Palos Grandes
Caracus
Venezuela

Entry Deadline: varies

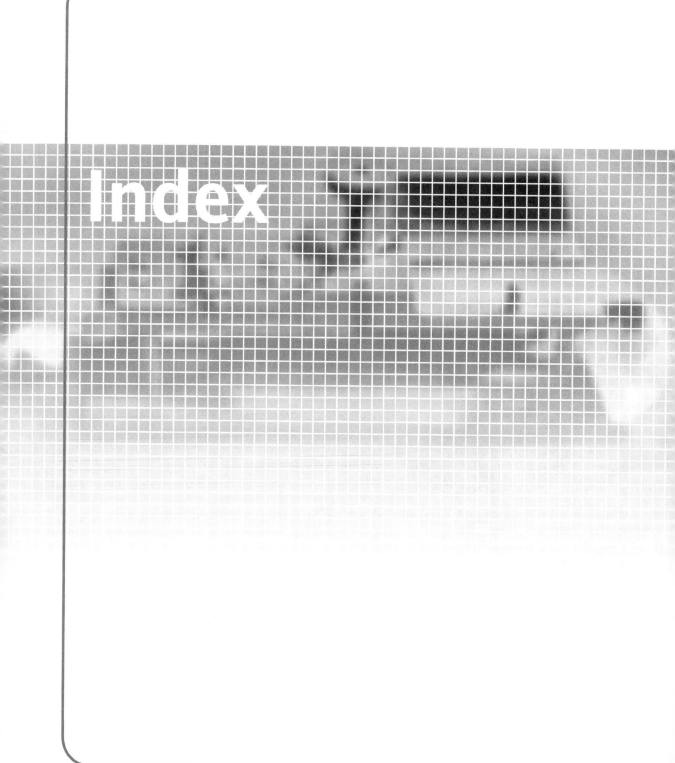

Index

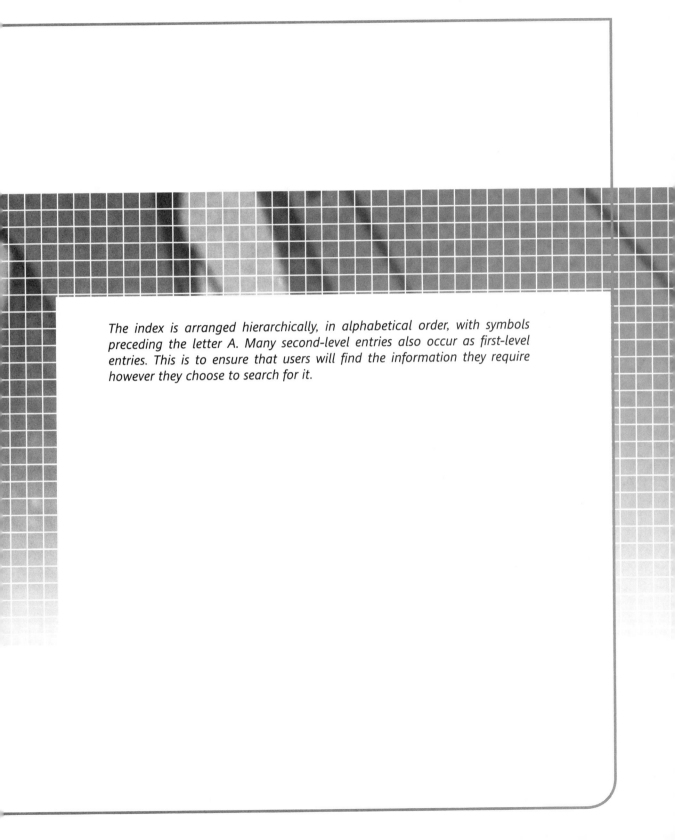

The index is arranged hierarchically, in alphabetical order, with symbols preceding the letter A. Many second-level entries also occur as first-level entries. This is to ensure that users will find the information they require however they choose to search for it.

DESIGNER TO DESIGNER™

friends of ED writes books for you. Any suggestions, or ideas about how you want information given in your ideal book will be studied by our team.

Your comments are valued by friends of ED.

For technical support please contact support@friendsofed.com.

Freephone in USA   800.873.9769
Fax   312.893.8001

UK contact: Tel: 0121.258.8858
Fax: 0121.258.8868

Premiere 6 - Registration Card

Name ....
Address ....
City ....State/Region ....
Country ....Postcode/Zip ....
E-mail ....
Profession: film student   ☐ freelance filmmaker ☐
             part of an agency ☐ inhouse editor   ☐
             other (please specify) ....
Age: Under 20 ☐ 20-25 ☐ 25-30 ☐ 30-40 ☐ over 40 ☐
Do you use: mac ☐ pc ☐ both ☐
How did you hear about this book?...
Book review (name)...
Advertisement (name) ....
Recommendation ....
Catalog ....
Other ....
Where did you buy this book? ....
Bookstore (name) ....City.............................
Computer Store (name)...
Mail Order...
Other...

How did you rate the overall content of this book?
    Excellent ☐   Good ☐
    Average ☐   Poor ☐
What applications/technologies do you intend to learn in the
near future?...
....
What did you find most useful about this book? ....
....
What did you find the least useful about this book? ....
....
Please add any additional comments ....
....
What other subjects will you buy a computer book on soon?
....
....
What is the best computer book you have used this year?
....
....

*Note: This information will only be used to keep you
updated about new friends of ED titles and will not be used for
any other purpose or passed to any other third party.*

DESIGNER TO DESIGNER™

NB. If you post the bounce back card below in the UK, please send it to:

friends of ED Ltd.,
30 Lincoln Road,
Olton,
Birmingham.
B27 6PA